LACROSSE
Team Strategies

LACROSSE
Team Strategies

Jim Hinkson

Warwick Publishing

Toronto Los Angeles

Published by:
Warwick Publishing Inc.
24 Mercer Street, Toronto, ON M5V 1H3
1424 North Highland Boulevard, Los Angeles, CA 90027

ISBN: 1-895629-55-1

Cover and text design: Kimberley Davison
Editorial Services: Harry Endrulat

Distributed in the United States and Canada by:
Firefly Books Ltd.
3680 Victoria Park Avenue
Willowdale, Ontario
M2H 3K1

Printed and bound in Canada by Webcom.

I dedicate this book to the person who started me in lacrosse:
my former coach, my mentor, and my good friend,
"Mr. Lacrosse," Jim Bishop.

Preface

The ideas I have presented in this book have come from my background as a player under Jim Bishop's famous Oshawa Green Gaels teams (seven Canadian Jr. A Lacrosse Championships); from trial-and-error as a coach; and from many contacts with lacrosse and basketball coaches. Not only have I been involved in lacrosse, as a player and coach for 30 years, but also I have coached basketball for more than 25 years in a Toronto high school. From this lacrosse-basketball background I have had a chance to play against some great coaches and also meet them at many camps and coaches' clinics all over the United States and Canada.

This book is an extension of my first work, *Lacrosse Fundamentals*. I felt at the beginning that I could not put both *Lacrosse Fundamentals* and *Lacrosse Team Strategies* together since the result would be too bulky and too expensive. So, this text is the continuation. Both books are connected and follow the same philosophy. Consequently, a reader of *Lacrosse Fundamentals* will be reinforced by reading *Lacrosse Team Strategies*.

I have tried to make this book simple enough for a new coach to understand and challenging enough for an experienced coach to get new ideas. I have tried to make the breakdown of the team strategies, the concepts of the different team strategies, and the system of play philosophies progressive and simple. The drills for all strategies are also progressive from simple to difficult.

Yet, this book is not merely a collection of drills. It is one with a definite philosophy of systems backed by drills that will help a coach teach and reinforce the principles of offense and the rules of defense. These are drills we have tested, proven, and been successful with over time.

I believe the first thing a coach, especially a beginner, has to do is to evolve a personal coaching philosophy. Then, he can derive his system of play philosophy to help reinforce the former. Lastly, team drills, through proper execution and high repetition, will also reinforce this philosophy and system of play.

Each chapter begins with pertinent terminology to make my meanings clear; then I talk about the philosophy of my systems, i.e., what I am trying to accomplish; then I give the rules or principles involved in building the different team strategies; and finally, at the end of each chapter, I provide the drills to practice and reinforce these same rules and principles.

In teaching team systems and team strategies, this is what "I believe in": Understand this is not the be-all or end-all for lacrosse coaches, but a well-proven system and strategy that has been good to me. I hope this book will make you question some things about your own philosophy and systems.

This book is quite technical and it's unlikely one will want to apply everything in it. So, take what you feel is comfortable at the level you coach and stay with the KISS philosophy–Keep It Simple Stupid.

Introduction

It takes a system and a sound philosophy to be successful at most everything we do. Jim Hinkson brings to you his many successful years in lacrosse via this lacrosse book. Every player, spectator, or coach will find the following chapters interesting and valuable as they master their particular situations in this fast-paced game.

Coach Hinkson's book is a virtual road map of how to play, coach, or understand this purely North American sport. Jim Hinkson is eminently qualified as a player-coach to impart his ultimate knowledge of this great game.

Since the 17th century when European explorers witnessed this game for the first time, lacrosse has grown in sophistication. A way of life for Native Americans has developed internationally into one of the best games for spectator and athlete alike. The Canadians in 1920, for example, adapted this Native American game to fit the many idle ice hockey rinks in the off-season.

This Native American/Canadian game is a gift from the Creator. Prior to the French name of *La Crosse,* the Native Americans had different names for this sport translated as "bump hips." The game has developed in two directions in the 20th century: the box and the field game. Both are quick and furious; both require great stamina and ball control.

Coach Hinkson masters both types of games in this text. He has fully explained all the individual skills in his first book, *Lacrosse Fundamentals.* He now covers team play both defensively and offensively with a great system and philosophy. The book imparts the spirit and the skills of the game in clear detail. The coaches' drills are outstanding for the novice and pro alike. Understanding Coach Hinkson's ideas will prepare you to win–in this, the fastest game on foot.

Coach Hinkson believes in the beauty of the sport itself for participants and spectators. He builds an arena of dreams and purpose for all. Take advantage of this, the most important book of its kind, explaining why lacrosse is a tradition that continues.

Coach Roy Simmons Jr.
Syracuse University
NCAA Div. 1 National Lacrosse Champions ('83, '88, '89, '90, '93, '95)

CONTENTS

CHAPTER II: ZONE OFFENSE

CHAPTER III: THE FAST-BREAK SYSTEM 99

CHAPTER IV: MAN-TO-MAN TEAM DEFENSE   173

CHAPTER V: 1-4 ZONE DEFENSE

CHAPTER VI: MAN SHORT (5-ON-4 SITUATION)   241

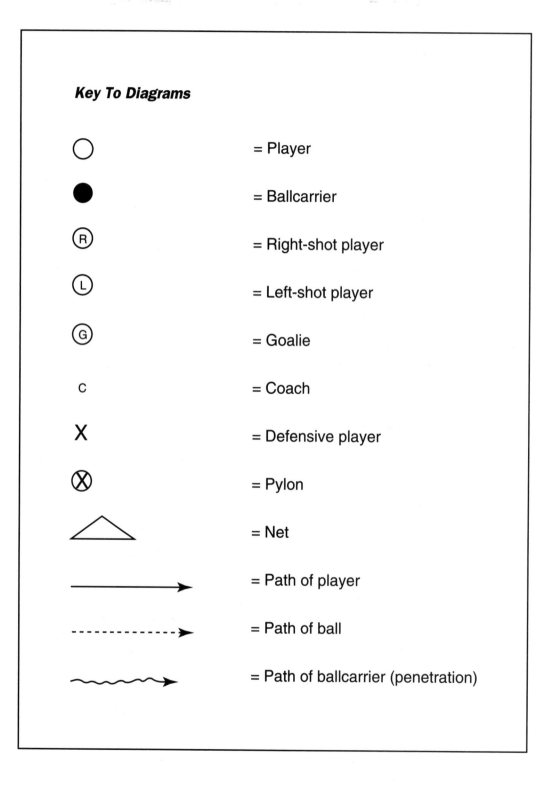

Key To Diagrams

◯	= Player
⬤	= Ballcarrier
Ⓡ	= Right-shot player
Ⓛ	= Left-shot player
Ⓖ	= Goalie
c	= Coach
X	= Defensive player
⊗	= Pylon
△	= Net
⟶	= Path of player
⇢	= Path of ball
∿⟶	= Path of ballcarrier (penetration)

CHAPTER 1: MAN-TO-MAN TEAM OFFENSE

I. OFFENSIVE TERMINOLOGY

1. Strong Side—the side of the floor with three players of the same shot.

2. Weak Side—the side of the floor with only two players of the same shot.

3. Ball Side—the side of the floor where the ball is.

4. Off-Ball Side—the side of the floor opposite the ball.

5. "Passing" or "Shooting" Pass—the perfect pass, i.e., high and outside on the stick side.

6. Getting in the "Clear" to Receive a Pass—popping back out to get open to receive a cross-floor pass or a down pass. The receiver now can pass to a cutter, execute a one-on-one, or set up a play.

7. Cut—movement to get "open" for a scoring opportunity. A player runs in front of his check through the middle of the floor looking for a pass and shot on net.

8. Backdoor Cut—movement to get "open" for a scoring opportunity. A player runs behind his defender looking for a pass and shot on net. The defender is either overplaying or playing even with the cutter.

9. Give-and-Go—when the ballcarrier passes the ball to a teammate and then cuts to get "open" for the return pass and a possible shot on net.

10. Go—used as an element of surprise when a non-ballcarrier just cuts—to the ball or the net—for a pass and a shot on net.

11. One-on-One Move or Penetration Move—the ballcarrier tries to beat his defender for a scoring opportunity.

12. Picks—when an offensive player goes to his teammate's area and sets, with his body and stick, interference on his teammate's defender to set his teammate in the clear for a pass or shot on net.

13. Screens—when an offensive player in his own area interferes with his own defender so his teammate can use this screen to rub out his check to get in the open for a pass or shot on net.

14. Names of Players' Positions on Offense—Creaseman, Cornerman, Pointman.

15. Names of the Playing Surface:

Offensive Zone—the area where the attacking team tries to score. This area is inside the Offensive Zone Line.

Defensive Zone—the area where the defensive team plays to stop the offensive team from scoring. This area is inside the Defensive Zone Line .

Neutral Zone—the area between the Defensive Zone Line and the Offensive Zone Line.

Corner Area of the Arena—the circular area at the end of the arena.

Defensive Face-Off Circles—the two Face-Off Circles located on the side of the floor in the Defensive Zone.

Offensive Face-Off Circles—the two Face-Off Circles located on the side of the floor in the Offensive Zone.

Center Face-Off Circle—the main Face-Off Circle in the center of the floor.

Note: The Official Face-Off Rules of Lacrosse:
1) Small Face-Off Circle Rule—the ball must come out of the small circle before any other player can enter the large circle.
2) Large Face-Off Circle Rule—if a player enters the large circle before the ball comes out of the small circle the non-offending team will be awarded the ball.
3) Face-Off Circle Restraining Line Rule—the centerman's feet cannot move either across the line prior to the start of the draw or until the ball comes out of the small circle.

Defensive Zone Line—the line across the width of the arena from side board to side board to distinguish the defensive area. Also used as a "ragging line" (See CHAPTER IV: MAN SHORT).

Offensive Zone Line—the line across the width of the arena from side board to side board to distinguish the offensive area.

Imaginary Center Line—an imaginary line down the middle of the floor, parallel to the side boards, which makes the shooter aware of shooting around this line. This line also breaks the offensive area into ball side and off-ball side.

Prime Scoring Area—the best position on the floor to score from (see diagram 5).

Imaginary Three Lanes—imaginary lines which divide the floor into three lanes: the Middle Lane and the two Outside Lanes. The Middle Lane consists of two imaginary lines parallel to the side boards and as wide as the goal crease; the two Outside Lanes are measured from these two imaginary lines to the boards. These three lanes help to teach offensive positioning, Fast-Break positioning, and defensive positioning (see diagram 5).

Imaginary Semicircle Shooting Line—an imaginary line that players should be aware of because around this 15-foot line a ballcarrier should be a threat to score (see diagram 5).

Crease—nine-foot radius from the center of the goal line in a semicircle pattern. Offensive players cannot step on this line or they lose possession of the ball.

Net or Goal—made up of two metal goal posts (4 feet long) and a metal cross bar (4 feet long) covered with a netting made of heavy string.

Goal Line—a line from goal post to goal post. If the ball goes past this line it is a goal.

Change Area—a rectangular area made up of two lines (4 feet wide) extending out from the boards and another line as long as the player's bench.

Note: Player Change Rule—a player coming off the playing surface must have one foot in the Change Area before the substitute player comes on the floor.

II. QUESTIONS A COACH SHOULD ASK HIMSELF WHEN PUTTING AN OFFENSIVE SYSTEM TOGETHER

> Do you want the players to fit the system or do you want the system to fit the players?

> Do you give the offensive positions names or numbers?

> How do you start your offense?

> Do you have good floor balance?

> Do you have good line balance, i.e., two left-handers and three right-handers or vice versa?

5   *Prime Scoring Area*
For Left-shot (Shaded Area)

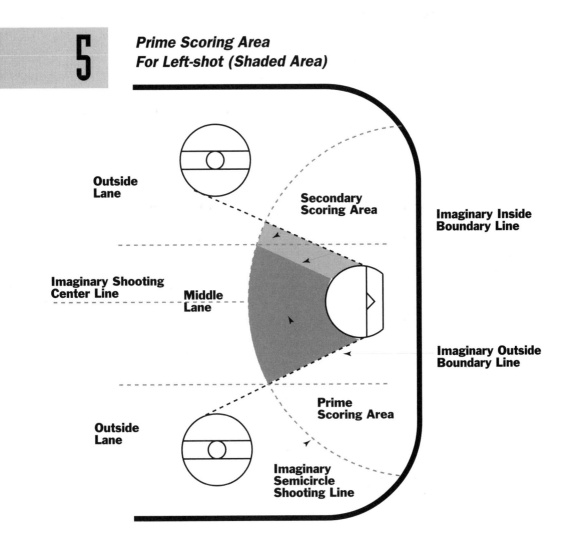

Outside Lane

Secondary Scoring Area

Imaginary Inside Boundary Line

Imaginary Shooting Center Line

Middle Lane

Imaginary Outside Boundary Line

Prime Scoring Area

Outside Lane

Imaginary Semicircle Shooting Line

> What would you do if you had four lefts and one right on a line?

> Do you try to put three equal lines together?

> Do you put your best five players together?

> Do you try to put your best three players together?

> Do you try to complement your goal scorers with good defensive players?

> Do you know how to get your best offensive players "open" against tough checking?

> Does each player on a line know his role?

> Do you have defensive responsibility on a shot?

> Does each player know what a good shot is?

> Do you have "keys" and/or signals to run your set plays?

> Do you have off-ball action while the play is being run on the ball side or vice versa?

> Do you practice the basic offensive fundamentals every day, i.e., passing stationary or on the run, cutting, screening, setting picks, shooting, and one-on-one moves?

III. TYPES OF OFFENSES

A coach has to answer these questions when putting in any type of system: Do you coach according to the talent you have? Do you coach according to your style? Or do you do both?

A. THE CONTINUITY OFFENSE

1. This is an offense that can be reset over and over again.

2. The team could have one of the following general guidelines:
   a. If a player passes down, he must set a Down Screen.
   b. If a player throws a cross-floor pass, he must set a Cross Pick-and-Roll on his side of the floor.
   c. If the ballcarrier does not pass, his teammate on his side of the floor must run an Up Pick-and-Roll.
   d. Or vice versa—pass down, set Cross Pick-and-Roll
   　　　　　　　　—pass across, set Down Screen.

B. SET PLAY OFFENSE

1. A team runs set plays so teammates can anticipate what is going to happen before it happens, and thereby, teammates do not end up running into each other. Usually, if the ball side players work the play, the off-ball side players stay out of their way by exchanging positions or moving. Sometimes it is best if players not directly involved in the play do not move at all and stay where they are.

2. It's not the play as much as the execution of the play. So, do not force the play, let it develop. Players must have patience in working a set play.

3. Set plays give the players something to play out of. But a lot of times by trying to run a set play the players end up getting a "broken" play.

4. Many times the defense will know what the players are trying to accomplish, so it's a matter of timing and execution. It is important that set plays have options and that the players "read the defense."

5. Set plays are run to get the ball to the shooters or to get the goal scorers in the clear.

6. If the set play does not work, the players should go immediately into their normal offense.

7. Some keys for initiating set plays:
   a. Some sort of hand or stick signal.
   b. Eye contact.
   c. A verbal command, such as the name of a color, a number, an animal, etc.

C. THE MOTION OFFENSE

1. The Motion Offense (or "The Passing Game" as it is sometimes called) is made up of passing and cutting (Give-and-Go). Cutters are constantly cutting through the middle of the floor to the point where two cutters cut, one off the tail of the other. It is an offense that gives players freedom within the structure of the offense.

2. This offense is continuous. It is always an ongoing offense of constant motion. It consists of lots of player movement and ball movement. But it is neither a free-lance offense where there is no structure nor a static offense where players have to stop and think to run the plays.

If the team has a problem moving and passing, they go into what is called "a grapevine motion" of passing the ball around the outside of the defense with the passer cutting between the receiver and his check.

Note: One of the major problems with this offense is that the ballcarrier looks to pass too much and consequently, takes himself out of the play. The ballcarrier should always be ready for an opportunity to go one-on-one as determined by the way the defender is playing him or by the situation (no back-up). In this offense, he sometimes looks to pass too much rather than reading the defensive situation.

3. It is a spontaneous offense where the offense is always "reading the defense"; i.e., the defense will tell the offense what to do. There is no defense for the unexpected. That is why deception and the element of surprise are a big part of this offense.

4. With all this passing, a player must be willing to give up the ball. The Motion Offense, then, is based on unselfishness. A lot of ball movement keeps a team happy. The ballcarrier looks to pass first and shoot second.

5. Yet, like most offenses, this Motion Offense does not give equal opportunity on offense. Although the offense still has to be balanced and everybody has to be a threat, individuals must be aware of playing through their star players, i.e., the stars have to handle the ball. Then, they can make the decision of either going one-on-one or passing the ball.

6. The team can have rules, such as "the offense must throw three passes before any player thinks shot"; or "the ball must change from one side of the floor to the other (cross-floor passes) before any player thinks shot."

D. THE PENETRATION OFFENSE OR THE BALL-CONTROL OFFENSE

1. The main emphasis of this offense is based on going one-on-one with teammates clearing out for the ballcarrier. In this offense the ballcarrier looks to shoot first and pass second, which is opposite to the Motion Offense philosophy.

2. This offense is very patient. The team wants to play a slower game, a "half-floor" game, i.e., five-on-five versus a quick running game.

3. The team wants to control the tempo of the game through its offense. If they cannot get a good shot on net within the 30-second rule, the ballcarrier will drop the ball in the corner of the arena to stop any quick breakout by the opposition off a bad or hurried shot.

4. This offense wants to wear the opposition team down by making them work longer on defense by rerunning their plays.

5. Ball control is very important in this offense. Players are very concerned about not turning the ball over easily. The face-off becomes extremely important because this is where everything starts. By getting possession of the ball, the team now controls the tempo of the game and forces the opposition to play defense.

6. This offense likes to work the ball out of the corner of the floor. It initiates its offense with a pass into the corner or the ballcarrier running the ball into the corner. It feels it puts more pressure on the defense by having the ball in the corner: 1) because the defensive players have to turn their backs to their checks to watch the ball, and as a result, their checks cut to the net open; 2) because if the ballcarrier loses the ball in the corner area, the team has three to four players to get back on defense and will be in good shape to stop any odd-man situation (defensing the Fast-Break).

If a player cuts and does not receive a pass, he continues around behind the net and sets up in the corner area for a possible pass and one-on-one.

7. This offense is a more deliberate one where the players run specific plays. They work a lot of Cross Pick-and-Rolls on the ball, and Down Pick-and-Rolls on the ball. During the Pick-and-Roll play, the ballcarrier is always looking to go one-on-one. Therefore he is definitely taking a hit from his defender, which helps to make the Pick-and-Roll play work better.
Remember: The ballcarrier does not leave until the pick is set.

As an element of surprise and to keep the opposition defense honest, this offense will also run a Cross Pick-and-Roll off the ball.

E. THE COMBINATION OFFENSE

1. The Combination Offense Philosophy
a. The Combination Offense is made up of the Motion Offense and the Penetration Offense.
b. The team wants to score the "easy" goals from defensive pressure, defensive steals, defensive hitting, loose balls, and Fast-Breaks. The team then wants to score from their 5-on-5 offense, which is the hardest part of the game to play.
c. The team likes to start the offense in the Outside Lane from the cornerman's area rather than in the corner area or at the top of the offense. This philosophy complements the Fast-Break. (see CHAPTER III: THE FAST-BREAK SYSTEM—Filling the Lanes)

d. The team wants an offense built around getting shots in the Prime Scoring Area from inside the Imaginary Semicircle Line, complemented by shots outside the Imaginary Semicircle Line, i.e., in a 60 percent to 40 percent ratio.

e. The team works for the highest percentage shot, i.e., within the Prime Scoring Area and unmolested (nobody checking the shooter).

f. The combinaton offense team's options are:

1. One-on-One.
2. Give-and-Go or Go Play.
3. Pick-and-Roll on the ball.
4. Pick-and-Roll on the off-ball.
5. Screen on the ball.
6. Screen on the off-ball.

g. The team looks for 50 percent one-on-one play and 50 percent team play.

h. The team wants to attack on offense, i.e., make an action to get a reaction, so that the defense will end up a split second behind them.

i. The offense has to learn to "read the defense," i.e., the defense will tell the offense what to do, by reacting to defensive mistakes.

j. The team runs a basic offense. The team does not do fancy things but rather runs simple plays that do not take much time to set up and are fundamentally sound.

k. The team does not believe in equal opportunity while on offense. They stress roles for players (passers, scorers, checkers, and loose ball players).

l. The team believes that the two best things a player can offer on offense are the perfect pass and help to set a teammate in the clear with a pick or screen.

2. Major Tips for Executing the Combination Offense

a. Players must penetrate, i.e., go one-on-one.

b. Players must go one-on-one from the side of the floor rather than from the middle.

c. Players must start the offense from the Side Lane rather than from the Middle Lane. This is especially true in minor/youth lacrosse.

d. Players must play on their proper side of the floor. Another major problem in minor/youth lacrosse is playing on their wrong side of the floor.

e. Players must move or cut. If players stand and watch the ballcarrier, nothing will happen.

f. Players must pass the ball around the outside of the defense. If they pass through the middle of the defense the ball will be intercepted. A good offensive rule is "players cannot pass into the defense unless a teammate is cutting towards them, or unless nobody is guarding the receiver."

g. Players must look to go one-on-one first and look to pass second.

h. Players must cut through the center, or cut so that their check cannot stay with them easily. They must not just "go through the motion" of cutting but "cut with authority."

i. Players must work to get in the clear.

j. Players must help their teammates get in the clear by setting "solid" screens.

k. Players must "pick" their shots from the Prime Scoring Area. They should not "bomb" their shots at the goalie from anywhere.

l. Players must shoot from their proper side of the floor.

m. Players must play and work together as a team.

3. Things to Ask Players in the Combination Offense

> Did you throw a "shooting" pass?

> Did you go one-on-one when your defender had no backup (defensive help)?

> Did you cut?

> Did you fake the opposite way before you cut?

> Did you set a pick or screen to set a teammate in the clear?

> What did you do after you set a pick or screen?

> If you are the ballcarrier and you pass the ball, what do you do next?

> If you are playing on the off-ball side in the creaseman's position and your cornerman cuts, what do you do?

> How did you initiate the offense?

> If you are playing the creaseman's position, what are you supposed to do after a shot?

> If you are playing the cornerman's or pointman's position, what are you supposed to do after a shot?

> Did you keep your eye on the ball all the time while on offense?

IV. BUILDING THE COMBINATION OFFENSE

Twelve principles a coach must consider when putting this offense together:

A. THE CONCEPT OF THE "GAME" OF LACROSSE

B. BALL MOVEMENT

C. PLAYER MOVEMENT

D. PENETRATION (ONE-ON-ONE)

E. GOOD SHOT SELECTION

F. REBOUNDS ON MISSED SHOTS OR OFF THE GOALIE

G. DEFENSIVE RESPONSIBILITY

H. FLOOR BALANCE (SPACING)

I. FAST-BREAK

J. TURNOVERS

K. INITIATION OF OFFENSE

L. PICKS AND SCREENS

A. THE CONCEPT OF THE "GAME" OF LACROSSE

1. A Mixture of Basketball and Hockey

The game of lacrosse is played much like basketball. Once a team has possession of the ball everybody should be an offensive threat by moving, cutting, and going one-on-one to make it difficult for the defense to defend.

Many hockey coaches also coach the game of lacrosse. Unfortunately, they often coach their defensemen to play back, like in hockey, which hinders the offense as these defensemen do not get involved in the offense as cutters or as a threat when they have the ball. As a result, the defenders guarding them back off and help their defensive teammates.

Accordingly in lacrosse, once a team loses possession of the ball everybody should come back to play defense.

2. The Names of the Players' Positions (see diagram 1)

Again the tendency for coaches is to name the positions of the players as in hockey, such as forwards, centers, and defensemen; although "defensemen" implies playing back on defense. As we have stated this should not be the case in lacrosse when the team is on offense.

It would be a good idea to use new names to designate players' positions. In the Fast-Break System, the following are the names used for positions:

a. Left Creaseman, Right Creaseman—these players play in the so-called forward position, and are usually near the net at the front of the break or on offense.

1

Players' Positions

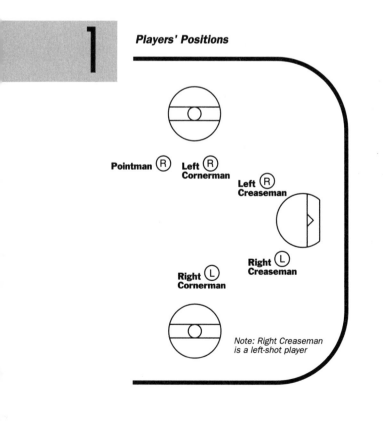

Pointman ®   Left ® Cornerman   Left ® Creaseman   Right Ⓛ Creaseman   Right Ⓛ Cornerman

Note: Right Creaseman is a left-shot player

b. Left Cornerman, Right Cornerman—these players play behind the creasemen with about 15 feet of spacing and bring the ball up the floor most of the time. One of these players is usually the center-man on the team.

c. Pointman—the player can be either a left- or right-hand shot and creates the strong side for that particular line. He lines up behind one of the cornermen.

The offensive players run to predetermined spots on the floor and start their plays out of these spots—one-on-one, cutting, setting picks, or just exchanging positions. Remember that the positions are similar to hockey, but the concept of the game is played similar to basketball.

3. Proper Side of the Floor

The most important principle in playing lacrosse is that players must play on their proper side of the floor. This means a right-handed shot plays on the left side of the floor and a left-handed shot plays on the right side of the floor. From these specific sides the ballcarrier is in a better position to score because his stick is facing the middle of the floor. This gives him a better angle to shoot the ball. Also, a player plays on his proper side of the floor because he will be in a better position to protect his stick with his body from his defender and still see the whole floor.

4. A Contact Sport

Contact in the game of lacrosse is similar to hockey with the body-to-body contact and stick check-ing, but lacrosse has one more element: cross-checking, the main means of stopping the ballcarrier.

When playing lacrosse there is always the threat of being hit. Thus, a player has to learn to relax when taking a hit, to concentrate on playing, and to run the plays with complete abandon.

Certain areas in the game of lacrosse make for great plays due to the contact aspect, such as:

a. When catching a ball, cutting through the middle of the defense and knowing one is going to get hit.

b. When beating a defender, knowing one is going to get hit.

c. When taking a step out in front of the net to get a high percentage shot, knowing one is going to get hit.

d. When going into the corner for a loose ball with a defender, knowing one is going to get hit.

e. When setting up a teammate with a perfect pass, knowing one is going to get hit.

B. BALL MOVEMENT

1. Movement of the Ball on Offense (see diagram 2)

The offense must move the ball around the outside of the defense and especially pass the ball from one side of the floor to the other. The cross-floor pass is one of the toughest passes to complete because of the threat of the defense intercepting the pass and getting a breakaway. Because the offense must swing the ball around the outside of the defense, players must know how to get into the clear. A player should not pass through the middle of the defense as this is another type of pass in which the ball will get picked off. A player passes into the middle of the defense only when a cutter is coming to the ball or when the receiver is all alone.

2. How the Passer Gets in the "Clear" to Start the Give-and-Go (see diagram 3a)

Give-and-Go—when the ballcarrier passes the ball to a teammate and cuts to the ball or net for the return pass and shot on net.

Ball Movement

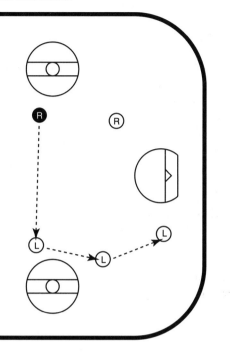

Getting In The Clear

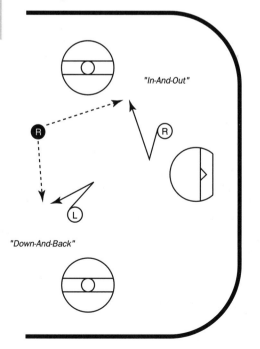

"In-And-Out"

"Down-And-Back"

Go—used as an element of surprise when a non-ballcarrier just cuts to the ball or the net for a pass and shot on net.

Note: The player is just getting in the clear to receive the ball to pass to someone else or make a return pass. He is not cutting to the ball or the net to score.

a. "Down-and-Back" V-Cut (see book *Lacrosse Fundamentals:* CHAPTER 4–PASSING DRILLS)

b. "In-and-Out" V-Cut (see book *Lacrosse Fundamentals:* CHAPTER 4–PASSING DRILLS)

3. The Passer in the "Give-and-Go" or "Go" Play (see diagram 3b)
Good execution of the "give-and-go" play depends on timing, anticipation of the cutter by the passer, and a perfect pass.

a. Movement of the ball in any offense is important rather than holding onto it too long. This delay of hanging onto the ball too long gives the defense time to get into good position to back up the defender checking the ballcarrier. Yet, the passer cannot pass the ball too quickly, as he must allow time for the play to develop.

b. On passing to a cutter through the middle:
(1) The key is to give a "shooting" pass to the stick target and to get the ball to the receiver as soon as possible where he can be a threat.
Remember: A "shooting" pass is one where a receiver does not have to move his stick to receive the pass and then move it again to shoot.

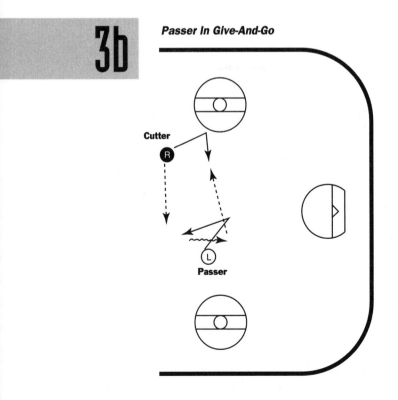

3b   *Passer In Give-And-Go*

Cutter

Passer

(2) The passer must pass away from the defender. If the receiver is closely guarded, the passer must throw the ball out from the receiver's body and away from the defender. The passer becomes the eyes of the receiver as he can see defensively what is happening around him.

(3) The passer wants to get the ball to the cutter before he crosses the Imaginary Center Line of the floor or as he enters into the Middle Lane. Thus, he will have plenty of time to make good decisions and to select his spot on the net and still be in the Prime Scoring Area when he shoots. The offensive rule for the passer is "to pass early, not late" to the cutter.

c. To give this good pass, the passer has to free his stick from defensive pressure by:

(1) Keeping his feet moving. If he stands still, he is easier to check and pressure.

(2) Faking like he is going to go one-on-one, then stepping away to avoid contact and passing unmolested.

(3) Pushing into his defender with his upper arm, then stepping back and passing unmolested.

(4) Setting up the defensive man with his eyes by looking one way to pass, which will draw the defender's stick over to that side to interfere with the pass, then passing the other way unmolested.

(5) Turning his body sideways and using his upper arm to protect his stick. He then leans into his defender and relaxes his body to equalize the pressure created by the defender cross-checking him. Once he stabilizes the checking, he is now in a position to pass.

Note: Holding his stick high and to the side of the body will help keep his hands away from defensive interference. Also, if he is being checked, he should not turn his back to the play, but receive the check on his shoulder pads while looking over his shoulder.

Remember: The ballcarrier is the quarterback on the floor and should be watching what is happening on the whole floor.

d. For best results the passer should be on the same plane as the cutter. By being in the cutter's line of vision, the passer makes it easier for the cutter to see both his defender and the ball.

e. One way of establishing communication between the passer and the cutter is eye contact. Other forms of initiating the play are verbal signals, hand signals, or prearranging which side of the floor to work the play first. The key to the success of the give-and-go play is the anticipation of the cutter by the passer and the skill level to catch the ball by the cutter.

f. To try to get more movement in the offense use this offensive rule: "The passer does not pass to a teammate if the receiver is standing still."

g. The passer must also be a scoring threat as a one-on-one player. He becomes a threat by:

(1) Playing the ball from the side of the floor—the Outside Lane—rather than in the Middle Lane. This position gives him more room to beat his defender and enables him to still end up in the Prime Scoring Area. Also, from this position the cutter will be at a better angle for him to see both the ball on the pass and his defender.

(2) Looking at the net rather than at the cutter. He can use his peripheral vision to see the cutter.

h. The speed of the pass depends on the distance of the receiver from the passer and the catching ability of the receiver.

Remember: It takes two to make a completed pass: the passer and the receiver.

C. PLAYER MOVEMENT

Players must learn to move without the ball. Getting in the clear to receive a pass and getting open to cut to the net are the two hardest things to do in lacrosse because they take hard work. One way of measuring a player's play is by the success he has in getting open.

Stress to players that movement and speed create fatigue in the opposition, loss of concentration by the opposition, and thereby great scoring opportunities for the offense.

Note: Sometimes on offense players do not always have to move. They may have to stay where they are so that they do not mess up the play, i.e., get in the way of a teammate.

1. The Cutter Passes the Ball to Start the Give-and-Go Play

a. Cross-Floor Pass
The receiver does a "Down-and-Back" V-cut to get in the clear for this cross-floor pass.

It is an excellent idea to move the ball from one side of the floor to the other. By "swinging the ball," the defense has to move from ball side defense to off-ball side defense making it harder for the defensive players to back up the defender checking the ballcarrier.

Also, moving the ball from side to side limits the goalie's ability to play good angles because he has to keep readjusting his position. This ball movement will not give him the time he wants to be set and in good position. This is especially important when the opposition goalie is large. If a team can get the large goalie moving laterally across the net, he will be even more vulnerable to being out of position when receiving shots on net.

b. Down Pass
The receiver does an "In-and-Out" V-cut to get in the clear for this down pass.

It is a good idea to pass the ball down to the corner area to draw the defense down, then the receiver can go one-on-one or pass back out to the top for a play.

c. The offensive rule is "If you pass, you must cut." On any pass—cross-floor or down—to a non-cutting player, the passer must cut for the return pass unless it is a set play. This rule gets rid of any standing around and creates movement.

2. The Cutter Cuts in the "Give-and-Go" or "Go" Play (see diagram 4a)

a. Why Pass and Cut:
(1) Players cut to get open for a pass and a shot. They either cut towards the net or towards the ball to receive a pass and hopefully get a good shot on net. It is just a matter of getting one step in front of the defender or just getting on the inside of the defender.
(2) Even if a player does not get into the open on his cut, at least he will keep his defender busy and thereby prevent him from helping out his defensive teammate who is checking the ballcarrier. Especially, if running a play on the ball side, the players on the off-ball side should keep moving and work their play (2nd option). Again, even if they do not get in the play, they will at least keep their defensive men busy who in turn will not be able to back up the ball.
(3) Stationary offensive players are the easiest kind of players to check. In addition, the lack of movement makes it easier for the defensive men to back up their teammate. Moreover, big players can do a lot of slashing and hard cross-checking when offensive players are not moving. By moving, it is harder for the big defender to stay with the offensive player especially if the offensive player is quicker. The big defender will have a tendency to overcommit and wear down as the game goes on. By moving, players stay away from heavy contact and, thereby, are freer to move. A team in offensive trouble is characterized by players standing around.

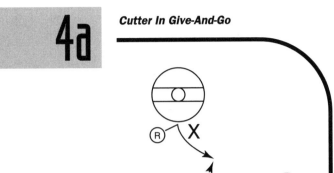

4a

Cutter In Give-And-Go

b. When to Cut:

In the "Give-and-Go" play timing is important. Perfect coordination must occur between the passer and the cutter, i.e., the passer must release the ball just as the cutter makes his cut.

(1) The cutter must use a degree of deception (fake), an element of surprise, and a move of quickness (first step), so that the defense will be a split second behind him. The cutter wants to get in front of his defender or at least on the inside of the defender's body.

(2) To time the pass and anticipate the passer (knowing when the cutter is cutting), the cutter must establish eye contact with the passer to let him know he is going to cut. The offensive rule "the cutter cuts late, not early" is to give the passer time to get ready to pass. All the cutting in the world will not help if the ballcarrier is not looking for the cutter.

(3) If the cutter is open and the ballcarrier does not see him, he calls "Ball" for the pass. This verbal communication could alert the defense and should only be done in an emergency, i.e., when the cutter is wide open.

(4) When the cutter cuts, he moves quickly and with a purpose.

(5) When a player cuts he must keep going to the ball until he receives it. If he stops to catch the ball, he might get intercepted or stick checked.

(6) When a player cuts, he must cut completely through the middle area and not stop halfway through to clog it up. The offense wants the Middle Lane clear for other cutters and, especially, for the ballcarrier, in case he wants to go one-on-one.

(7) If a cutter does not get the ball on a cut, he continues on behind the net or stops just past the Imaginary Center Line and returns to his proper side of the floor.

c. How the cutter gets open to cut to the net or to the ball:

Generally, players beat their defender the same way they would with the ball.

(1) Fake—the same movement as the ballcarrier is used by the cutter to get the defender leaning or moving sideways and thinking he is going one way while he goes the other way. The offensive rule

"if I cut, I fake first" reminds the players of the importance of the fake. To help their timing, the two give-and-go players can use precise patterns. For example, after the pass, the cutter will take three steps down and cut.

(2) Stutter Steps—the cutter runs straight at the defender then makes several quick steps to get the defender off balance then reacts accordingly. The cutter always tries to cut on the inside of the defender, but if he is overplayed, he can cut outside (backdoor) to the net.

(3) Pivot—this is just a quick spin move to end up on the inside of the defender.

(4) Backdoor Cut—this is usually executed when the defender overplays the offensive player and starts playing out higher on the defense in which case the offensive player cuts behind him (see diagram 4b).

(5) Change of Pace—usually the player starts with the ball and passes it. He relaxes and moves lazily, walking or jogging, towards the crease area. He then quickly breaks to the ball. Other options after the pass: he can just stand still (hesitate or delay) and then cut; or just cut right away.

(6) Knock opponent's stick down and break.

(7) Cross-Check—push off on the defender with his stick to get an advantage.

(8) Pick-and-Roll—with the non-ballcarrier on the same side of the floor.

(9) Use a Screen—cut off a screen set by a teammate.

(10) Fake a Pick-and-Roll and cut.

d. If Being Checked on the Cut:

When a player cuts he will either be one step ahead of his check or he will be cutting with his check right on him.

(1) When cutting always expect a pass and cut with the stick up ready to shoot.

(2) Always give a good stick target for the passer and concentrate on watching the ball all the way into the pocket, even though being hit.

4b

Cutter Cutting Backdoor

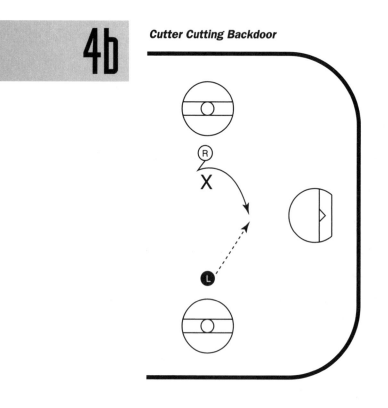

(3) When cutting always expect to get hit so that when it comes it will not be a surprise.

(4) Be prepared to get hit by being totally relaxed from the waist up. Do not shrink or tighten up on impact. If a player stiffens up on contact, he will be holding his stick too tight to catch the ball.

(5) On contact from the cross-check, the cutter should dip his inside shoulder and lean his body weight into his checker's stick to equalize pressure and stabilize his opponent's stick when catching the ball. The defender, from this body weight, will have a tough time pushing his stick forward to give the cutter a jarring cross-check.

(6) On cutting through the middle for a pass some players like to even shorten up on their grip on the stick, holding it at the throat with the top hand and in the middle of the shaft with the bottom hand. They feel this grip makes it easier to catch a pass and control the ball when being checked or when in a crowd.

e. The Shot

The cutter has to make a decision of taking either a quick shot or hanging onto the ball for a split second more. Do not just catch and shoot automatically without taking a slight look at the net. Players must learn to shoot quickly but not to hurry their shot.

f. Common Mistakes in Executing the "Give-and-Go"

(1) Poor timing; receiving the ball too late.

(2) Bad passing.

(3) No fake preceding the cut to get into the "open."

(4) Stick not in the shooting position; no target.

(5) Shooting too quickly; shooting without "picking"; or shooting off balance.

(6) Cutting into the middle, then standing, waiting for the pass with the possibility of the ball being intercepted, or just clogging up the middle of the floor for other cutters.

D. PENETRATION (ONE-ON-ONE)

1. The ballcarrier must be a scoring threat on offense to contribute to the team.

2. The best time for the ballcarrier to go one-on-one is when the play is still flowing into the Offensive Zone. The opposition defense will still be looking for their checks and will not be in the best position to back up their teammate checking the ballcarrier.

3. Once the five defensive players are in their zone and set, it is much tougher to go one-on-one. Therefore, in the 5-on-5 offense, more passing and player movement will create more chances of confusion and a better possibility of going one-on-one.

4. A one-on-one situation on a weak check takes precedence over anything else.

5. The offensive players can run set plays or a clear out for the ballcarrier to go one-on-one (to isolate the ballcarrier with no backup).

6. Make the ballcarrier hard to defend by teaching the players to go both ways, to have an inside shooting game, and to have an outside shooting game.

E. GOOD SHOT SELECTION

The team shooting objective for each game is 20 percent or approximately 12 goals on 60 shots. The shots on goal objective is 70 percent or roughly 42 shots on net on 60 attempts.

Do players understand what a good shot is?

1. Location on Floor
As the angle of the shot is important, the shooter should know the best position on the floor to score from—the "Prime Scoring Area" (see diagram 5).

2. Distance
The shooter should shoot in his range, i.e., whatever is comfortable. Some players like to shoot in close, some like to shoot from a long distance around the Imaginary Semicircle Line.

3. Defensive Pressure
If a shooter is "open," he will get a better shot off than if he is closely checked when shooting.

4. Shot Selection
Good shooters shoot relaxed, are confident, and have quick releases. They take good shots, "picking" for the open spots on the net rather than bombing their shots (just shooting at the net). They are very disciplined shooters and take only shots they can make; i.e., they understand that "hope" shots only lend hope to the opposition.

5. Who Shoots
Offense is not a game of equality. The coach must base his offensive attack around shooters who can shoot 25 percent or more in practice.

6. Shot Distribution
It is also important that each player knows his role on the team. Try to put two to three shooters on a line. Get a good idea of who the good shooters are by rating the shooting percentage at the shooting board in practice. Then rank the players offensively based on this shooting percentage.

The challenge for the coach is "to get the ball to the player who has the 'hot stick' in a game."

F. REBOUNDS ON MISSED SHOTS OR OFF THE GOALIE

Usually after a missed shot, send two players to the boards for rebounds and loose balls, as the team defensive philosophy is never to concede a loose ball to the opposition and to pressure the ball constantly.

G. DEFENSIVE RESPONSIBILITY
(See CHAPTER IV: MAN-TO-MAN TEAM DEFENSE)

Teaching players to get back on defense is hard to do; make sure this situation is drilled over and over. When the offense takes a shot, send one to two players instantly back on defense. On reacting back, physical quickness is important, but mental quickness is even more important. To come back every time on defense must become a habit which a player just does. It is believed that the ratio of physical quickness to mental quickness is one to five. This habit is learned through drills and verbal reinforcement.

Who comes back on defense:
1. A specific player can be designated so that it is his job to come back first.
2. The coach can verbally reinforce who is coming back on defense during a game.
3. The coach can have general guidelines:
   a. If the ballcarrier, in the cornerman's position, is only a passer, then his priority after he passes is to react back first on the shot.

b. If the ballcarrier, in the cornerman's position, is the shooter, then he must be ready to react back second on the shot.

c. The second player back is always the cornerman opposite to the first cornerman reacting back or the pointman.

d. If the cornerman is taking a close-in shot, then the creaseman on his side of the floor will drop back to take his spot, and consequently his defensive responsibility of coming back second.

H. FLOOR BALANCE (SPACING)

The players are given positions to keep them spaced out between 12 to 15 feet. This spacing gives the players more room to operate, stops them from running into each other, and prevents the defense from possibly double-teaming the ballcarrier. Players should be taught to play out of their spots on the offense, stay in their lanes, and know how and when to move (see CHAPTER I: MAN-TO-MAN TEAM OFFENSE—Initiation of Offense; CHAPTER III, THE FAST-BREAK SYSTEM—Filling the Lanes).

I. FAST-BREAK

A team must have a transition game in their offense (see CHAPTER III: THE FAST-BREAK SYSTEM).

J. TURNOVERS

It is a fact that Fast-Break Teams will have more turnovers than Ball-Control Teams. The law of averages would suggest that if a team passes the ball a lot, it will have more chances of errors, turnovers, or dropped passes. No matter what kind of system a team plays, the question is "How many turnovers can a coach live with?" A coach must know that for every turnover, there is a possibility of a two-goal difference—a possible goal for the opposition and a possible goal for his team. To help cut down on turnovers a team must have the right type of players carrying the ball up the floor.

K. INITIATION OF OFFENSE

1. How does a team start its offense? It is important to initiate the offense in a specific way so that the players on both sides of the floor know what is going on and do not run into each other.

2. The offense can be initiated when the ballcarrier is at the top of the Middle Lane of the offense, in the Outside Lane of the offense, in the corner area of the floor, or behind the net.

3. The offense can be initiated from a one-on-one situation, from a pass to the corner area, or from a cross-floor pass.
Recall: The receiver does a "Down-and-Back" V-cut to get in the clear for the cross-floor pass. The receiver does an "In-and-Out" V-cut to get in the clear for the down pass.

4. No matter how a team starts its offense, learning to "read and react" to what the defense gives them is the first priority all the time, even over a set play.

5. The team can initiate the offense from a specific side of the floor. That is, the right side of the offense always works their side of the floor first no matter where the ball is or vice versa.

6. The team can initiate the offense in regards to where the ball is. The ball side players work their side of the floor first. The players on the off-ball side run a delay play as a second option. Or the first option is the off-ball play and the second option is on the ball side.

7. The team can initiate the offense in regards to the weak side (the side with only two players) or the strong side (the side with three players). The first option could be the weak side with the second option being the strong side (no matter where the ball is) or vice versa.

8. The offense can be initiated as follows by the ballcarrier who is usually a cornerman or pointman:
   a. If he looks directly to the weak side (play initiated by eye contact), then he is looking for an off-ball play.
   b. If he looks down but does not pass down to the corner area immediately, then the bottom man comes up to execute a ball side play. On a ball side play, the off-ball side will run an interchange without a cut through the middle. This off-ball interchange will keep the defensive players busy.
   c. If he throws a cross-floor pass, he can cut to the net (Give-and-Go), go set a screen or pick for a teammate on his side of the floor, or pretend to cut and pop out for a return pass.
   d. If he throws a down pass to the corner area, he can set a Screen, set a Down Pick on the ball, or clear out for a one-on-one from the corner. If the defense sags when the ball is in the corner, then this creaseman can move the ball back out quickly to the top for a shot.

9. The offense can be initiated in regards to diagonal plays. If the ball is in the cornerman's position, then the first option is his teammate on the off-ball side kitty-corner to the ball. If the ball is in the creaseman's position, then the first option is his teammate on the off-ball side kitty-corner to the ball.

10. The offense can be initiated from the fast-break. As the team enters the Offensive Zone and there is no odd-man situation, the team runs their secondary break and goes right into their offense.

11. Other variations of initiating the offense:
   a. By eye contact.
   b. By a verbal command, such as actually calling "Pick," or camouflaging the play with a name such as "Bear."
   c. By hand signals.
   d. By numbering the players on the right side of the floor with even numbers and the players on the left side of the floor with odd numbers. When a player calls an even number, the team is going to run a play on the right side of the floor.
   e. By letting the pointman dictate the side of the floor the play will be run. If he goes down the right side, the team works that side first or vice versa.

L. PICKS AND SCREENS

Pick—when a player goes to his teammate's area and sets, with his body and stick, interference on his teammate's defender to put his teammate in the clear.

Screen—when a player in an area, close to his teammate, interferes with his own defender so his teammate can use this screen to rub out his check to get in the clear for a pass or at least create space to catch the ball and go one-on-one.

1. Pick and Screen Strategy

a. The main purpose of picks and screens is to set a teammate in the clear for a shot or a pass. These picks and screens are one of the main weapons for the coach to help get his goal scorers in the clear to make their task of scoring goals easier.

b. Usually the better checkers pick up the better scorers. So the offensive team has to use picks and screens to create mismatches by forcing a switch by the defense to get a poor checker on a good scorer or by forcing a smaller defender to check a bigger offensive player.

2. The Action-Reaction Principle

In lacrosse either the offense creates the action or the defense creates the action. If the offense creates the action, it will force the play and thereby create a reaction by the defense, which will be a slight physical delay with the defense chasing the offense.

If the offensive team sets a pick (action) and forces the defense to switch (reaction), something good will happen offensively; i.e., the defense will be trying to catch up. Some teams feel a successful pick is one which creates a "switch" by the two defensive players.

But if the offense sets a pick and the defense is ready to switch (action), now the defense dictates the action and the offense will react. In this situation the offense must still have another action (counter) to get a reaction from the defense.

So the question is: Is the offense creating the switch or is the defense initiating the switch?

Note: There are here many possibilities of pick and screen plays for the coach to try with his team. He can choose a specific pick or screen play on the strengths of his players or by trial and error. If he decides he wants to use picks and screens in his offensive scheme, his progression should be to start with one particular pick or screen play with one option only. When the players get this specific play refined, he can then work on the second option or counter play to the defense. Later, the coach can then add a second specific pick or screen play with one option, then two options. A coach should have only three or four pick and screen plays with one or two options.

Summary of the "Up Series" and the "Down Series" for Picks and Screens

Ball Side Up Series
The key—the cornerman keeps the ball.
a. Up Pick-and-Roll
b. Cross Pick-and-Roll
c. Up Screen
d. Fake Up Pick-and-Roll

Ball Side Down Series
The key—a down pass to the creaseman.
a. Down Screen
b. Down Pick-and-Roll

Off-Ball Up Series
The key—the ball side cornerman keeps the ball.
a. Up Pick-and-Roll
b. Up Interchange
c. Up Fake Pick-and-Roll
d. Up Screen
e. Cross Pick-and-Roll options:
    (1) Picker "Pops"
    (2) Picker "Cuts"
    (3) Picker "Curls"
    (4) Cutter cuts "Backdoor"
    (5) "Double" Pick—cutter sets second pick

Off-Ball Down Series
The key—the ball side cornerman keeps the ball.
a. Down Screen
b. Down Pick-and-Roll (versus the regular, sagging, or switching defense):
    (1) Picker "Pops"
    (2) Picker "Cuts" to net
    (3) Picker "Curls"
    (4) Cutter "Out"
    (5) Cutter cuts "Backdoor"
    (6) "Double" Pick—cutter sets second pick
c. Down Interchange
d. Down Fake Pick-and-Roll

3. Ball Side Up Series

a. Up Pick-and-Roll on the Ball (see diagram 6a, 6b)

Key for Initiating the Up Pick-and-Roll
If the top man does not pass down immediately, the bottom man comes up to start the play.

Setting an Up Pick:
(1) Inside-Out Theory
The picker starts to cut into the middle to make his check think he is cutting for a pass. He then changes direction and comes back to set the Up Pick. By running this V-pattern the picker comes up behind the defender checking the ballcarrier, making it harder for him to see the pick being set. If the picker runs up in a straight line, the checker on the ballcarrier will see him coming out of the corner of his eye (peripheral vision) and anticipate the play.
(2) Floor Position
The players like to work the Up Pick-and-Roll play on the side of the floor rather than in the middle of the floor to give themselves more room to operate. It also helps before the pick is set that the ballcarrier is in the Prime Scoring Area.
(3) "Headhunt"
Stress making physical contact when setting the pick on the defender. Common mistakes made by players include not setting the pick well by "picking air" or setting a half pick on the defender rather than a full pick, i.e., making physical contact on his teammate's defender. When setting the pick do the following: face the defender; take a stance wider than shoulder width apart; keep the knees bent; cut the defender in half by straddling the defender's back leg; and place the stick in a cross-checking position on the side of the defender's body to block the path of the defender. Another major mistake made by players is placing their stick on the defender's back, thereby giving the defender room to squeeze through the Up Pick and staying with the ballcarrier.
Note: Some players like to set the pick with their back to the defender, but in this position they have a hard time maintaining contact.
(4) Angle of Pick
Setting the proper angle is key to making the Up Pick-and-Roll work. Besides straddling the defender's back leg, place the body directly in front of the defender's path, which is usually towards the net.
(5) Picker's Move
After the ballcarrier cuts by his outside shoulder, the picker turns (rolls), faces the direction of the ballcarrier, and follows the ball with his eyes and his body (versus turning his back to the ballcarrier, then cutting to the net). Follow the offensive rule of "never taking one's eyes off the ball." Also by turning this way the picker will not get the head of his stick caught up in the defender's body. A major problem in setting the Up Pick-and-Roll is that the picker starts to roll to the net before the

6a

Up Pick-&-Roll (On The Ball)

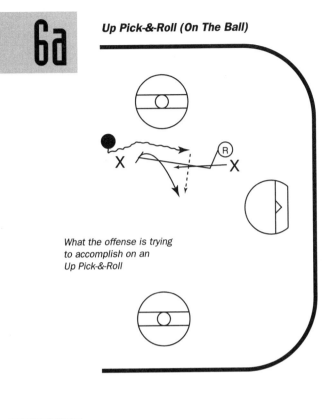

What the offense is trying
to accomplish on an
Up Pick-&-Roll

6b

Defending Against Up Pick-&-Roll

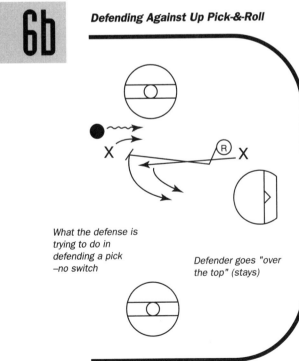

What the defense is
trying to do in
defending a pick
–no switch

Defender goes "over
the top" (stays)

ballcarrier is past his shoulder. As a result, the defender "goes over top" of the pick and stays with the ballcarrier. The picker's job is to block the path of the ballcarrier's defender to prevent him from staying with the ballcarrier. The offensive pick rule is "the picker does not leave early and holds the defender for a count of '1,000...2,000.'"

Even though the picker is trying to set the ballcarrier in the clear, with all the confusion, the picker ends up being in the clear. Consequently, the picker gets the pass and shot on net. So, players should follow the philosophy: "By helping someone else, they help themselves."

Using the Up Pick:
(1) The Way to Cut
It is the picker that designates which way the ballcarrier will go. In the execution of the "Up Pick-and-Roll" the picker sets the pick behind the ballcarrier's defender signaling the ballcarrier to cut to the outside and towards the net.
(2) Wait
The ballcarrier must wait for the pick to be set before using it. If the ballcarrier leaves too soon before the pick is set, the ballcarrier's defender will have enough space between the picker and the ballcarrier to go over top of the pick. Also, if the picker is moving when trying to set the pick, he might be called for a moving pick (interference). Besides, it is much harder to set a pick on a moving defender than a stationary defender.
(3) Fake First
To set his check up, the ballcarrier must keep his defender busy by making it look like he is actually trying to beat him and by faking in the opposite direction he wants to go. In this case, he fakes as if he is going to cut across the top of the floor, then cuts back to the outside of the defender. By just moving slightly, the ballcarrier gets the attention of his defender as the pick is being set rather than his defender seeing or anticipating the pick being set.
(4) Touch Shoulders
When using the Up Pick the ballcarrier cuts close to his teammate and tries to touch his teammate's outside shoulder to "rub out" his defender.
(5) Coming Off the Up Pick
The defenders will tell the offensive players, by their movement (reaction to the pick), what kind of play they should make. Once the ballcarrier is past the picker, he has to read the situation ("read the defense") to decide what he is going to do, i.e., hang on to the ball or pass to the picker cutting to the net.
    (a) If the ballcarrier's defender is picked off, the ballcarrier cuts to the net looking to score rather than fading away looking to pass. If he fades away looking to pass, the other defender (the defender that was checking the picker) will only stay in the middle of the two offensive players looking to intercept the pass and nothing offensively will happen.
    (b) If the defense switch assignments, i.e., the ballcarrier draws his teammate's defender, the ballcarrier can now throw a lob or "rainbow" pass to the picker cutting towards the net who is now a step in front of his new defender. Or at least with the space created on the switch, the ballcarrier can take a shot or, with his momentum, go one-on-one (see diagram 6c).

b. Cross Pick-and-Roll on the Ball (see diagram 7)

Setting the Cross Pick
This is the same as setting the Up Pick-and-Roll except:
(1) On the Inside-Out theory the picker comes up beside or on the inside of the defender checking the ballcarrier.
(2) When "Headhunting" the picker cuts the defender in half by straddling his front or inside leg. Make sure the stick is placed on the side of the defender's body.

6c

Up Pick-&-Roll

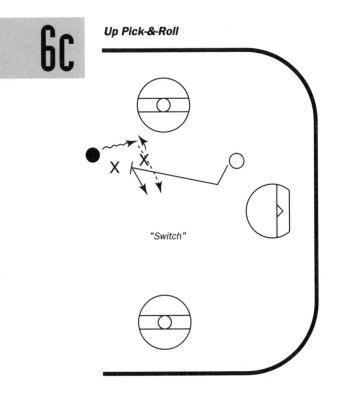

"Switch"

7

Cross Pick-&-Roll (On The Ball)

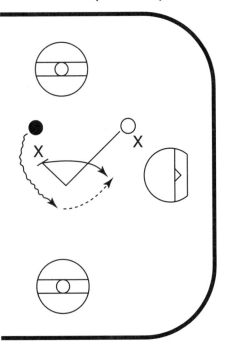

(3) To get a good angle the picker puts his body directly in front of the defender's path which is usually in the direction of the net.

(4) As soon as the ballcarrier passes his shoulder, the picker rolls facing the direction of the ballcarrier so he never loses sight of the ball.

Variation: As soon as the picker makes contact with the defender, he rolls right away and does not wait for the ballcarrier to make his move. Because this is a quicker move, the picker will get the element of surprise.

Using the Cross Pick
This is the same as using the Up Pick-and-Roll except:

(1) The picker determines the direction the ballcarrier will go by setting the pick on the inside side of the defender's body signaling the ballcarrier to cut across the top and towards the net.

(2) To set his check up the ballcarrier fakes as if he is going to go outside, then cuts back across the top of the floor.

(3) The ballcarrier has the same options as in executing the Up Pick-and-Roll: shooting, passing to the picker rolling to the net, or going one-on-one. In the Cross Pick play the ballcarrier has good momentum going across the top, so even if the defenders slow down the Cross Pick-and-Roll, the ballcarrier still can make a good one-on-one move with the space created by the pick.

c. Up Screen on the Ball

Setting the Up Screen
(1) The bottom offensive man (creaseman) fakes as if he is going to set an Up Pick to get the attention of his defender.

(2) Two things can happen here:
   (a) The defender will push him out of the way trying to prevent him from setting the so-called pick. As a result, the defender could get tied up when cross-checking (see diagram 8a).
   (b) The bottom offensive man on the way up to set the so-called pick ties up his check by suddenly pivoting on his inside foot and swinging his outside foot backwards. Thus, he ends up below his defender and blocks his path with his back, thereby creating a screen. This move helps prevent the screener's defender from switching to help his defensive teammate as the ballcarrier cuts outside of the screen (see diagram 8b).

Using the Up Screen
(1) Two things should be noted here:
   (a) The ballcarrier reads the situation and, seeing his teammate being tied up by his check, uses it as a screen and cuts outside, rubbing his defender out of the way.
   (b) Or on a verbal signal the bottom offensive man (creaseman) sets an actual Up Screen for the ballcarrier.

d. Fake Up Pick-and-Roll on the Ball (see diagram 9)

(1) The Fake Up Pick-and-Roll is best accomplished when the picker's defender is cheating, i.e., staying slightly behind the picker anticipating an Up Pick-and-Roll play and thereby prepared to switch with his defensive teammate.

(2) As the creaseman goes up to set the pick, he reads his defender backing off, i.e., he feels or sees his check back off. He then cuts towards the net without making any contact.

(3) Seeing this move by his teammate the ballcarrier breaks quickly to the outside of his check, hopefully to draw both defenders, and then throws a "lob" pass to the faking picker who is now cutting to the net.

8a

Up Screen (On The Ball)

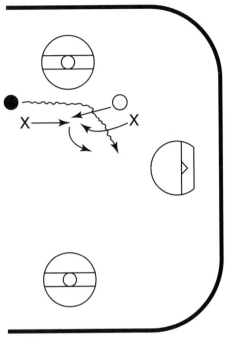

8b

Up Screen (On The Ball)

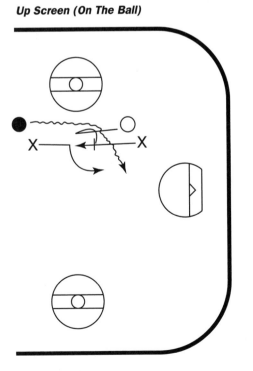

9 *Fake Up Pick-&-Roll (On The Ball)*

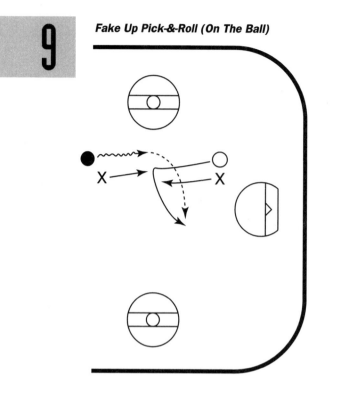

4. Ball Side Down Series

a. Down Screen on the Ball (see diagram 10)

Key for Initiating the Down Screen—the cornerman passes to the creaseman.

Setting the Down Screen
(1) To set a good Down Screen the screener does not run a straight line down to the ballcarrier but cuts in the direction of the net. It is important the screener gets inside his defender by faking a cut to the net and by looking as if he wants a return pass from the ballcarrier. He should make the cut look like he really wants the ball, even to the point of putting his stick out in front of himself, looking at the ballcarrier, and calling for the pass. If he cuts like a real threat, his defender will have to play him seriously and turn his back to the ballcarrier. The result of this fake cut is to prevent his defender from anticipating what is going to happen and thereby prevent him from switching.

Note: If the screener can't get on the inside of his defender, he continues on the outside of his defender, then spins back around and blocks him out (see diagram 11).
(2) The screener wants to set the screen around the inside edge of the Outside Lane and near the area of the ballcarrier.
(3) The screener on his cut is not trying to beat his defender. He should go slowly, letting his defender stay with him.
(4) The screener, on reaching a point close to the Prime Scoring Area and the ballcarrier, stops and steps in front of his check to interfere with his path in case he tries to switch checks. When setting the screen face the defender, take a wide stance, and put the stick over the opponent's stick to prevent him from switching off to help his teammate if he gets screened off.

10 ***Down Screen (On The Ball)***

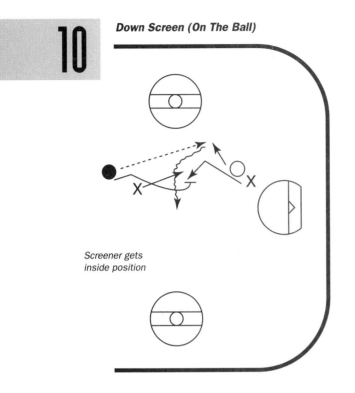

*Screener gets
inside position*

11 ***Down Screen (On The Ball)***

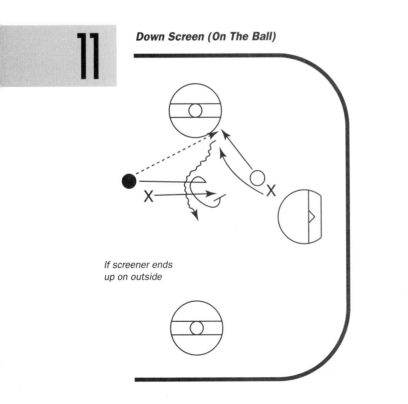

*If screener ends
up on outside*

Note: The defensive man may create a screen himself by trying to tie up the screener.

Using the Down Screen
(1) Timing and the element of surprise are important for the success of the play; i.e., as the screener cuts to the net the ballcarrier is starting his move towards the spot where the screen is going to be set.
(2) While the player is setting up the screen the ballcarrier must set up his check to come off the screen properly. The ballcarrier starts his move as soon as he gets the ball. He does not wait for the screen, but when he finishes his move, hopefully the screen will be set for the purpose of rubbing out his check. It is the responsibility of the ballcarrier to take his defender to the screen rather than waiting for the screen to come to his area. However, both the screener and the ballcarrier can meet simultaneously or half way.
(3) It is up to the ballcarrier to use the screen by rubbing shoulders with his teammate.
(4) If the ballcarrier's check is impeded by the screen, the ballcarrier will be "home free" because his check's teammate will be tied up and will not be able to help out by switching.
(5) If the ballcarrier's check goes behind the screen, the ballcarrier will have some space to shoot, fake a shot and go one-on-one, or have momentum to beat his check.

b. Down Pick-and-Roll on the Ball (see diagram 12a)
(1) This is similar to the Up Pick-and-Roll.
(2) On setting the pick, the picker uses the Inside-Out theory; "Headhunts"; sets the pick straddling the inside leg; places the stick across the side of the defender's body; rolls to the net facing the ball after the ballcarrier passes his outside shoulder; and cuts with his stick in front of his body.
(3) The ballcarrier must wait for the Down Pick; fake the opposite way he wants to go; rub his teammate's shoulder; and, if there is a defensive switch, pass to the picker "leading" him with a soft lob pass.
(4) Variations:
   (a) The picker fakes a Down Pick, then pivots to get the inside position and runs besides his defender creating interference for the ballcarrier. The picker pivots to interfere with his own check so there is no defensive switch. The best time to pivot is just before the cutter goes by him (see diagram 12b).
   (b) The picker sets a phony Down Pick, letting the ballcarrier's defender go over the top of the screen, and then he sets a second pick (see diagram 13).

5. Off-Ball Up Series
a. Up Pick-and-Roll on the Off-Ball (see diagram 14a, 14b)
(1) Set the Pick the same way as the Up Pick-and-Roll on the ball.
(2) The cutter uses the pick the same way as the Up Pick-and-Roll on the ball. The ballcarrier looks to pass to the cutter first, picker second.
(3) The offensive spacing rule is "the cutter cuts to the net and the picker cuts (pops) or steps to the ball." This rule creates good spacing for both players so that they will not get in each other's way.
(4) The ballcarrier's passing rule against a switching defense is "to look to pass to the picker first, the cutter second."

b. Up Interchange on the Off-Ball (see diagram 15)
(1) Rather than waiting for the Up Pick, the cornerman starts to move towards the creaseman.
(2) The creaseman on his fake Up Pick aims for the inside of his teammate's defender's body.
(3) The cornerman cuts hard outside forcing a switch and picks up the creaseman's check. The creaseman already has the inside position on his new defender and cuts to the ball.

c. Up Fake Pick-and-Roll on the Off-Ball (see diagram 16)
(1) The same motion as the Up Pick-and-Roll is used, but just before setting the pick, the picker cuts to the ball.

Down Pick-&-Roll (On The Ball)

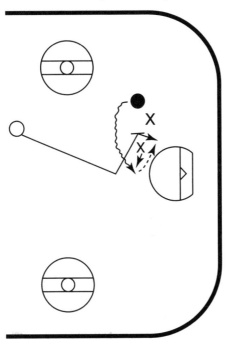

Down Pick-&-Roll (On The Ball)

Pivot

13

Down Pick-&-Roll

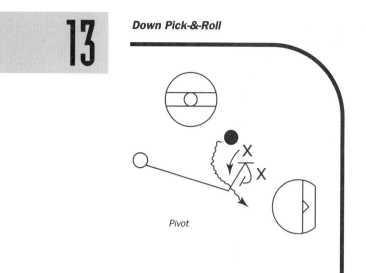

Pivot

14a

Up Pick-&-Roll (On The Off-Ball) - 1st Option

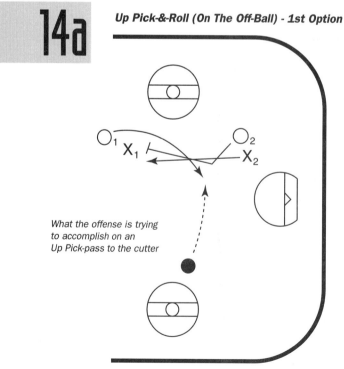

*What the offense is trying
to accomplish on an
Up Pick-pass to the cutter*

14b

Up Pick-&-Roll (On The Off-Ball) - 2nd Option

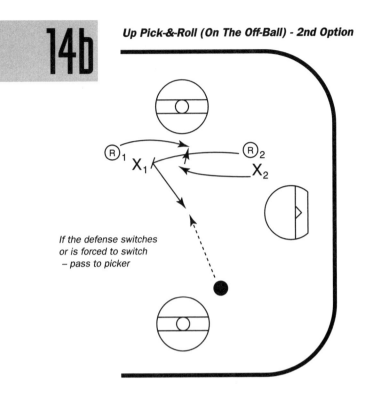

*If the defense switches
or is forced to switch
– pass to picker*

15

Up Interchange (On The Off-Ball)

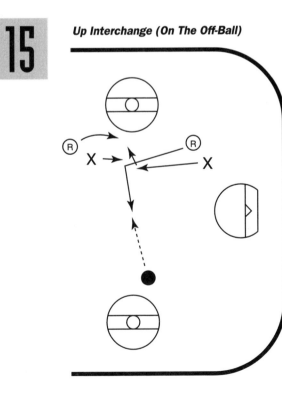

16 *Up Fake Pick-&-Roll (On The Off-Ball)*

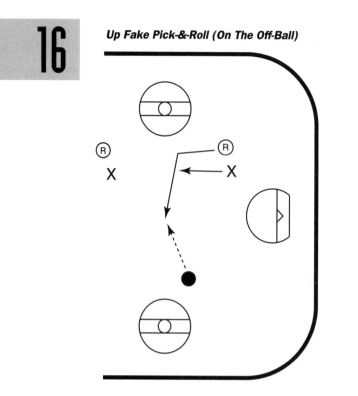

(2) This is a surprise move as the picker reads his defender, i.e., the defender is playing off him anticipating an actual Up Pick-and-Roll.

d. Up Screen on the Off-Ball
(1) The creaseman ties up his check on the way up to set a phony Up Pick (see diagram 17a).
(2) He sets this screen by doing a reverse pivot on his check as his teammate approaches (see diagrams 8a, 8b: Up Screen on the Ball). He does this to prevent his check from switching.
(3) Another way a screen is formed is when the checker just gets tied up trying to prevent him from setting the pick (see diagram 17b).
(4) The cornerman reads the situation and cuts outside of the screen (backdoor). The teammates can also run it as a set play.

e. Cross Pick-and-Roll on the Off-Ball
(1) This is the same technique as the Cross Pick-and-Roll on the ball.
(2) The picker can read his teammate (cutter) or they can run a set play between them.
(3) Options on the Cross Pick-and-Roll on the off-ball:
   (a) Picker "Pop" Option (see diagram 18a)
   This is the same movement for the picker as setting the Cross Pick-and-Roll on the ball. The creaseman fakes a cut to the ball, then just past the inside boundary of the Outside Lane, he comes back to set a pick for the cutter to cut into the middle of the floor. The cutter cuts to the net while the picker pops (cuts) to the ball after his teammate passes his shoulder. The picker rolls in the same direction as the ballcarrier, i.e., behind the ballcarrier. He must remember to rotate his stick upwards and hold it vertically as he rolls so it does not get caught on his teammate's defender's body. The passer passes to whoever is open. This option works against non-switching or switching defenses, or as a set play.

17a

Up Screen (On the Off-Ball)

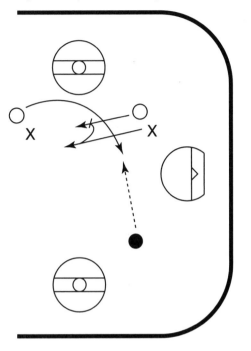

17b

Up Screen (On The Off-Ball)

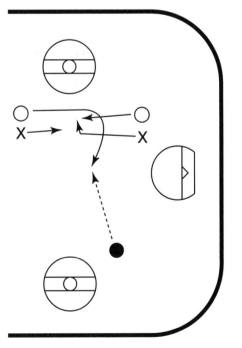

Cross Pick-&-Roll (On The Off-Ball)
Picker "Pops" Option

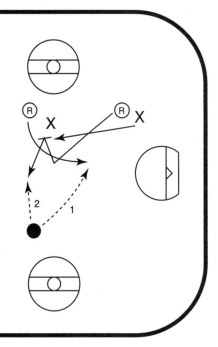

(b) Picker "Cut" Option (see diagram 18b)

This time the cutter cuts to the ball for a clear out for the picker. The picker turns (the opposite way to the cutter) and pushes off the defender, going straight to the net for the pass.

(c) Picker "Curl" Option (see diagram 18c)

Both the cutter and picker cut to the net. The picker rolls right behind the cutter.

(d) Cutter cuts "Backdoor" Option (see diagram 18d)

The cornerman or cutter sees that his check is starting to "cheat" on receiving the pick by moving up early so it is easier to step over the top of the pick. To counter this defensive move, the cutter fakes to cut across the top and then cuts behind the pick (backdoor or to the outside) and goes to the net.

(e) "Double" Pick Option (see diagram 18e)

The cutter, when cutting past the pick, calls the picker's first name indicating he is setting a second pick for him. The picker cuts to the ball coming off the second pick. The picker now has an advantage as he ends up with his defender on his back or behind him. To give the picker or second cutter room to get the pass and still take a high percentage shot, start the play as close to the side boards as possible.

Generally, on most Pick-and-Roll plays, first the cutter reads the picker by where he places himself for an Up or a Cross Pick. Then, the picker reads the cutter whether he goes to the net or to the ball and does the opposite.

6. Off-Ball Down Series

a. Down Screen on the Off-Ball (see diagram 19)

(1) Set the screen similar to the Down Screen on the ball.

(2) If the cutter gets the ball off the screen for a shot, the screener's options are: (a) to go to the net for a rebound off the goalie or the boards; (b) to step back as a defensive safety; or (c) to step back as a release man for the passer.

18b

Cross Pick-&-Roll (On The Off-Ball)
Picker "Cuts" Option

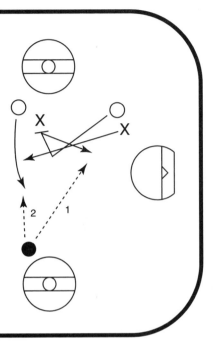

18c

Cross Pick-&-Roll (On The Off-Ball)
Picker "Curl" Option

*Very effective
in minor/youth lacrosse*

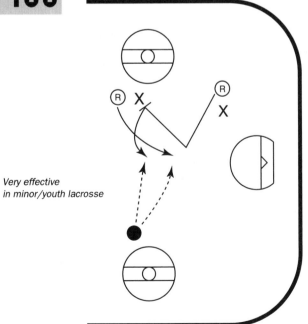

Cross Pick-&-Roll (On The Off-Ball)
Cutter Cuts "Backdoor" Option

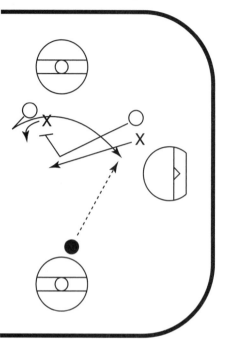

Cross Pick-&-Roll (On The Off-Ball)
"Double" Pick Option

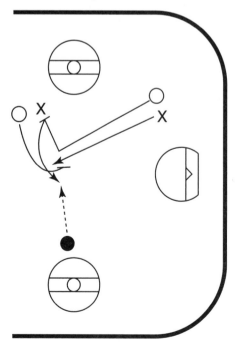

Down Screen (On The Off-Ball)

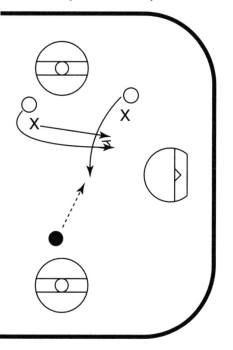

(3) If the cutter does not get the ball, he can continue on around the net or stop around the Imaginary Center Line and come back to the side where he started. The screener can step back as a release or safety valve for the passer.

(4) If the cutter's defender starts to cheat over top of the screen, the cutter can cut behind the screen (backdoor) for the pass.

b. Down Pick-and-Roll on the Off-Ball

(1) Use the same principles as setting and using an Up Pick-and-Roll.

(2) Options on the Down Pick-and-Roll:

(a) Picker "Pop" Option (see diagram 20a)

The cutter tries to cut tight to the pick, rubbing out his defender while going to the net. The picker pops or steps towards the ball after the cutter passes his shoulder as the second option. The picker turns in the direction of the shoulder the cutter just passed. By turning in this direction the picker keeps his defender on his back and picks up the sight of the ball quickly.

Remember: The offensive Pick-and-Roll rule is "one player cuts to the net, the other player cuts to the ball" for good spacing.

Against a switching defense: If the cutter cuts to the net he will be covered so the picker becomes the first option. The ballcarrier should know that against any switching defense he keeps his eye on the picker (see diagram 20b).

(b) Picker "Cut" Option (see diagram 20c)

The counter against a switching defense is for the cutter to cut high to the ball to pull his teammate's defender away to give room for the picker to cut low to the net.

(c) Picker "Curl" Option (see diagram 20d)

After the cutter cuts by the picker he follows the cutter (curls) to the net.

Variation: The picker rolls at the same time as the cutter.

(d) Cutter "Out" Option (see diagram 20e)

Down Pick-&-Roll (On The Off-Ball)
Picker "Pops" Option

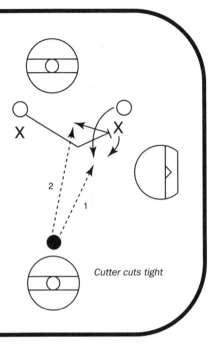

Cutter cuts tight

Down Pick-&-Roll (On The Off-Ball)
Versus Switch Picker "Pops" Option

Cutter still cuts tight

20c

Down Pick-&-Roll (On The Off-Ball)
Versus Switch Picker "Cuts" Option

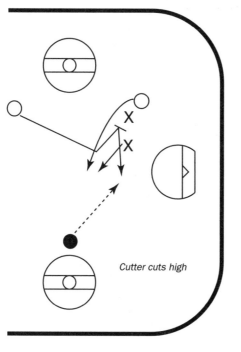

Cutter cuts high

20d

Down Pick-&-Roll (On The Off-Ball)
Cutter "Out" Option

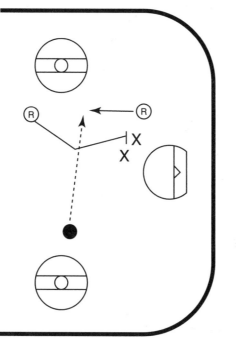

**Down Pick-&-Roll (On The Off-Ball)
Cutter "Out" Option**

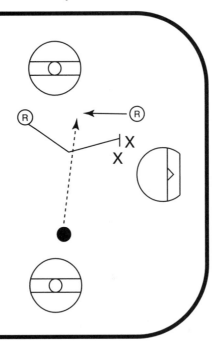

The ballcarrier looks for a quick cross-floor pass to the cutter who is stepping back from his defender to create a gap. The cutter can take a quick shot off the Down Pick or fake a shot and go to the net. This play works best against a defense that sags a lot on the off-ball side, looking to help on the ballcarrier.

(e) Cutter cuts "Backdoor" Option (see diagram 20f)

The cutter cuts behind the defender when the defender fights to go over top of the pick; when the defender starts high, in relation to the cutter, to go over top before the pick is set; or just as an element of surprise.

(f) "Double" Pick Option (see diagram 20g)

The cutter coming off the first pick calls his teammates first name to key that he is going to set a second pick. The cutter has to get on the inside of his defender to get good positioning to set the second pick properly. The closer to the side of the floor the second pick is set, the better it is to give the cutter coming off the second pick more room to catch the ball and still be in a good scoring area.

c. Down Interchange on the Off-Ball (see diagram 21)

(1) The cornerman starts to run straight down as if to set a Down Pick.

(2) Rather than waiting for the Down Pick to be set the creaseman starts to move up towards the cornerman.

(3) The cornerman aims for the inside of the body of the creaseman's defender.

(4) The creaseman cuts hard around the cornerman trying to force a switch.

(5) During this interchange by the offensive players, hopefully the would-be picker (the cornerman) will end up on the inside of his new defender and cut to the ball.

d. Down Fake Pick-and-Roll on the Off-Ball (see diagram 22)

(1) The cornerman runs down as if to set a Down Pick.

(2) The picker's defender, anticipating the Down Pick, starts to play off him and gets ready to switch and pick up the cutter.

20f

Down Pick-&-Roll (On The Off-Ball)
Cutter Cuts "Backdoor" Option

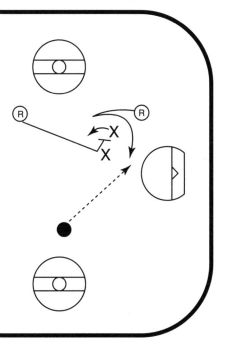

20g

Down Pick-&-Roll (On The Off-Ball)
"Double" Pick Option

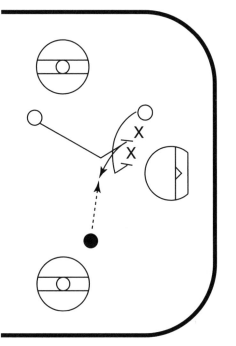

Down Interchange (On The Off-Ball)

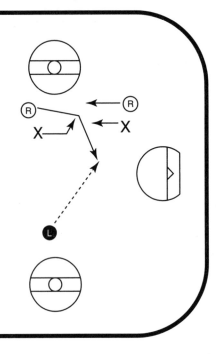

Down Fake Pick-&-Roll (On The Off-Ball)

(3) The picker, reading his defender, cuts 90 degrees to the net. This is called an "L-cut" and can be done as an element of surprise.

V. BUILDING THE COMBINATION OFFENSE THROUGH DRILLS

A. TIPS FOR COMBINATION OFFENSIVE DRILLS

1. Team offense, because it is the most complicated phase of the game of lacrosse, is the hardest part of the game to teach. So, as a coach, be patient.

2. It is important to remember that it is not what type of system a team runs on offense, but how it executes on offense. Stress fundamentals:
   a. Players must be able to pass and catch.
   b. Players must be able to go one-on-one.
   c. Players must be able to pass the ball while being pressured, i.e., being bothered, not cross-checked, by a defender.
   d. Players must learn to play on their own side of the floor and out of their position.
   e. Players must be able to cut through the middle of the floor and catch the ball with a defender right on them.

3. Create drills that get the players to react more and think less on offense.

4. Create drills that get the players in the habit of passing and cutting.

5. Teach the "Whole-Part-Whole" method. Walk through a 5-on-0, then progress with breakdown drills of the offense: 2-on-1, 2-on-2, 3-on-1, 3-on-2, 3-on-3, 4-on-2, 4-on-3, 4-on-4, and 5-on-5.

6. Drills should be broken into teaching drills and competitive drills. Eventually make the competitive drills tougher than any game situation.

Note: During practices coaches do not want the balls all over the floor where a player may accidentally step on one and sprain his ankle. To keep the balls available for the players and still keep the drills flowing, all coaches, assistant coaches, and ball-boys should wear ball bags in front of their waist to pick up any loose balls. In a drill, when a player drops a ball, the ball-boy can throw a new one to him to keep the drill going.

B. INDIVIDUAL OFFENSIVE DRILLS

1. 1-on-1 Drills (see book *Lacrosse Fundamentals:* CHAPTER 6: INDIVIDUAL OFFENSE)

C. TEAM OFFENSIVE DRILLS

2. 5-on-0 Drill
a. Five players walk through the offense with coaches explaining and demonstrating what they do. A good idea is to have the players write down what their role is on the offense.
b. Players now run through the offense without the ball.
c. Players work on offensive positioning by moving the ball around slowly. Stress to the players to stay in the proper position, stay on the proper side, keep good floor balance, and initiate the offense quickly.

3. 2-on-2 "Give-and-Go" Drills

a. 2-on-0 Drill

This drill starts with two lines—one line of right-hand shots with balls and another line of left-hand shots with no balls. The right-hand shots pass and cut to the ball or the net for a return pass and shot.

b. 2-on-1, 2-on-2 Drills

This offensive drill is run with an offensive right-hand shot and an offensive left-hand shot. Now and then run two left-hand shots or two right-hand shots together.

Defensive progression:

    (i) Start with one defender on the cutter.

    (ii) Then one defender on the passer.

    (iii) Then a defender on both players.

Defensive variations:

(1) The defense has no sticks. They can push with their hands.

(2) The defense plays with their sticks held the wrong way.

(3) The defense puts their sticks on the cutters, but they only ride with them.

(4) The defense can push the cutters, but they cannot cross-check them.

(5) The defense can cross-check the cutters. However, the defense uses old sticks.

(6) The offense sees how many cross-floor passes they can make.

(7) The cutter works on different ways of beating his defender with the defender playing token defense. Include the following in the drill:

    (a) Fake or change of direction.

    (b) Stutter step to a fake.

    (c) Pivot—use a drop step to get the defender on one's back.

    (d) Cut backdoor—use this maneuver when the defender is trying to steal a cross-floor pass.

    (e) Change of pace—change from a lazy trot to a quick break.

    (f) Knock the opponent's stick down.

    (g) Cross-check—push off with the stick.

(8) Live Defensive Drill—opposite shots check the two offensive players. Stress to the offensive players to work on deception and quickness and that the cutters should try to get on the inside of their defenders. The offensive passer's rule is to "pass early, not late, to the cutter."

The offensive cutter's rule is to "cut late, not early."

(9) Work on the Give-and-Go, but if the cutter does not get the pass he continues across the floor and sets a Cross Pick for the ballcarrier.

(10) Give-and-Go Game—two teams of partners composed of a left- and a right-shot must score off a Give-and-Go. They play to four goals.

Variation: Both players are right-hand shots or both are left-hand shots . They work a Give-and-Go on the same side of the floor.

c. 2-on-3 Drill

The defense has a numerical advantage. Therefore, the offense has a more difficult time executing on offense. Only run this drill at a Junior or Senior level. In minor/youth lacrosse always give the advantage to the offense.

4. 2-on-2 "Picks and Screens" on the Ball Side Drills

a. 2-on-1, 2-on-2 Drills

2-on-1—teach the offensive players how to set and use a pick or screen properly.

2-on-2—teach the offensive players how to set and use the pick or screen properly.

2-on-2—work on the Up Series (see diagrams 6 to 9) and Down Series (see diagrams 10 to 13).

Defensive progression for picks and screens:

    (i) The defender is on the ballcarrier only.

    (ii) Then the defender is on the picker or screener only.

(iii) Then the defenders are on both offensive players.
Defensive variations:
(1) The defense has no sticks.
(2) The defense plays with their sticks the wrong way.
(3) Token defense is maintained with four variations:
    (a) The defense plays their check tight with their back to the ball (closed stance) and are not allowed to switch on picks.
    (b) The defense plays their check tight with their back to the ball (closed stance) and are allowed to switch on picks.
    (c) The defense plays a helping defense (open stance) and are not allowed to switch on picks.
    (d) The defense plays a helping defense (open stance) and are allowed to switch on all picks.
(4) Live defense.

b. 2-on-2 Screen Out Drill
The drill is for use against a team that plays a zone. This is where a defensive player automatically goes to the crease area before his check gets there, and the next defensive player goes to the top of the zone box. The first offensive player screens out the top defensive man as the ballcarrier comes in behind him. If the defensive man goes one way the screener lets him go that way and stops him from coming back, while the ballcarrier goes in the opposite direction.
c. 2-on-3 Drill
In this drill the offense has a more difficult time to execute since the defense has a numerical advantage.

5. 3-on-3 "Picks and Screens" on the Off-Ball Side Drills
a. 3-on-1, 3-on-2, 3-on-3 Drills
3-on-1—the players work on setting and using a pick or screen properly.
3-on-2—the players work on the Up Series (see diagrams 14 to 18) and the Down Series (see diagrams 19 to 22).
Defensive progression for picks and screens:
    (i) Start with one defender on the cutter.
    (ii) Then place one defender on the picker or screener only. The cutter learns to read the defender.
    (iii) Then place defenders on the two off-ball offensive players.
Defensive variations:
(1) The defense has no sticks.
(2) The defense holds their sticks the wrong way.
(3) Token defense is applied with four variations:
    (a) The defense plays their check tight with their back to the ball (closed stance) and are not allowed to switch on picks.
    (b) The defense plays their check tight with their back to the ball (closed stance) and are allowed to switch on picks.
    (c) The defense plays a helping defense (open stance) and are not allowed to switch on picks.
    (d) The defense plays a helping defense (open stance) and are allowed to switch on all picks .
(4) 3-on-3 with live defense is practiced. Combinations of two lefts and one right, two rights and one left, three rights, or three lefts are used.

b. 4-on-2 Drill
In this drill there are two passers, two offensive off-ball players, and two defensive players guarding the off-ball players. The offensive off-ball players run different plays against the two defenders. The two passers, each with a ball, wait for the play to develop with one passer passing to the cutter going to the net, and the other passer passing to the player coming towards him. Sometimes the goalie may end up trying to stop two balls at the same time.

6. 3-on-3 Offensive Cut Throat Drill (4-on-4)

The drill consists of three groups of three or four players. Because the coach wants to stress offense in this drill, a team can only get points while on offense. If the offense scores, they stay on offense and get one point while the defense goes off the floor. After the offense scores, they must pass the ball to the coach who then passes it back to the offense to start the drill while a new defensive group comes on the floor. If the defense stops the offense, the defense goes on the offense and the offense goes off the floor to sit out a turn while a new group of defensive players comes on the floor. The first group to three points is the winner.

7. 3-on-3 Game

(see CHAPTER III: THE FAST-BREAK SYSTEM, Drill #29)

Split the whole team equally into two. The two teams are further divided into groups of three players who play full-floor and run continuously for 45-second shifts. On the whistle three players from each team run off the floor while three new players from each team run on the floor. The ballcarrier on hearing the whistle must drop the ball right where he is and run off the floor. The game is played to a designated score with the losers running sprints.

8. 3-on-4 Drill

This is a half-floor drill in which the defense has a numerical advantage to make it harder for the offense to execute.

9. 4-on-4 Passing Game

The coach counts the number of passes completed by the offense. The drill is over if the ball touches the floor or the defense steals the ball. Once this happens the defense goes on offense and tries to beat the number of catches completed by the former offensive unit.

10. 4-on-4 Offense with Offensive Restrictions Drill

The offense huddles to call the restriction. The restrictions are:

(1) The offense can score after 5 passes.
(2) The offense must score off a one-on-one.
(3) The offense must score off a Screen.
(4) The offense must score off a Pick-and-Roll.
(5) The offense must score off a cut (Give-and-Go or Go).
(6) A certain player must score.

11. 4-on-5 Drill

This is a half-floor drill in which the defense has a numerical advantage to make it harder for the offense to score.

12. 5-on-5 Offense with Offensive Restrictions Drill

The same restrictions apply as in the 4-on-4 drill.

13. 5-on-5 Offense with Defensive Restrictions Drill

The following restrictions may be applied:

(1) The defense has no sticks.
(2) The defense uses their sticks the wrong way.
(3) The defense plays token defense. Four variations of the defense are:

    (i) The defense plays their check in a tight man-to-man with their back to the ball (closed stance) and are not allowed to switch on picks. Here the offense can work on their 1-on-1 moves in a controlled game situation.

(ii) The defense plays their check in a tight man-to-man with their back to the ball (closed stance) and are allowed to switch on all picks.

(iii) The defense plays a helping, sagging defense (open stance) and are not allowed to switch on picks.

(iv) The defense plays a helping, sagging defense (open stance) and are allowed to switch on picks.

(4) The defense slashes the ballcarrier and the off-ball players.

14. 5-on-5 Borden Ball Drill (see CHAPTER III: THE FAST-BREAK SYSTEM, Drill 45; CHAPTER IV: MAN-TO-MAN TEAM DEFENSE, Drill 40)

Play this game full-floor or half-floor.

The rules are:

1) The ballcarrier can only take three steps with the ball before he must pass it.

2) The ballcarrier must pass in three seconds. Any violation of these two rules gives the other team the ball.

3) If the offensive team drops the ball, it loses possession.

This game reinforces the Give-and-Go play, the need to work to get open for a pass, the need for the ballcarrier to see the whole floor, and the need to avoid panicking when being pressured.

15. 5-on-5 Scrimmage Drill

Play a half-floor game with live defense. Each team is given five possessions to score. Play to five points. The coach gives feedback to the offense.

16. 5-on-6 Drill

Practice this half-floor drill in which the defense has a numerical advantage to make it harder for the offense to execute .

17. 5-on-5 "One Shot" Game Drill

Allow the offense one shot while playing full-floor. The offense can react back on defense or press.

D. OFFENSIVE SPOT SHOOTING DRILLS

18. Shooting Off a "Give-and-Go"

19. Shooting Off a "Go"

20. Shooting Off a "Cross-Floor" Pass

21. Shooting Off an "Up Pick-and-Roll" On the Ball

22. Shooting Off an "Up Pick-and-Roll" Off the Ball

23. Shooting Off a "Fake Up Pick-and-Roll" On the Ball

24. Shooting Off a "Fake Up Pick-and-Roll" Off the Ball

25. Shooting Off a "Cross Pick-and-Roll" On the Ball

26. Shooting Off a "Cross Pick-and-Roll" Off the Ball

27. Shooting Off a "Down Pick-and-Roll" On the Ball

28. Shooting Off a "Down Pick-and-Roll" Off the Ball

29. Shooting Off a "Down Screen" On the Ball

30. Shooting Off a "Down Screen" Off the Ball

31. Shooting After "Swinging the Ball" Off the Ball (see diagram 23)

32. Shooting Off a "Down Pick-Pick-and-Roll" Off the Ball

33. Shooting Off a "Cross Pick-Pick-and-Roll" Off the Ball

23 Shooting after "Swinging The Ball" 4-on-0 Drill

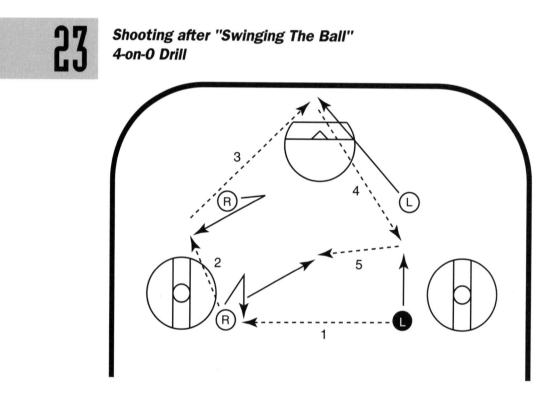

CHAPTER II: ZONE OFFENSE

I. ZONE OFFENSE TERMINOLOGY

1. Strong Side—the side of the floor with three players of the same shot.

2. Weak Side—the side of the floor with only two players of the same shot.

3. Ball Side—the side of the floor where the ball is.

4. Off-Ball Side—the side of the floor opposite the ball.

5. Penetration (One-on-One Move)—the ballcarrier beats his defender for a scoring opportunity or at least tries to go to the net for a possible shot.

6. Gap—standing in between two defenders. People have a tendency to gravitate to people (stand beside them) making it easier for the zone defenders to play defense.

7. Swing—passing the ball from one side of the floor to the other side.

8. Overload—placing offensive players where they will outnumber defensive players in an area.

II. PHILOSOPHY

1. The zone offense likes to run a passing-game type offense to complement their man-to-man offense. This gives the offensive players lots of freedom regarding player movement and ball movement.

2. The zone offense likes to run an offense that can be reset again and again. It is called a continuity offense.

3. The zone offense watches the middle defender to see what he does. If the ball is brought up the Middle Lane, does the middle defender play the ballcarrier or does one of the top defenders play the ballcarrier? If the ball is in the middle of the overload side, does the middle defender come out to the side to defend the ballcarrier, or does the top defender drop down to play the ballcarrier? Who covers the first pass down the side: the top defender or the middle defender?

4. The zone offense stresses poise and lots of patience when attacking the zone defense. Zone defenders have a tendency to lose their concentration the longer they stay in the zone.

5. A coach can instill confidence in his players by explaining that the opposition cannot play them man-to-man so they have to play zone.

6. The zone offense never attacks with five players but runs a two-man or three-man game while eliminating the other defenders by occupying them or screening them.

III. WHY TEAMS PLAY ZONE DEFENSE

1. Opponents don't like it. It irritates teams to play against zone defenses because they lose their rhythm, as in their man-to-man offense, and have to attack more systematically.

2. Zones force long (outside) shots.

3. A zone is a great equalizer, especially against a team that likes to go one-on-one.

4. A team can hide a poor checker in the zone.

5. Zones seem to hurry the offense.

6. Zones are set up perfectly to run the fast-break.

7. Zone defenses change the tempo of the game. The zone offense cannot be executed as quickly as a man-to-man offense.

8. If a coach does not want to use a lot of players, he can play a zone defense to rest them.

IV. WEAKNESSES OF A ZONE DEFENSE

1. All the defenders are following the ball.

2. The defenders are flat-footed and, thereby, easier to beat one-on-one.

3. The defenders have a tendency to get mentally lazy and/or lose their concentration the longer they stay in the zone defense.

V. ZONE OFFENSIVE PRINCIPLES

A. ALIGNMENT

B. MOVEMENT OF THE BALL

C. MOVEMENT OF PLAYERS

D. PENETRATION

E. ATTACKING THE ZONE

F. THE MIDDLE DEFENDER

G. OFF-BALL PLAYS—PICKS AND SCREENS

H. SHOOTING

I. FAST-BREAK

J. SET PLAYS

A. ALIGNMENT

The offensive players align between two defenders to create indecisiveness. They stand in these gaps to create problems in defensive coverage and to create uncertainty in the defenders' minds: "Who takes the man?" Usually, players gravitate to players, i.e., offensive players have a tendency to line up beside their defenders which makes the defense's job much easier.

There are seven spots the players can play out of to give them reference points. As well, these spots help players keep good spacing. Players should be at least 15 feet apart to make the zone move and spread out (see diagram 24).

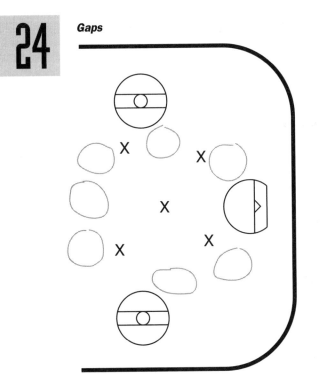

24 *Gaps*

B. MOVEMENT OF THE BALL

A pass can move a lot faster than a defender can move. So, by doing a lot of passing, a team can pick apart a zone defense.

1. "Swinging the Ball"

The offense wants to attack the zone defense by passing the ball around the outside of the zone defense. It wants to reverse the ball quickly from one side of the floor to the other side to give them a numerical advantage or even get a player wide open for a shot. Although quick movement of the ball is important, the zone-offense players should always make the easy pass rather than forcing the ball.

The first pass to the side is usually a decoy. Because all the defenders are facing the ballcarrier, the offensive players make it look like they are attacking on this ball side. In reality they are looking for the off-ball side play by attempting to swing the ball followed by cutters. The zone-offense players do not shoot on the first pass (unless the player is wide open), but want to swing the ball at least two times before looking for a scoring opportunity.

2. Passing
The zone offense want only "shooting" passes, i.e., passes right into the stick target (high and outside) without the receiver having to move his stick. The passes should be accurate so the offensive player does not waste precious time getting away his shot or pass. Short, snappy, accurate passes are recommended.

Because smart defenders are always looking for the steal, a player should constantly fake before actually passing to keep the defender at "home." He fakes one way to pass, but goes back the other way on the pass. So it is important that, after a player passes, he steps in for a possible return pass and shot because the teammate he just passed to might fake the pass and pass back to him. However, if the ballcarrier cannot get the ball to him, he must then make himself available by popping out for the pass or cutting to the open spot or net.

3. Receiving the Pass
Players should receive the ball in a shooting position, i.e., with knees bent and the stick ready to shoot. Players should catch and shoot all in one motion.

4. Types of Passes Against the Zone Defense
a. Skip pass—by-pass the next logical offensive player as he is being overplayed by a defender.
b. Cross-floor pass or "swing" pass—pass from one side of the floor to the other side. This pass makes the zone shift and opens up the zone defense. Speed, as well as accuracy, is important. The zone offense can also swing the ball with a player at the top of the offense.
c. Diagonal pass—a pass from the creaseman to the opposite cornerman cutting towards him or to the net; or a pass from the cornerman to the opposite creaseman cutting towards him or to the net.
d. Down pass or up pass

5. Passing Options
a. Pass and stand.
b. Pass and go away from the pass.
c. Pass and cut to the ball.
d. Pass and pick on the ball.

The zone offense cannot just pass, pass, pass, and shoot. They must have a combination of passing and player movement with the ballcarrier attempting to go to the net to score (Penetration).

C. MOVEMENT OF PLAYERS

1. Off-Ball Cutting
Players flash into the gaps or open areas of the zone. They must be a threat when cutting with their sticks up and ready for a pass. This concept is the simplest and probably most effective play against a zone. This concept works best when the cutter cuts from the off-ball side and he is on the weak side (two players) of the floor (see diagrams 25a, 25b).

2. Cut and Replace
This concept is also worked from the off-ball side of the floor which seems to be the best way to attack a zone.

Cutters

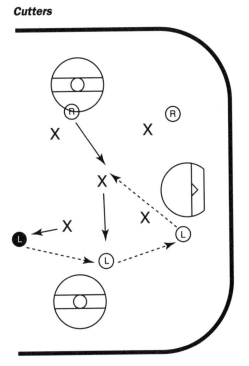

Cutters

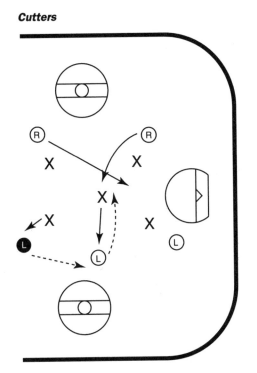

Cut and Replace Principles:
a. Cut to make yourself available for a pass. Look for the open spots.
b. Swing the ball either around the horn or by cross-floor passes.
c. Follow the rule "leave a spot, fill a spot."
d. Run the "cut and replace" concept continuously.

On the first pass to the side, the opposite cornerman cuts in front of his defender followed by the creaseman. The creaseman moves up and cuts from the cornerman's spot, not from his crease position. Players move in this triangular rotation following the principle of "leave a spot, fill a spot." (see diagrams 26, 27)

Variation: Players can cut from behind the zone defense into an open area. The creaseman cuts into the middle and is replaced by the cornerman moving down the side of the zone for a pass, or he cuts into the middle of the zone behind the first cutter. Here, the zone offense always wants somebody leaving and somebody coming from behind (see diagram 28).

3. Versus Overplay on the Cross-Floor Pass
a. The cornerman can cut behind the top defender looking for the pass. If the defender plays him on the cut, the creaseman fills and cuts behind him (see diagram 29).
b. The cornerman fakes a backdoor cut and V-cuts out for the pass (see diagram 30).
c. Players can interchange (see diagram 31).

26

Cut & Replace

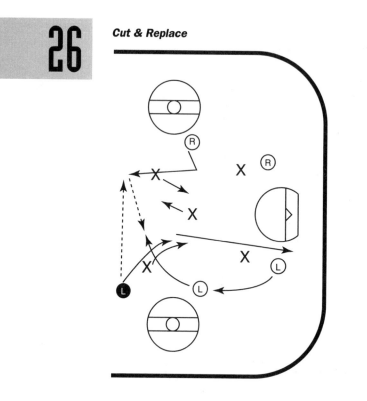

27

Cut & Replace

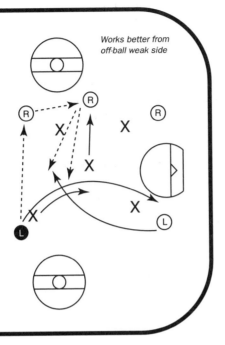

Works better from off-ball weak side

28

Cut & Replace From Behind

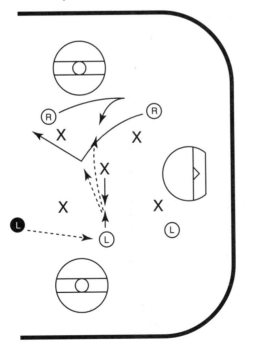

**Versus Overplay On Cross-floor Pass
- Cut Backdoor**

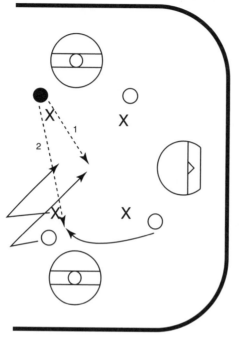

**Versus Overplay On Cross-Floor Pass
- Fake Backdoor & V-Cut Out**

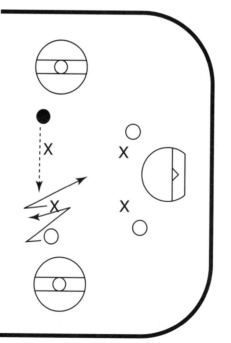

**Versus Overplay On Cross-Foor Pass
- Interchange**

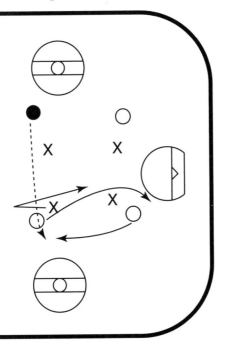

4. Players Interchange Positions
Players on the same side of the floor interchange positions to occupy their defenders. This can usually happen when the offense is running a set play. The players opposite to the play will interchange positions to keep their defenders busy.

D. PENETRATION
Players penetrate to draw two defenders and pass off, to shift the zone, or to beat their defender and score.

1. Direct Penetration into the Gaps
The ballcarrier penetrates from the top or penetrates from the side with the idea of drawing two defenders and passing off. If the middle defender stays in the center of the defense, the receiver must think shot (see diagrams 32a, 32b, 32c).

2. Penetrate Rotation (Fill a Spot)
The ballcarrier penetrates a gap with the idea of drawing a defender so he shifts the zone. The next offensive player to the ballcarrier fills in his spot, ready to receive a pass and shoot. These angle penetrations, towards the corner of the floor or to the top of the zone, are used quite often during ball reversals. The ballcarrier penetrates taking the defensive man as far as he will go and creating a gap for a teammate to fill.

a. Penetrate Down
When the ballcarrier penetrates down the side of the floor, this movement keys his teammate behind to rotate (follows him) and replace the ballcarrier's former position looking for a pass and shot. If this teammate is covered, the ballcarrier then skip passes and hits the next receiver (see diagrams 33a, 33b).

32a   *Direct Penetration Of The Gaps*

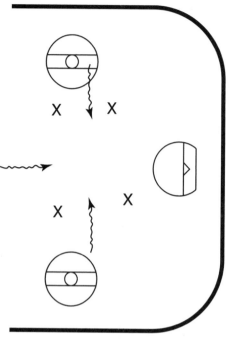

32b   *Direct Penetration From Side*

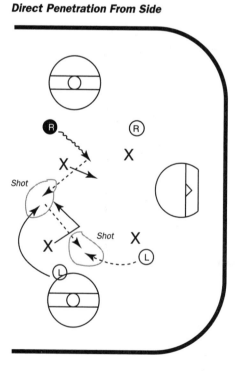

Direct Penetration From The Top

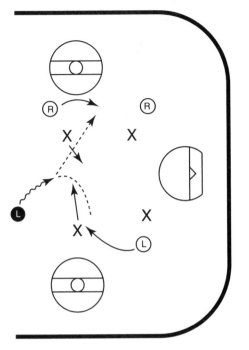

Penetrate Down - Shift Zone With
Penetration - Creating Overload By Shifting

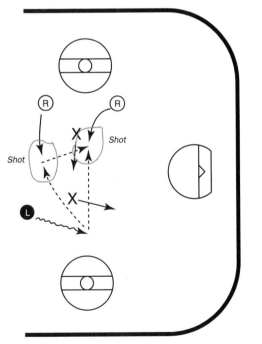

33b *Penetrate Down*

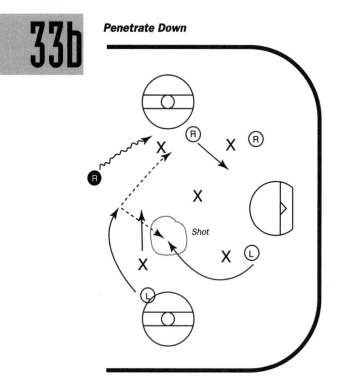

b. Penetrate Over
When a ballcarrier penetrates across the top of the zone, the teammate behind just moves over (follows him) and fills in the ballcarrier's former position looking for a pass and shot (see diagrams 34a, 34b).
c. Penetrate Up
When a ballcarrier penetrates away from a teammate, the teammate just moves up (follows him) and fills in the ballcarrier's former position looking for a pass and shot.
d. Penetrate and Swing
This is just a continuous combination of penetration and ball passing around the outside while looking for a good scoring opportunity (see diagrams 35, 36).

3. Circling or Looping (Exchange Positions)
When the ballcarrier penetrates towards a teammate on his side of the floor, this movement keys the teammate to rotate and replace the ballcarrier's former position. This teammate who filled in the spot when he receives a pass must read the far top defender to see what he is going to do about playing him. If the top defender comes over to play him, he passes over to the off-ball teammate who made himself available for a pass. If the top defender stays, the receiver shoots.

This movement is different than the other penetration moves because there is no teammate following him to fill the open spot. The teammate whom he penetrated towards circles behind and fills in the open spot looking for the pass and shot (see diagram 37).

E. ATTACKING THE ZONE DEFENSE
The zone offense likes to attack the zone defense mainly from the side but will attack from the top to give the zone defense a different look. Other options are to attack from the crease or from behind the net.

34a *Penetrate Over - Shift Zone With Penetration*

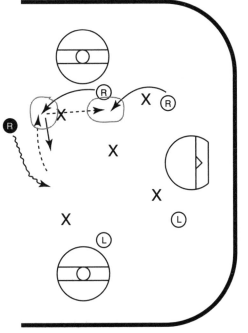

34b *Penetrate Over - Fill Vacant Spot*

35

Penetrate & Swing

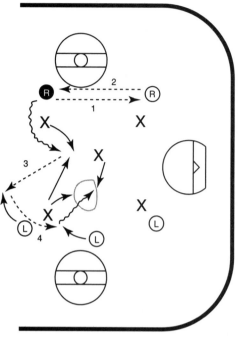

36

Penetrate & Swing

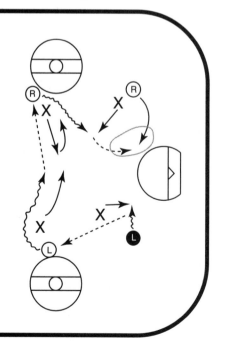

Circling (Penetration Rotation)

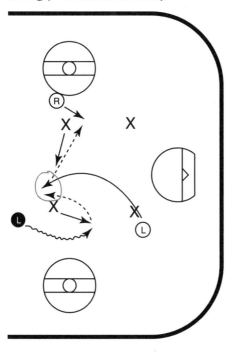

F. THE MIDDLE DEFENDER (OVERLOAD)
The zone offense must be aware of doing something with the middle defender.

1. The zone offense can attack the defense like a power play with a pointman at the top moving the ball back and forth and providing some penetration. So in this situation the zone offense isolates the middle defender.

2. The zone-offense team likes to attack the zone defense from the strong side creating an overload on that side. Attacking from this side and putting the ball in the middle to the offensive player draws the middle defender out of the middle of the zone (see diagram 38).

3. Another way to occupy the middle defender is to put an offensive player in the middle of the zone to neutralize the middle defender. This offensive player can then screen the middle defender or interfere with his defensive slides.

4. Another way of doing something with the middle defender is to put a player at the top of the zone offense to draw him out of the middle of the zone defense or at least to occupy him (see diagram 39).

5. Another way of getting the attention of the middle defender is to put a player behind the net.

G. OFF-BALL PLAYS—PICKS AND SCREENS
Because all the defenders are following the ball, the zone offense runs many off-ball plays.
1. Off-ball Up Pick-and-Roll (see diagram 40).
2. Off-ball fake Down Pick-and-Roll (see diagram 41).
3. Off-ball fake Up Pick-and-Roll (see diagram 42).

38

Overload

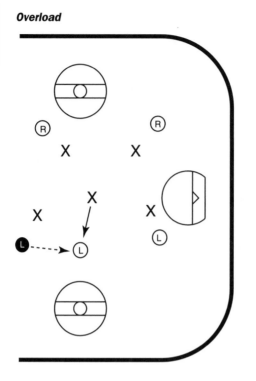

39

Overload

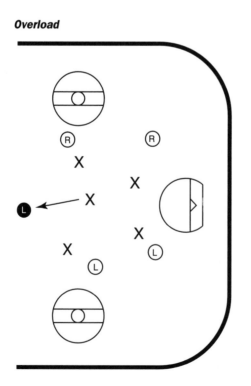

40

Off-Ball Weak Side Up Pick-&-Roll

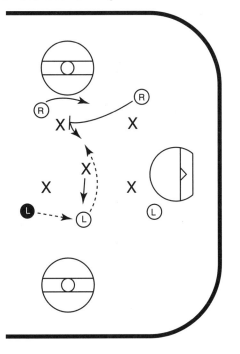

41

Off-Ball Fake Down Pick-&-Roll

Off-Ball Fake Up Pick-&-Roll

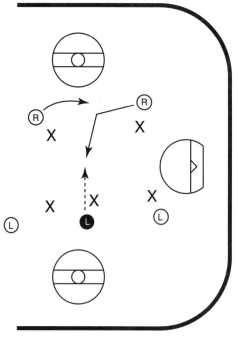

Ball Side Up Pick-&-Roll Ballside

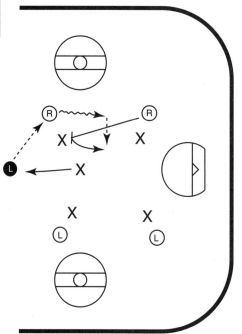

4. Ball side Up Pick-and-Roll (see diagram 43).

5. Pick the top defender from the same side as the ball or from the off-ball side.

6. Neutralize the middle defender by picking him.

H. SHOOTING

1. The receiver must be physically ready to shoot the ball before he receives it. He must turn his upper body to face the passer, have his knees bent and feet planted wide, and have his stick ready to catch and shoot the ball all in one motion.

2. If the defender charges the shooter, he must fake a shot to freeze the defender, then go around him. Shot fakes are important against a zone defense because players are usually flat-footed and play in an upright position.

3. The zone offense must take only good shots against a zone defense. The coach must explain and reinforce what a good shot is.
Shooting Rule: "If you are within your range in the Prime Scoring Area and you are uncontested without any interference placed on your shot, shoot!"

I. FAST-BREAK

Fast-break before the opposition can get set up in their zone.

J. SET PLAYS

The zone offense runs special plays to capitalize on their good shooters. The zone offense occasionally likes to run set plays just for a different look. One way of running a set play is to put a player on his wrong side of the floor (see diagram 44). A coach can make up his own set plays for special players.

VI. ZONE OFFENSE DRILLS

1. 5-on-0 Drill
Put cones on the floor to represent a 2-1-2 zone defense. Talk to the players about the principles of attacking a zone defense.

2. 3-on-3 Drills
a. 3-on-3 Swing the Ball Drill
Teach all the zone concepts while executing against a token defense.
b. 3-on-3 Cut from the Off-Ball Side Drill
c. 3-on-3 Swing, Cut, and Replace Drill
Execute this principle 3 times before the zone-offense players can shoot, or have them make 10 passes before they can shoot.
d. 3-on-3 Direct Penetration of the Gaps Drill
Align in the gaps; make two defenders play you; penetrate also to score. Just keep penetrating and swinging the ball.
e. 3-on-3 Penetration Rotation (Down, Over, Up) Drill
f. 3-on-3 Circling Drill
g. 3-on-3 Off-Ball Pick-and-Roll Drills

3. 4-on-4 Drills
a. 4-on-4 Swing the Ball Drill

Set Play

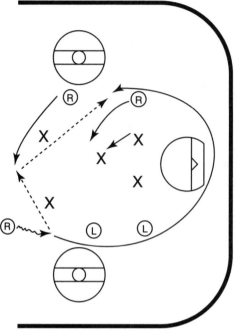

Teach all the zone concepts versus a token defense.

b. 4-on-4 Cut from the Off-Ball Side Drill

c. 4-on-4 Swing, Cut, and Replace Drill

Execute this principle 3 times before the zone-offense players can shoot, or have them make 10 passes before they can shoot.

d. 4-on-4 Direct Penetration of the Gaps Drill

Align in the gaps; make two defenders play you; penetrate also to score. Just keep penetrating and swinging the ball.

e. 4-on-4 Penetration Rotation (Down, Over, Up) Drill

f. 4-on-4 Circling Drill

g. 4-on-4 Off-Ball Pick-and-Roll Drill

4. 5-on-4 Drill (No Middle Defender)

5. 5-on-5 Drills

a. 5-on-5 Swing the Ball Drill

Teach all the zone concepts versus a token defense.

b. 5-on-5 Cut from the Off-Ball Side Drill

c. 5-on-5 Swing, Cut, and Replace Drill

Cut and replace with the cornerman cutting.

Cut and replace with the creaseman cutting (attacking from behind the zone).

Passes can be from the pointman, the cornerman, or from the creaseman. Do not become predictable.

   1) Execute this principle 3 times before the zone-offense players can shoot.

   2) Or have them make 10 passes before they can shoot.

   3) Or have the player who started the drill end up shooting.

d. 5-on-5 Direct Penetration of the Gaps Drill

Align in the gaps; make two defenders play you; penetrate also to score. Just keep penetrating and swinging the ball.

e. 5-on-5 Penetration Rotation (Down, Over, Up) Drill

f. 5-on-5 Circling Drill

g. 5-on-5 Off-Ball Pick-and-Roll Drill

CHAPTER III: THE FAST-BREAK SYSTEM

I. WHAT IS THE FAST-BREAK SYSTEM?

One or two players running up the floor is *not* Fast-Break Lacrosse. Five players running up the floor as quickly as possible in an organized manner to create an odd-man situation *is* Fast-Break Lacrosse.

We call the fast-break "a system" because it is not just a case of running up the floor, but running up the floor in an organized manner. In this disciplined system, players get to their right spots at the right time so that teammates can anticipate each other's movements, giving them the ability to play together. The success of the fast-break lies in its simplicity in which players do not have to think as much as react to situations on the floor.

The Fast-Break team looks for the high percentage shot (the highest percentage shot is being all alone in front of the net). This usually comes from obtaining an odd-man situation in the Offensive Zone.

The Fast-Break team wants a five-man breakout with speed and ball control. They want to get the ball up the floor as quickly as possible in an attempt to outnumber the opposition at the other end.

II. WHY FAST-BREAK?

1. Good teams fast-break to score the so-called "easy goals." Easy goals are those scored by players who do not have to take a lot of heavy hitting to get them. But these "easy goals" are usually hard to get in another way because a player has to run all out. In a tough game a team must have the ability to score the easy goals.

2. Good teams fast-break to wear the opposition down. A team does this by opening up the game and forcing the opposition to run. It emphasizes speed to make "conditioning" a crucial factor. Speed creates fatigue, loss of concentration, as well as good scoring opportunities. A Fast-Breaking team pushes the ball even when there is not an odd-man situation to keep offensive pressure on the opposition at all times, to control the tempo of the game, and to wear the opposition down.

3. If a team does not run and gets behind in a game, it is difficult to catch up unless it can fast-break.

4. The threat of the fast-break is important. The constant threat of the break makes the opposition cautious on offense, i.e., they do not play with as much abandonment and risk on their offense because they are always worrying about getting back on defense.

5. The fast-break creates a lot of one-on-one situations. It is easier for the ballcarrier to go one-on-one before the defense can get settled down and provide backup for each other. It is harder to play against a set, organized defense as opposed to a defense in transition, i.e., in the process of getting back on defense.

6. Players enjoy playing in a fast-tempo game.

7. Spectators enjoy watching a fast-tempo game. Fast-Break lacrosse is entertaining and exciting lacrosse.

8. Fast-Break lacrosse gives an advantage to a team that is in excellent physical condition.

9. This aggressive form of play will carry over and help the team on offense and defense.

10. Teams "fast-break" to prove that quicker players can beat bigger players and to prove that the game of lacrosse is a transition game and not a half-floor game.

11. Even if a team does not use the fast-break in a game, the drills which it uses in practice will help to develop skills in passing, catching, and shooting on the run. The drills will also improve conditioning.

12. Players learn how to make quick and good decisions under pressure.

13. A pressing defense and a running offense give more players a chance to play.

14. The most important reason to play Fast-Break lacrosse in youth/minor leagues is because it gives the parents an opportunity to see their child playing often and aggressively, rather than giving them a chance to wonder about their child's playing time.

III. WHEN TO FAST-BREAK

The fast-break starts: from the goalie after he makes a save; from obtaining loose balls from playing a tough defense; from intercepting forced passes from a pressure defense; from pressuring the ball-carrier into a turnover; and from rebounds off the boards from forced shots.

IV. QUESTIONS A COACH SHOULD ASK HIMSELF WHEN PUTTING A FAST-BREAK SYSTEM TOGETHER

> What is your fast-break philosophy?

> What are the names of the players' positions?

> What type of players do you want in the creaseman's position?

> What type of players do you want in the cornerman's position?

> What type of players do you want in the pointman's position?

> What starts or signals the fast-break?

> Where do you want your players to go on the breakout?

> Who brings the ball up the floor?

> What are the goaltender's responsibilities on the breakout?

> What are the cornerman's responsibilities on the breakout?

> What are the creaseman's responsibilities on the breakout?

> What are the pointman's responsibilities on the breakout?

> What does a breaking team do if they are denied the outlet pass on the breakout?

> What are the creaseman's responsibilities when running up the Outside Lane?

> What are the cornerman's responsibilities when running up the Outside Lane?

> How do the players execute a 2-on-1 situation?

> How do the players execute a 3-on-2 situation?

> How do the players execute a 4-on-3 situation?

> How do the players execute a 5-on-4 situation?

> What do the five offensive players do if all five defenders are back?

> How does the team execute a line change?

V. REVIEW OF THE PARTS OF THE FAST-BREAK

A. BREAKOUT (THE BEGINNING)
1. Possession of the Ball
2. Breakout Positions
3. Breakout Responsibilities
4. Breakout Versus Pressure Defense

B. FILLING THE LANES (THE MIDDLE)

C. PRIMARY BREAK (THE ENDING)
1. Scoring Priorities Off the Break
2. Odd-Man Situation Rules
3. Prime Scoring Area Positions and Responsibilities
   a. 2-on-1 Situation
   b. 3-on-2 Situation
   c. 4-on-3 Situation
   d. 5-on-4 Situation

D. SECONDARY BREAK (THE ENDING)

VI. PARTS OF THE FAST-BREAK

A. THE BREAKOUT (THE BEGINNING)
The first step and quick reaction at the beginning of the break are the keys for a successful Fast-Break. The Fast-Break is determined largely during the first two seconds after possession.

1. Possession of the Ball
a. General Rule #1: "Nobody breaks until the team has complete possession of the ball."

Some teams like to "cheat" or send a player up the floor early on the shot, but this play could be costly if the ballcarrier fakes a shot, then passes to an open offensive man, or if the opposition team retains possession of the ball after a shot and ends up with an extra-man advantage for a better scoring opportunity.

But, if a team sends a "cheater" or floater up the floor, make sure the ball is in the air before he goes. This release man should be on the defensive strong-side of the floor so that his teammates can form a quick box-zone defense easily in case the opposition gets possession of the ball off the shot.

b. General Rule #2: "Players never pass back or run back on the breakout; they always pass and run forward up the floor."

2. Breakout Positions

Players run to specific spots on the floor so that the ballcarrier or goaltender will know exactly where everybody's stick is going to be and so that the players are balanced and spread out. At the beginning of the season, have specific players run to these designated positions, but later on in the season allow the players to interchange positions depending on who is closest to it. There are advantages of running to specific breakout positions where everybody has to be in definite spots: (1) Players do not have to make any decisions, they just go to their spots; (2) Players can get organized quicker; (3) Through repetition players can refine the breakout (see diagram 45).

Be conscious of position when beginning to teach the Fast-Break. The most important thing in the Fast-Break system is how quickly the team moves the ball out of their Defensive Zone. Players should take two seconds to get to their spots on the breakout. Here, the keys are mental quickness, mental reaction, and physical reaction.

45 *Breakout Positions*

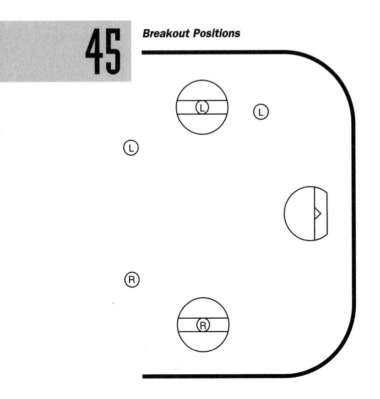

If a player is on the wrong side of the floor on defense, he must cross over on the breakout to get to his proper side of the floor and his proper spot. One of the major problems the ballcarrier has in lacrosse, especially in minor/youth lacrosse, is bringing the ball up the wrong side of the floor.

The "Named" Fast-Break:

Cornerman's Position
The cornerman flares out to the Side Face-Off Circle and stops on the Center Dot. He goes close to the side area because the most congested part of the floor is in the middle. In the beginning, the cornerman holds for the pass, but as he gets more comfortable with this position, he can receive the outlet pass from the goalie on the run (see diagram 46).

Creaseman's Position
The creaseman breaks to the Defensive Zone Line in alignment with the far crease and waits to see what happens with the ball.

46   **Breakout Names**

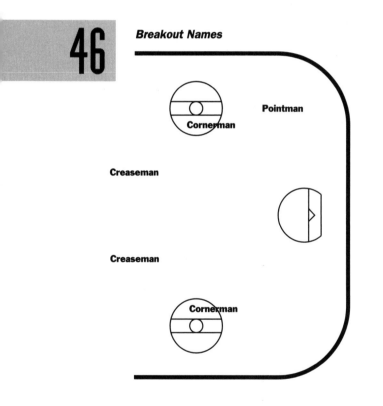

Pointman's Position
The pointman will play even with the goalie as a safety valve in case the cornermen and creasemen are covered.

Note: Some teams on the breakout move everybody up one position on the strong side of the break; i.e., the pointman stops in the Face-Off Dot, the cornerman goes to the Defensive Zone Line, and the creaseman breaks all the way down the floor.

The "Numbered" Fast-Break:

#1 and #2 are the creasemen's positions.
#3 and #4 are the cornermen's positions.
#5 is the pointman's position.

3. Breakout Responsibilities
It is important that all players know their responsibilities on the breakout.

a. The Goaltender's Responsibilities On The Breakout
(1) The goalie starts a lot of the Fast-Breaks from stopped shots. Once he makes the save and obtains the rebound he yells "Ball," which tells his teammates to get to their spots.
(2) The key to a successful Fast-Break is how quickly and accurately the goalie can release the outlet pass. This ability takes a lot of practice and the goaltender must be one of the best passers on the team. When using the stick to stop the ball, think of "catching" the ball to start the Fast-Break, rather than just stopping the ball.
(3) The Goalie's Pass Options:
    (a) The first pass the goalie looks for is the breakaway pass to a creaseman breaking up the floor.
    (b) The second pass the goalie looks for is the outlet pass to the cornerman. This is the most common pass option.
    (c) The third pass the goalie looks for is the safety valve pass to the pointman.
(4) On a line change the goalie passes to the cornerman opposite the bench because this side of the floor is not as congested as the bench side where players are changing.

Note: On a normal breakout (not a line change), the goalie looks for the weak-side cornerman first no matter what side of the floor he is on, but he can hit the other cornerman or anybody else if they are open first.

(5) If the Fast-Break is slow moving, the goalie has the option of running up the floor with the ball to pick up the tempo.

b. The Cornerman's Responsibilities On The Breakout
(1) Qualities for the cornerman's position:
    (a) He handles the ball well.
    (b) He has mental quickness to make good decisions with the ball.
    (c) He is disciplined; i.e., tell him to do something and he does it.
    (d) He is a good athlete with speed who can beat or outrun his check to create an odd-man situation.
    (e) He has a good outside shot, but this is not a major concern.
    (f) He is a centerman, but again this is not a major concern.
    (g) He is a right-hand shot, but again this is not a major concern.
    (h) He plays on the weak-side of the line (only two players on that side of the line), but again this is not a major concern.
    (i) He plays with poise and has the ability to anticipate well (plans ahead). He knows a relaxed, loose player performs his best. Consequently, he does not panic, does not play out of control, does not play "tight," and does not try too hard because he knows he will end up making mistakes. He knows by being calm and controlled, he will execute and think at his best.
(2) Like a quarterback in football, the cornerman "runs" the break, i.e., brings the ball up the floor most of the time. Therefore, he has to be a good ballhandler and a good long-ball shooter. Coaches want only specific players to handle the ball on the break.

(3) The cornerman, while waiting for the outlet pass, faces the inside of the floor with his back to the boards. He turns his upper body to receive the ball over his stick shoulder. He keeps the face of the stick in the direction of the pass.

(4) On receiving the ball, the cornerman turns and looks up the floor. If there is daylight between the defender and the breaking creaseman, he will pass the creaseman the ball. This can be a diagonal pass to the opposite creaseman (see diagram 47) or a pass straight up the sideline to the creaseman on his side of the floor (see diagram 48a). This pass to either creaseman is usually given immediately or not until the end of the break.

47   *Cornerman's Responsibilities*

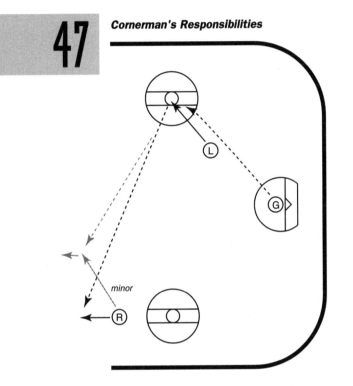

The cornerman's pass options to the creasemen are:

(a) The pass to a creaseman on the run up the floor and on the opposite side of the floor can be made. This is a difficult pass to make. The creaseman who is running up the side boards will not only have his stick behind him but also will be running away from the pass. So, the timing of the pass between the passer and the receiver is important. The passer can throw a level pass to the receiver or a semi-lob pass depending on his distance away from him. The passer must anticipate where the target will be and throw a pass to that area. "He must pass not where the receiver is, but where he is going to be." Thus, he has to aim the ball so it will be passed ahead of the receiver, yet when it arrives it will hit the stick target, which is held behind him; i.e., over his inside shoulder. Therefore, he must aim slightly in front of the receiver so that when the ball arrives it will make contact with the stick, which is held behind him.

(b) The cornerman can throw a semi-lob ("rainbow") pass to the creaseman running up the same side of the floor as himself. His job is to pass the ball ahead of the receiver so that as the creaseman runs up the floor he will run into the pass catching the ball over his inside shoulder without breaking stride. The stick is held horizontally in front of his body and in front of his inside shoulder (tip pointing to the far end boards) with the "face" of the stick open to the approaching ball.

48a   *Cornerman's Responsibilities*

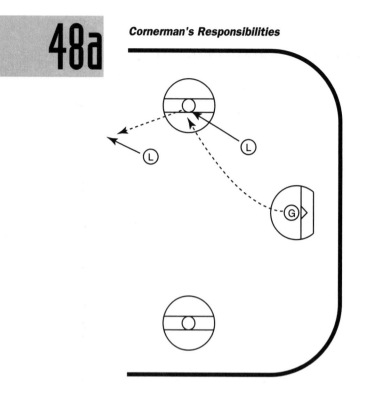

Variation: The cornerman can cut into the Middle Lane of the floor to create a better passing angle to the ball side creaseman (see diagram 48b). Here, he would throw a crisp, level pass, but to the stick which is held behind him.

Note: Throwing these passes becomes more difficult if the cornerman is also on the run.

Stress that if the cornerman passes the ball up the floor, he must then follow up the play by running hard to beat his check down the floor. One of the major problems of the cornerman passing the ball up the floor is that after he passes the ball, rather than running, he either jogs up the floor or stands and watches the play. Another major problem is that once a cornerman passes the ball to a crease-man he never sees the ball again—creasemen have a tendency to go one-on-one no matter what the situation is.

c. The Pointman's Responsibilities On The Breakout
The pointman is a safety valve. He will get the outlet pass if the weak-side cornerman or the strong-side cornerman are covered, or if the pointman has just beaten his check to get in the clear.

d. The Creaseman's Responsibilities On The Breakout
(1) The creaseman should be a good goal scorer, quick, fast, aggressive, and a "hustler."
(2) When the creaseman should look for a pass on the breakout while running up the floor:
First Option—the creaseman should look for the breakaway pass immediately from the goalie on the break (usually before or around the center area of the floor).
Second Option—the creaseman then looks for a pass from the cornerman. If the creaseman gets this pass and it's an odd-man situation, he takes the ball to the crease area trying to draw a defender. If it's strictly a one-on-one situation, he tries to beat his defender.

48b

Cornerman's Responsibilities

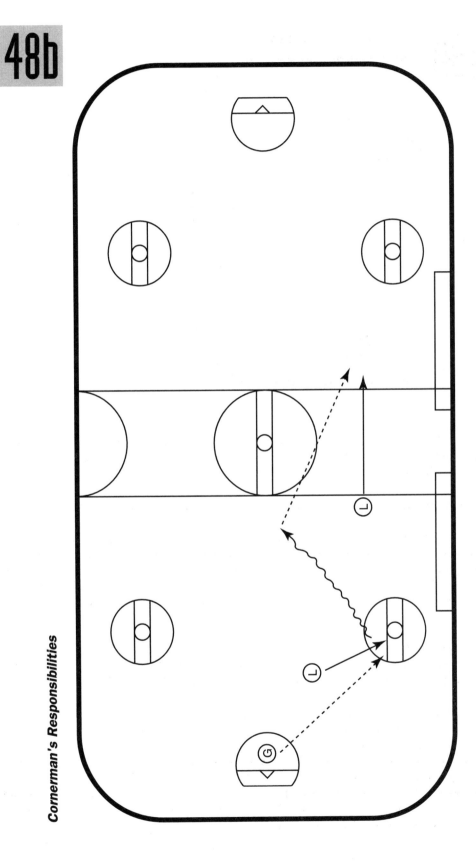

Third Option—the creaseman keeps his eye on the ball, but once over center he knows he will not get the ball until the end of the break unless it's a broken play. A broken play occurs when a defender attacks the ballcarrier in the Neutral Zone or just over the Offensive Zone Line.

(3) A creaseman receiving a breakaway pass on the run from the goalie should hold his stick horizontally (with the tip pointing to the far end boards or facing into the middle of the floor, depending on the player's preference) in front of his body and in front of his inside shoulder. He should catch the ball over his inside shoulder with the "face" of the stick open to the approaching ball.

(4) An off-ball creaseman receiving a pass on the run from the cornerman should turn his upper body and receive this level pass over his inside shoulder. He should give a target with the "face" of the stick turned facing this passer. He must make sure he waits with the stick for the ball to come to the pocket, and that he "gives" with the stick on impact of the ball.

(5) A ball side creaseman receiving a "rainbow pass" from the cornerman catches the ball almost the same way he catches a breakaway pass. He holds the stick horizontally, pointing the tip to the side boards this time, and catches the ball over his inside shoulder.

4. Breakout Versus Pressure Defense

The best way to beat defensive pressure is for the goalie to throw a quick outlet pass. This will not give the pressers the time they want to set up their press. In other words, run the typical Fast-Break.

a. Pressuring the Outlet Pass

Five options a team can use to counter an opposition team which likes to press or forecheck to stop or interfere with the outlet pass to the two cornermen (see CHAPTER VI: MAN SHORT - Press Breaker Against the Ten-Second Press):

(1) The Outside Exchange

The cornermen and the creasemen exchange positions (with the cornermen running up the floor on the outside of the creasemen and the creasemen running on the inside of the cornermen towards the goalie and the outlet area). The goalie has the option of passing to either the player in the outlet area or to the breaking player. It is amazing how often the cornerman ends up in the clear down the floor with all this confusion (see diagram 49).

(2) The Inside Exchange

The cornermen this time run up the floor but on the inside of the creasemen (see diagram 50a).

(3) The Up Pick-and-Roll

Both cornermen run an Up Pick for their respective creasemen and roll into the middle of the floor for a possible pass from the goalie (see diagram 50b).

(4) The Safety Valve

The pointman stays even with the goalie for a safety valve pass (see diagram 51).

(5) Off-the-Bench Play

The creaseman and cornerman on the same side of the bench break to the defensive door on the bench. Two new teammates break out quickly through the offensive door to get a jump on the opposition players. (see CHAPTER III: THE FAST-BREAK SYSTEM - Line Changes)

(6) The Goalie Runs the Ball

The goalie runs the ball down the floor until he is going to be checked. At this time, he passes off to an open teammate.

b. Pressuring the Ballcarrier

In this situation the goalie has already made the outlet pass, but the defense still has time to set up their press.

(1) The Ballcarrier Runs the Ball

Give the ball to the cornerman and let him run the ball out of the Defensive Zone. The rest of his teammates should just clear out.

49

Breakout Versus Pressure Defense - The Outside Exchange

50a

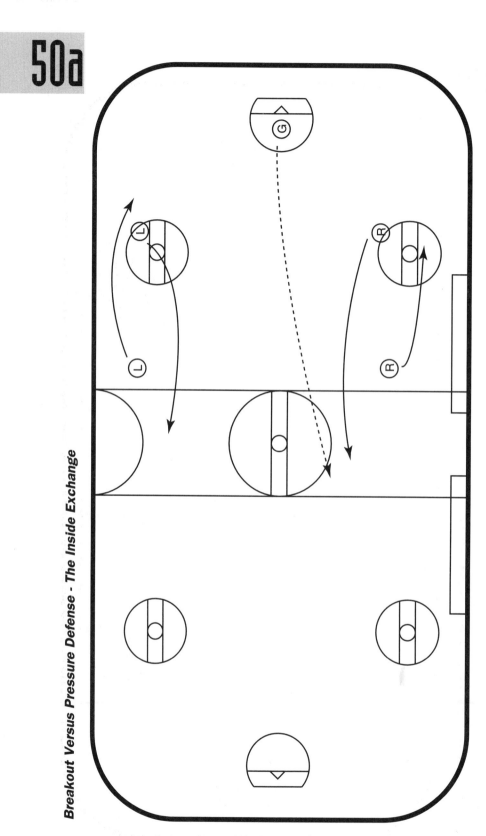

Breakout Versus Pressure Defense - The Inside Exchange

50b

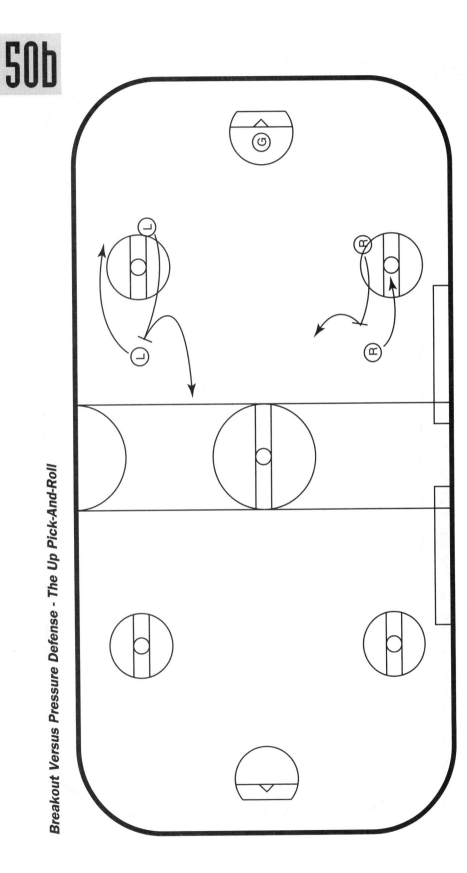

Breakout Versus Pressure Defense - The Up Pick-And-Roll

51

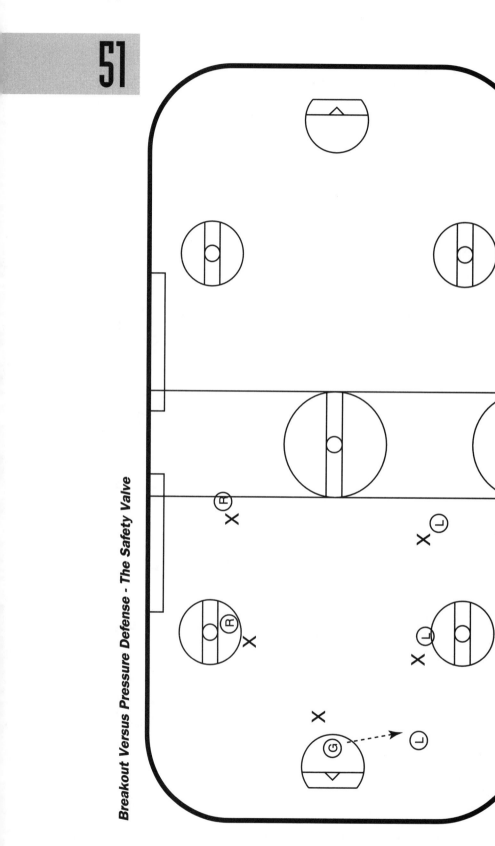

(2) The Ballcarrier Passes the Ball

The ballcarrier can pass the ball out of the Defensive Zone. He should keep his poise and not be rushed by the opposition's pressure to make frantic passes. He should look for either creasemen to button hook and run back to meet the pass so there is no chance of an interception. The creaseman on the ballcarrier's side can break straight back to the ball, while the creaseman on the off-ball side can break diagonally back to the ball into the center area of the floor. Against pressure, a receiver should never stand and wait for a pass. The ballcarrier can also look deep down the floor or to the bench area for a new teammate coming on the floor. Finally, the ballcarrier can look to pass to the goalie who has stepped out of his crease.

B. FILLING THE LANES (THE MIDDLE)

To teach the process of filling the lanes, divide the lacrosse floor into three lanes or alleys. Fast-Break lacrosse teams are not like basketball and hockey teams (sports teams which like the ball or puck in the Middle Lane of the playing surface). Fast-Break lacrosse teams prefer the ball in one of the two Outside Lanes.

a. The Cornerman's Responsibilities When Filling the Outside Lane

(1) The main weapon for a Fast-Breaking team is to have the cornerman run the ball up the Outside Lane into the Offensive Zone. Even though the ball can move up the floor quicker by passing it than running it, the best option is to run the ball up the floor. This option is the best especially if the cornerman has the ability to beat his defender, thereby creating an odd-man situation at the other end of the floor. This philosophy complements the Combination Offensive System (see CHAPTER I: MAN-TO-MAN TEAM OFFENSE) with regards to starting the offense from the cornerman's position rather than the creaseman's position (see diagram 52). In minor/youth lacrosse, the better option might be a short pass up the floor.

(2) The cornerman's rule is to run the ball from the Defensive Face-Off Circle to the Offensive Face-Off Circle. When carrying the ball up the floor, he must be aware of what is happening around him, i.e., in front of him, behind him, and to his sides.

(3) When running with the ball up the floor keep the stick in close to the body (always being aware of protecting the stick with the body) and hold it high in a passing position while cradling the ball to "feel" the weight (thereby knowing the ball is in the stick).

(4) Once over the Offensive Zone Line, it is decision time for the ballcarrying cornerman, who must read what the defense is giving him.

b. The Creaseman's Responsibilities When Filling the Outside Lane

(1) The creaseman runs a narrow pattern up the floor in the Outside Lane in line with the far crease (see diagram 53).

(2) When the creaseman should look for a pass when filling the Outside Lane:

First Option—the creaseman looks back immediately for the pass, but if he does not receive the ball by the time he is over center, he continues to run directly to the crease and holds this threat position for a possible pass.

Second Option—if the odd-man situation does not materialize and if he is the creaseman on the ball side, he can pop out for a pass into the corner area; if he is a creaseman on the off-ball side, he waits for a Down Pick.

C. THE PRIMARY BREAK (THE ENDING)

In the Fast-Break System, players run to create odd-man situations, with the following results:

    (i) A direct shot on net by the ballcarrier may occur.

    (ii) One pass and a shot may result. This is an excellent play, but is usually executed against teams poorly prepared in stopping the fast-break.

52

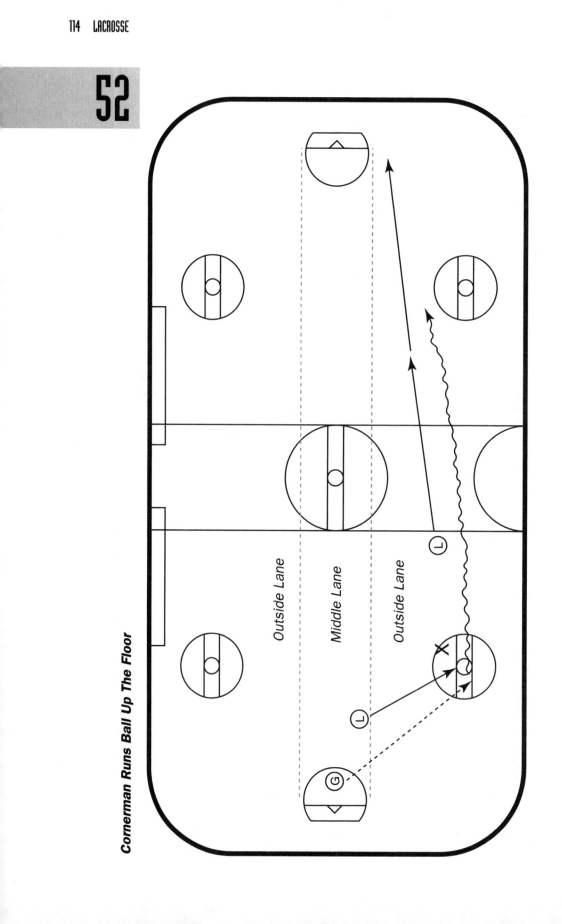

Cornerman Runs Ball Up The Floor

Outside Lane

Middle Lane

Outside Lane

53

Creaseman's Pattern On Breakout

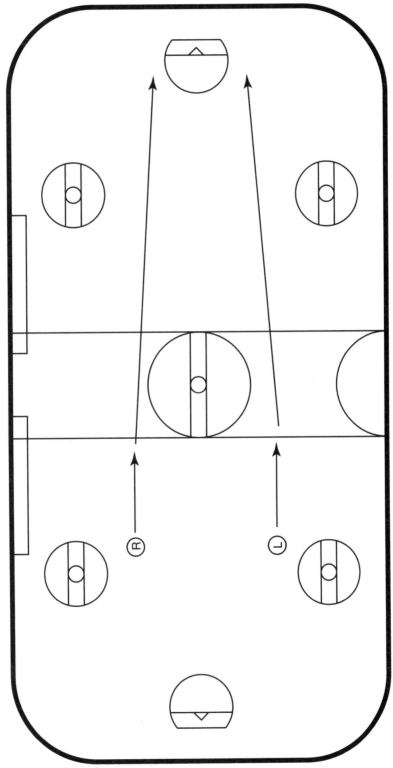

(iii) Two passes and a shot is the best result which gives the offensive team time to execute a good play.

(iv) A fast-breaking team might get in three good passes at the end of the break, but any more passes will give the defensive team time to get back on defense.

So, the end of the break is a series of short passes (looking for the open man) and a good shot on net.

Note: It should take about five seconds from the beginning of the fast-break (possession of the ball) to the end of the fast-break (good shot on net). Here, a coach has to determine the best time to get the ball up the floor considering his player's age level.

1. Scoring Priorities Off the Break

First Scoring Priority—an uncontested close-in shot from a breakaway or from an odd-man situation.
Second Scoring Priority—an uncontested long shot (cornerman's spot) from an odd-man situation.
Third Scoring Priority—a one-on-one situation when the defense is still in transition (moving back).
Fourth Scoring Priority—a shot off the Down Pick (Secondary Break).

2. Odd-Man Situation Rules

Rule #1—The cornermen and creasemen must hold their positions until the fast-break is over.

Rule #2—The cornerman and creaseman on the same side of the floor must maintain good spacing between themselves so that one defensive player cannot cover both of them at once. Good spacing also gives the cornerman with the ball enough time to make the best play selection; i.e., if the defensive player "cheats" or moves up early on the opposite cornerman for a possible interception on a pass, this spacing will leave the opposite creaseman open for a diagonal cross-floor pass from the ballcarrying cornerman.

Rule #3—The ballcarrier or the player creating the odd-man situation must yell "odd" to let his teammates know.

Rule #4—The ballcarrier thinks shot (score) first, pass second. It is easier to adjust one's thinking from shooting to passing than from passing to shooting. In addition, if the ballcarrier is thinking pass, he doesn't look like a real offensive threat. As a result, the defender will play off him and look to intercept the pass. By looking at the net, actually thinking shot, and taking the ball to the net, the ballcarrier becomes more of a scoring threat. Then, when the defender commits himself, the ballcarrier passes to the open man.

Rule #5—The ballcarrier in an odd-man situation does not take a hit when in the process of passing. He must back off, i.e., back pedal. Now and then, however, he might have to take a hit to set up a teammate. This is an important rule especially in minor/youth lacrosse.

Rule #6—Never pass the ball up to a creaseman unless he can either score or is in an odd-man situation where a score will occur.

3. Odd-Man Prime Scoring Area Positions and Responsibilities
a. 2-on-1 Situation (see diagram 54)
(1) Good spacing between the two offensive players is important because one defensive player cannot play them both. A rule of thumb for a 2-on-1 situation is that the two players stay as wide as the crease, i.e., along the boundary lines of the Middle Lane, so that they are a good scoring threat as soon as they get the ball.
(2) Basically the ballcarrier's responsibility is to take the ball to the net until he is played; i.e., the ballcarrier is thinking shot first and pass second. If a defender commits to him, he passes off to his open teammate.

54 **2-On-1 Spacing**

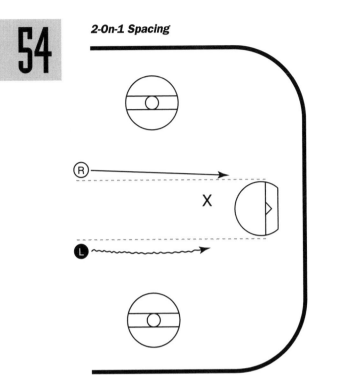

(3) As the ballcarrier runs towards the net, he must read the defensive man. If the defensive man commits himself, the ballcarrier passes to the open man. If the defensive man stays in the middle of the floor, the ballcarrier must shoot or think shot once in the Prime Scoring Area.

(4) The ballcarrier shouldn't pass to his teammate when the defensive man is standing in the middle of the floor between them since this is a good position for an interception.

b. 3-on-2 and 4-on-3 Situations (see diagram 55)

(1) Be conscious of positioning when ending the fast-break. The three offensive players form a right-angle triangle while the four offensive players form a box. The creasemen station themselves beside the crease and the cornermen station themselves behind the creasemen and far enough back to give themselves time to make the right play. Insist that each player runs to his spot in the triangle or box.

(2) The Ballcarrying Cornerman's Responsibilities:

(a) The primary responsibility of the ballcarrier is first to look to score, and secondly, to draw a defensive man and pass off to an open teammate.

(b) His role involves a lot of decision-making skills. He has to make quick, good decisions on what to do, plus have the technical skill of making the perfect pin-point pass. He is like a quarterback in football who has to "read" the defense and react accordingly.

(c) His options are:

(i) The ballcarrying cornerman can move in for a shot, if no defender picks him up to check (see diagram 56).

(ii) The ballcarrying cornerman can pass across to the off-ball cornerman, if the off-ball cornerman's defender leaves him to check the ballcarrier, or if the top defensive player plays him immediately (see diagram 57).

(iii) The ballcarrying cornerman can pass to the creaseman on his side of the floor, if this ball side creaseman's defender charges to check him (see diagram 58).

55

3-On-2

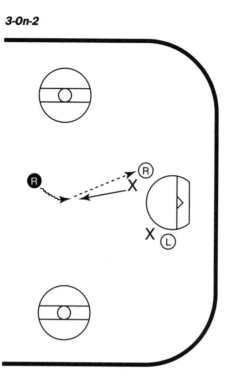

56

4-On-3 Options -
Ballcarrier Shoots

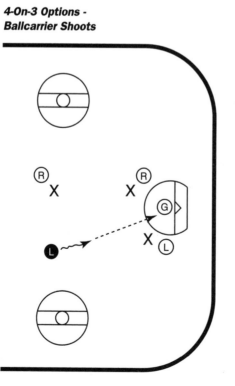

57

4-On-3 Options
Pass To Off-Ball Cornerman

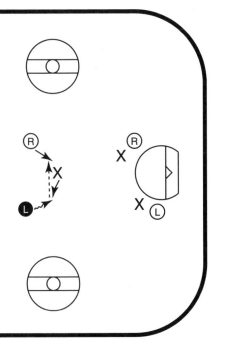

58

4-On-3 Options
Pass To The Same-Side Creaseman

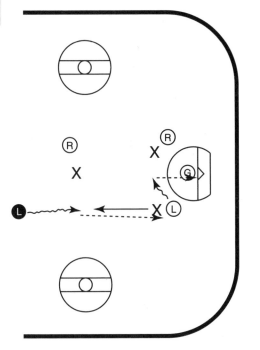

(iv) The ballcarrying cornerman can pass diagonally to the off-ball creaseman, if the ball side creaseman's defender has started his move to check the ballcarrier and the off-ball creaseman's defender has started to "cheat" or move across early to play the ball side creaseman for the anticipated pass to him, leaving the off-ball creaseman open (see diagram 59).

(v) The ballcarrying cornerman can pass diagonally to the off-ball creaseman, if the top defender picks up the ballcarrier and if the off-ball creaseman's defender starts to "cheat" or move up early to the off-ball cornerman for the anticipated pass (see diagram 60).

(vi) The ballcarrying cornerman can fake a pass to the off-ball creaseman to draw the defender over and then pass to the ball side creaseman on his side of the floor. This works best in a 3-on-2 situation (see diagram 61).

(d) Most times the ballcarrier will run to the cornerman's spot on his proper side of the floor, but he will fill in the open spot in the box formation wherever it is. (Sometimes this is the other cornerman's spot.)

(e) The ballcarrier stays on the side of the floor at the beginning of the play. He cuts to the middle of the floor if no defender challenges him and shoots at the net. If he draws a defensive man, he will pass to the open man.

(f) If the ballcarrier passes to the off-ball cornerman, he holds his position! Most players at the beginning want to cut for a return pass, but this is a bad idea because if the former ballcarrier cuts and does not get the pass, the odd-man situation is over. By holding, he is in a better position to receive a possible return pass and shot.

(3) The Off-ball Cornerman's Responsibilities:

(a) He goes to his proper side of the floor and fills in the open spot on the box formation.

(b) The off-ball cornerman must be in a good position, i.e., good spacing between himself and the creaseman on his side must occur, so that when he receives the ball he will have time to make a play without hurrying.

59

4-On-3 Options
Pass To The Off-Ball Creaseman

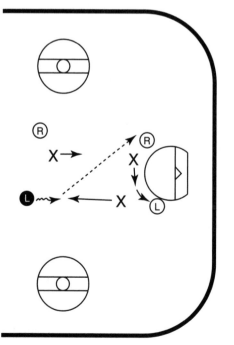

60

**4-On-3 Options
Pass To The Off-Ball Creaseman**

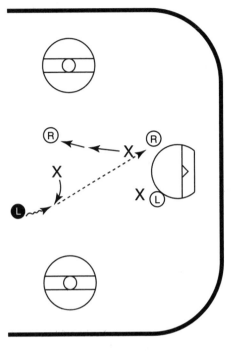

61

3-On-2

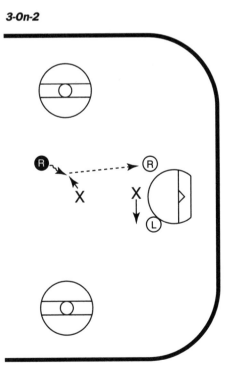

(c) He must put himself in a good shooting position by stepping slightly into the middle of the floor. He must also physically prepare himself to shoot before he receives the pass, by putting his stick up in a shooting position and taking a slightly wider stance.

(d) On receiving the ball the off-ball cornerman's options are:

(i) Move in for a shot, if nobody picks him up to check.

(ii) Pass to the creaseman on his side of the floor, if he draws this creaseman's defender.

(iii) Pass back to the original ballcarrier, if the top defender recovers to pick him up.

(iv) Pass diagonally to the opposite creaseman, if the opposite creaseman's defender starts to "cheat" or move across the floor early.

(4) The Creasemen's Responsibilities:

(a) Basically their job is to draw their checks to the crease by running hard to the crease and standing there to keep their checks occupied.

(b) They line themselves up along the side of the crease in a position to score, so that when they get the ball, they can catch and shoot in one motion (which is called a "quick stick").

(c) They now wait and are physically and mentally prepared to receive a pass.

(d) Their feet are staggered with the outside foot forward, so that they can take a step out quickly with this foot to get in front of the net. This step provides a better position to see the whole net and, thereby, a better opportunity to score.

(e) The creaseman's options on receiving a pass:

(i) He shoots quickly at the net. His check has either charged the cornerman with the ball on his side of the floor, has charged the cornerman without the ball anticipating a pass to him, or has charged the opposite creaseman. So, this "scoring" pass can come from the opposite crease-man, the cornerman on his side of the floor, or from the opposite cornerman.

(ii) He steps out in front and takes a shot to the far side of the net.

(iii) He steps out in front and fakes a shot to the far side, then shoots to the near side.

(iv) He passes to the opposite creaseman as he is being pressured by the opposite creaseman's defender coming across the crease.

(v) He passes back to the opposite cornerman.

(vi) He passes back to the original ballcarrying cornerman on his side of the floor.

d. 5-on-4 Situation

(1) The same rules as the 4-on-3 and 3-on-2 situations are used.

(2) The team does not practice the 5-on-4 situation as much because it doesn't occur as often in a game.

(3) The options for the off-ball cornerman on the strong side:

(a) He can cut in front of the defender at the top of the four-man zone. He will be either open for a pass or will draw the defender with him leaving an open spot for the pointman to fill in for a possible pass and shot (see diagram 62).

(b) He can screen out the top defender of the zone, allowing the pointman to cut behind him for a possible pass and shot.

D. THE SECONDARY BREAK (THE ENDING)

From the primary fast-break, the team should run its offense when the odd-man situation becomes an even-man situation. Flowing into its offense is called the secondary break. Fast-Breaking Teams do not like to bring the ball up the floor and set up deliberately into their offense as this becomes too slow and predictable.

1. Down Pick Option

a. The creaseman on the ball side pops out for a pass and a possible Down Pick.

b. The creaseman on the off-ball side holds on the crease also to receive a Down Pick.

c. The ballcarrier options are:

1) Passing to the creaseman coming off the off-ball Down Pick. Coaches likes this option because it is

62

5-On-4

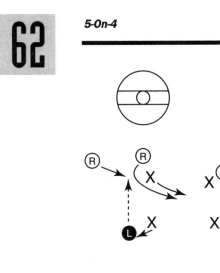

a good maneuver to swing the ball from one side of the floor to the other to make the defense move and thereby making it harder for the defense to back each other up.

2) Passing down to the creaseman who popped out, and then going down and setting a Down Pick. This play will set him free for a shot or a pass across to the opposite creaseman coming off his Down Pick (see diagrams 63a, 63b).

2. Double Pick Option
The pointman and cornerman on the strong side set Down Picks for the creaseman who comes off both of them for a possible pass and shot from the ballcarrying cornerman (see diagram 64).

3. Cut Through Option
The pointman cuts through, drawing his defender, with the cornerman on the strong side cutting right behind him (see diagram 65). The passer hits either the first or second cutter, whichever is open.

VII. LINE CHANGES

When to change lines:
a. Change lines by a coach's gut feeling when he thinks his players are tired.
b. Change lines by the tempo of the game. In a fast game use quick changes; in a slow game use longer shifts.
c. Change lines on the breakout or when bringing the ball out from the Defensive Zone. The coach wants his players fresh on offense.
d. Change lines when the fast-break is over in the Offensive Zone (players then come off).
e. Change lines when the team loses possession of the ball and is coming back into the Defensive Zone. The coach wants his team fresh on Defense.

63a

Secondary Break - "Down Pick"

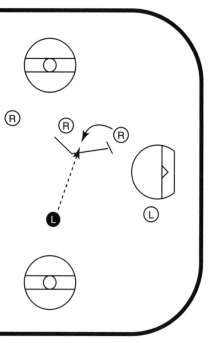

63b

Secondary Break - "Down Pick"

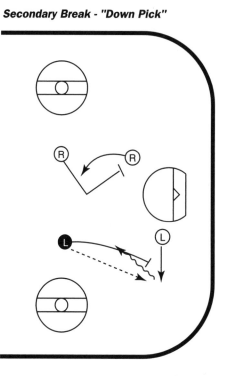

64

Secondary Break - "Double Pick"

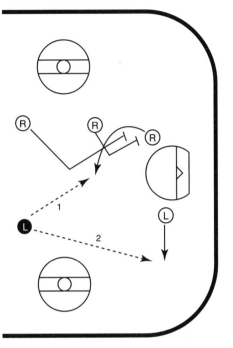

65

Secondary Break - "Cut Through"

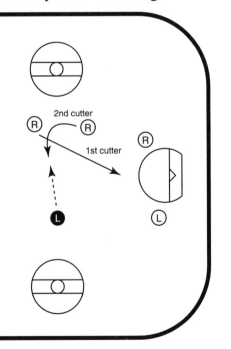

f. A general Line Change Rule is "Once up the floor and back and then off"; or "Twice up the floor and back and then off."
g. Change lines by timing the shifts. Players come off in 30 seconds no matter what they are doing, except when on defense.

To figure out his line change strategy a coach must answer the question: "Do you want your players fresh on offense or fresh on defense?"

1. The Fast-Break Line Change
The philosophy of a Fast-Breaking team is to keep offensive pressure on the opposition at all times. Therefore, the ability to change lines quickly helps the team to maintain this pressure.
a. Use an offensive door and a defensive door. Players can only go out the offensive door and only come in the defensive door. Players never go over the boards to change unless it is only a one-man line change. Letting players go over the boards on a wholesale line change could result in a penalty for too many men on the floor. Note: It is important to man these doors with coaches who under-stand what is happening in the game and who can stay mentally alert on the bench during the game.
b. On a complete line change, players do not change by positions, i.e., left-shot cornerman for a left-shot cornerman, but by the number of players coming off the floor; i.e., five players come off, five players go on. Usually three players come off the floor on the breakout: the creaseman, the point-man, and the cornerman on the bench side. The cornerman and creaseman opposite the bench stay on the floor until the primary break is over. On the offensive door are five players: the first three are in order of their shot and position. If the right-shot cornerman and creaseman stay on the floor, then the left-shot creaseman and cornerman, in that order, are at the offensive door ready to go on the floor along with the pointman. It does not really matter what type of shot the pointman is. Here, the offensive-door coach is not concerned with exchanging by proper positions, but by sending out the correct number of players on the floor as fast as the others come off the floor. So he is always watch-ing the number of players stepping into the Rectangular Change Area and pushing the exact number of players out the offensive door.

On a one-man line change, players change by position; i.e., if a left-shot cornerman comes off the floor, a left-shot cornerman goes on the floor. This player is allowed to go over the boards as this is a quicker method than trying to fight through his teammates to go out the offensive door.
c. On a line change never walk off the floor. Run!
d. Never come off the floor when on defense.
e. Basically, the team wants quick line changes—up the floor and back and off . It is important to time the line changes so that a coach knows whether the team is running all out. Usually 30 seconds is the criterion for the time required to make a line change, but a coach will have to experiment to find the best time for his team. Note: The length of the shifts will determine the length of the fast-break drills.
f. How the Fast-Break Line Change Works (see diagram 66):
    1) The coach calls "Line change" when the team is in the Defensive Zone or when the line is on its way back to play defense.
    2) The team tries to get 25 percent of their goals from the fast-break.
    3) The Fast-Break team does a "combination line change" of changing partly on the breakout and then changing the rest of the players when the fast-break is over.
    4) On the line change the team is going to go for the odd-man situation and still make changes at the same time.
    5) The creaseman, the cornerman on the same side of the players bench, and the pointman come off the floor every time.
    6) The first two players, who are the same shot and will be on their proper side of the floor when they go on, try to get an advantage by leaving the bench early, as soon as the first player coming off touches the Change Area. Make sure the two players coming off the floor are running hard to the bench.

66

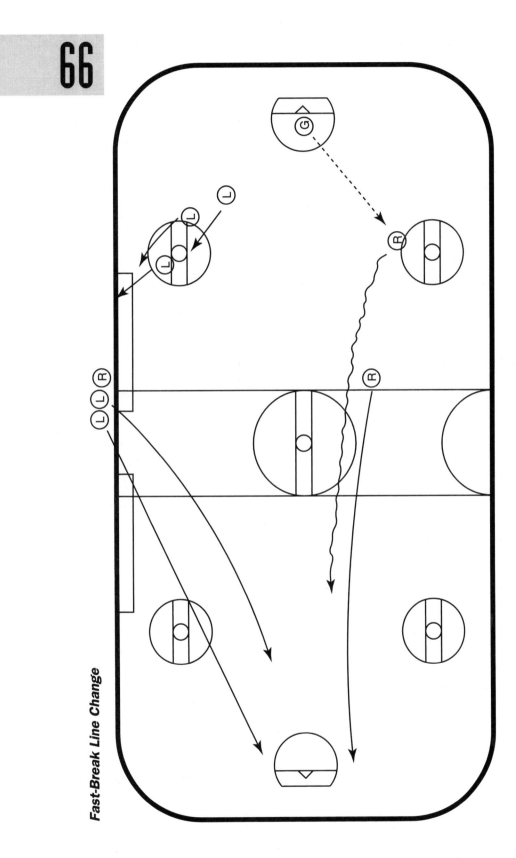

Fast-Break Line Change

Recall: The Official Change of Players Rule—A player leaving the playing floor must have one foot in the Rectangular Change Area before the substitute player can make contact with the playing floor.

7) The cornerman and creaseman on the opposite side of the bench stay on the floor until the fast-break is over. The off-bench cornerman on receiving the outlet pass looks for the first two breaking players off the bench while running the ball up the floor. If the goalie can hit one of these two players breaking off the bench then he should throw the ball to one of them rather than going to the off-bench cornerman.

8) If an odd-man situation does not materialize out of this line change, the team finishes the complete line change by having the other two players on the off-bench side come off the floor and two new players go on.

Remember: If the players are not called for a line change on the breakout, they run the primary break (the odd-man situation) into the secondary break.

VIII. THE RUNNING ASPECT OF FAST-BREAK LACROSSE

1. The Fast-Break team understands that they do not necessarily have to be faster than their opposition in order to fast-break against them. The fast-break game does not only depend upon speed, endurance, and quickness, i.e., mental quickness as well as physical quickness, but it also depends on habit. Thus running at every opportunity becomes "second nature."

2. The Fast-Break teams have to run all out in the first and second periods for the conditioning factor to take place in the third period. Because a Fast-Break team wants to keep intensity and pressure on the opposition to wear them down, a coach has to distinguish the difference between running all out and jogging to his players. Players should be coming off the floor after every line change exhausted.

3. Ball-control teams—teams that like to play five-on-five rather than transition lacrosse—will try to slow the game down. On the other hand, the Fast-Break teams will try to keep the game wide open forcing the opposition to run. It is only human nature to take the easy route and not run. This is what a coach must be aware of. Thus, he must fight the tendency of his players to slow down rather than speed up, i.e., the inconsistency of not going all out, all the time.

4. There are physical and mental stages a player goes through during a game. At the beginning of a game both these aspects do not usually come into play, but as the game goes on a player starts to suffer some physical discomfort and possibly physical pain in the stomach and back area. If a player keeps pushing himself through this discomfort he will get his "second wind"—a point during the game when all the pain and discomfort go away—at which time he feels like he could run forever. Since most players go through this painful process, some believe the harder they push themselves, the sooner they will get over this pain and the sooner they will feel better about playing. A player's conditioning will affect this stage.

Because of this suffering and pain, players must learn to play through it mentally. Players have to have mental toughness to force themselves to run when they are hurting.

5. It is one thing to have conditioning, it is another thing to have "heart," "courage," and "character" to use that conditioning. A player could be in the greatest shape, but if he does not have the intestinal fortitude to use it he will not be successful on the playing floor. Another player could be in the worst shape but because of his "grit," "heart," and "desire to win," he is very successful by running all out even though it hurts more than the conditioned athlete. Definitely the best combination is to have conditioning and the "heart" to use it.

IX. PROBLEMS IN TEACHING THE FAST-BREAK SYSTEM

1. The problem of turnovers: If a coach makes a commitment to this system he must be aware that he is going to have more turnovers, more mistakes, and more breakdowns than a slow-down, ball-control system. In the beginning of the season a coach must live with early turnovers. A coach must also know how many turnovers he can live with during a game.

2. The problem of players jogging up the floor and back in practice and in games: Players have to sprint from crease to crease. To get this intensity, time the players with a stopwatch.

3. The problem of players not wanting to give up the ball: It is imperative that players are unselfish in this system. They have no choice but to set each other up to make this system work.

4. The problem of spacing: The cornermen, by getting too close to the creasemen at the end of the break, allows one defender to cover both players. This poor positioning does not give the cornerman time to make the perfect play; rather he has to rush the play when he is so close.

5. The problem of creasemen running wide rather than in a straight line with the edge of the crease: If they get the ball when they are wide, they will not be an instant offensive threat.

X. BUILDING THE FAST-BREAK SYSTEM THROUGH DRILLS

A. TIPS FOR FAST-BREAK DRILLS

1. The coach should figure out what kind of Fast-Break System he wants to run, then break it down into drills. When teaching the fast-break start with the whole (5-on-0), then break it into parts (2-on-1, 3-on-2, 4-on-3, 5-on-4), then return to the whole (5-on- 5).

2. Build the fast-break every day with drills.

3. Stress a good beginning and a good ending to the fast-break.

4. Realize when a coach talks seconds, he is talking feet. Time the players running up the floor to give them a gauge on how hard they are running in a game. Not all teams run because executing the fast-break is hard to teach and hard work.

5. Run all drills at top speed with a ball and use the full length of the floor.

6. Understand that the success of the fast-break depends upon how quick a team gets into transition, i.e., from defense to offense. Work on the outlet pass.

7. End most drills with a score. This gives the players a good feeling and it conditions them to be persistent. Even if the goalie stops the shot in a drill, he must throw the ball into the corner for the offensive players to pursue.

8. Fast-break drills make players play hard against one another.

9. Give the offense an advantage in most fast-break drills so there is successful execution and, thereby, positive reinforcement.

10. Teach the fast-break by letting the players "do" the drill rather than by the coach talking theory.

11. At the beginning of teaching the fast-break do not give players options. Make them go to specific positions. As the system becomes more refined, the players can then exchange positions.

12. Passing on the run, which is one of the toughest skills in lacrosse, is practiced and taught every day in the Fast-Break drills.

13. In the shooting segment of the drills players can practice Close-In Shooting, usually from the creaseman's position, or Long-ball Shooting, which is often from the cornerman's position.

14. Get players to say what they are doing on the break : "I'm crease." "I'm corner." This communication gets rid of indecision and helps to build team cohesion.

15. Everybody does all the drills, although there are some specific drills for creasemen and some specific drills for cornermen.

16. Objectives of Drills:
    a. Teaching Drills
    To practice the skills start all drills with no pressure on the players so that they can concentrate on their form, technique, and execution.
    b. Pressure Drills
    After teaching the skill, put pressure on the players: to force them to concentrate in the drill; so that they can practice their execution of skills in a pressure situation; and to teach players to keep their composure in a pressure situation.

A coach puts pressure in the drill: by having the team trying to beat an objective of a certain number of passes caught; by having an objective of catching as many balls in a row without dropping any; by having players do a punishment (push-ups) for every dropped ball; by having an objective of beating a certain number of shots on net; by having an objective of trying to beat its last shooting percentage; by having right-handed shots competing against left-handed shots; and by putting a defensive chaser in an odd-man situation.

By setting an objective for each drill, the coach gives a player and the team something to compare themselves with and something to try to beat each time. This objective becomes a great challenge and thereby a great motivator.

(1) Passes Caught Cooperative Drill
In this drill the team keeps stats on how many passes are completed (no shots) for 3 to 5 minutes. The pressure comes from the whole team working together trying to beat the number of passes caught in the last practice (for example: Return Pass Drill, 2-on-0 Up Drill).
(2) Passes In a Row Cooperative Drill
The team just tries to beat the number of passes caught in a row (no time limit) without anybody dropping the ball (for example: Return Pass Drill, 2-on-0 Up Drill).
(3) Punishment Passing Drill
Every player who drops a ball during the drill will do one push-up for every dropped ball at the end of the drill (for example: 2-on-0 Up Drill).
(4) Time Limit Passing Drill
The team tries to complete the drill in a certain length of time (seconds). Everybody passes up and down the floor (to the stationary passers) trying to beat their last time (for example: Single Line Drill).

(5) Shooting Cooperative Drill

The team runs this drill for 3 to 5 minutes keeping stats on how many shots are taken on net. The pressure comes from the whole team trying to beat the number of shots on net from the last practice (for example: Single Line Drill, 2-on-0 Up Drill).

(6) Shooting Percentage Cooperative Drill

The team runs this drill for 3 to 5 minutes keeping stats on the percentage of goals scored in relation to the number of shots taken (trying to obtain an average of 20 percent). The pressure comes from the whole team competing to beat their shooting percentage from the last practice (for example: 2-on-0 Up Drill).

(7) Competitive Drill

This drill is a game with left-handed shots competing against right-handed shots or just two picked teams competing against each other. The winning team is the one which scores the most number of goals or is the first team to score 10 goals (for example: Single Line Drill, Return Pass Drill, 3-on-2 Continuous Drill).

(8) Defensive Pressure Drill

In all odd-man situation drills, the coach includes a chaser to put pressure on the offense. This chaser must touch a cone then get back into the play trying to pressure the fast-break players into mistakes (for example: 2-on-1 with a Chaser Drill, 3-on-2 with a Chaser Drill).

B. FULL-FLOOR WARM-UP DRILLS

1. Single Line Drill (see diagram 67)

Use six stationary players: three on each side of the floor spaced out along the boards; one player above the Side Face-Off Circle; one player at center; and the last player before the far Side Face-Off Circle.

At the end boards, all the left-handed shots with a ball line up on their proper side of the floor and all the right-handed shots with a ball line up on their proper side of the floor.

The first left-shot player passes to the opposite stationary passer above the Side Face-Off Circle and sprints up the floor looking for a return pass. He then passes to the next stationary passer and looks for the return pass, and does the same thing to the last passer. This is a no shot drill. When the runner has caught the ball from the last passer, he runs behind the net and lines up to come back the other way. Once the left-shot player leaves, the first right-shot player executes the same procedure. The lines alternate until everybody has practiced the "give-and-go" up the floor.

Variation: (1) All the left-handed shots go up the floor, then all the right-handed shots go. (2) Make it into a shooting drill where all the players end up shooting. The coach can stress Close-In shots, planted Long-Ball shots, or on the run Long-Ball shots.

2. Zig-Zag Rotation Drill (see diagram 68)

This drill has a similar formation as the "Single Line Drill," except this time there are three passers for the left-handed shots and three passers for the right-handed shots. Two are located in the middle of the floor near the Defensive Zone Line, two are located by the side boards across from each other near the Offensive Zone Line, and two are in the middle of the floor near the far crease.

The competitive drill has the right shots racing against the left shots. The drill begins with a player passing to the first passer, who he consequently replaces. The first passer then passes to the second passer and replaces him; the second passer passes to the third passer and replaces him; the third passer runs back along the side boards to the end of his respective line. All the lefts and rights do this rotation until the last player has gone.

67

Single Line Drill - All The Lefts, Then All The Rights

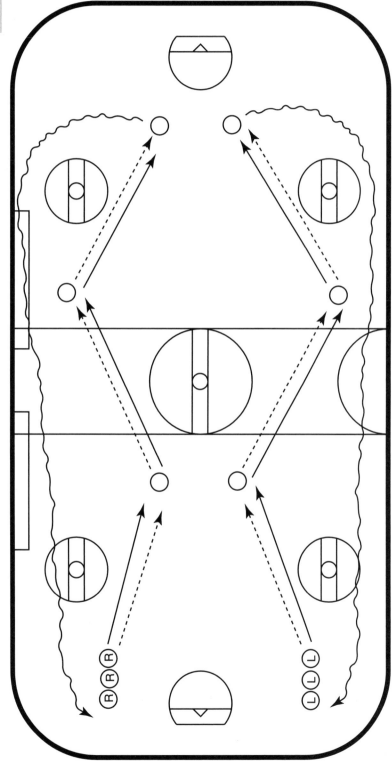

Zig-Zag Rotation Drill

Variation: Use six passers, but this time the whole team lines up on the right side of the floor. Players rotate up one side and rotate back down the other side. This is a cooperative drill where the whole team works together to beat the team objective of the number of passes in five minutes.

3. Return Pass Drill (see diagram 69)

This drill has a similar formation as the "Zig-Zag Rotation Drill," except there are only two passers in the middle of the floor near the Offensive Zone Line, and two passers in the middle of the floor near the Defensive Zone Line.

The right-hand shot passes to the first passer, gets the ball back, then passes to the second passer who gets the ball back, and then lines up at the far end boards. Once all the rights have gone up the floor they do the same thing coming back down the same side of the floor. The left-hand shots do the same thing on the other side of the floor. Run it as a competitive drill: rights versus lefts, or run it as a cooperative drill where the whole team tries to beat their last objective. Run the drill for 5 minutes, replacing the passers every minute.

C. BREAKOUT DRILLS

4. 5-on-0 Walk Through Drill
Players go to their breakout spots, then walk the ball up the floor where the players end up in their Primary Break spots. The coach explains the principles of the Fast-Break as they are walking.

5. 1-on-1 Full-Floor Breakout Drill
This drill helps to build confidence for the ballcarrier to beat a defensive man who might press him immediately on possession of the ball. He learns to create odd-man situations by beating his man. The defender lets him get the outlet pass from the goalie first, then tries to deny him from going up the floor.

Variation: The defender tries to deny the offensive player from getting the outlet pass first, then denies him all the way up the floor.

6. 1-on-0 Half-Floor Outlet Pass to Cornerman Drill (see diagram 70)
Start the drill with two lines, right shots and left shots. Have all the players with a ball line up along the side boards on their wrong side of the floor facing the goalie. Alternate with the first ballcarrier in each line running towards the goalie and rolling the ball to him. The player then continues running to his spot for the breakout—the Face-Off Dot—and receives the pass from the goalie. In the beginning players should take the short outlet pass standing stationary. Then progress with the player receiving the pass on the run. As the goalie's passing skills improve, add pressure by having a defender in front of him to interfere with his passing.

7. 1-on-0 Half-Floor Outlet Pass to Creaseman Drill
The same set up is used, except the difference here is the goalie throws a long level pass to the breaking creaseman in the area between the Defensive Face-Off Circle and the Defensive Zone Line.

8. Four Corners (1-on-0) Breakaway Pass from Goalie Drill (see diagram 71)
This is a teaching drill to get the timing down between the breaking player and the goaltender's pass. Four groups of players stand in the four corner areas of the arena. One player breaks from one line from one end of the floor, then another player from the same end but different side breaks. The receiving player runs to the other end of the floor and takes a shot on the other goalie. Once these two players have gone and taken a shot, then two players from the other end break alternately. The drill continues with players alternating sides and alternating ends.

69

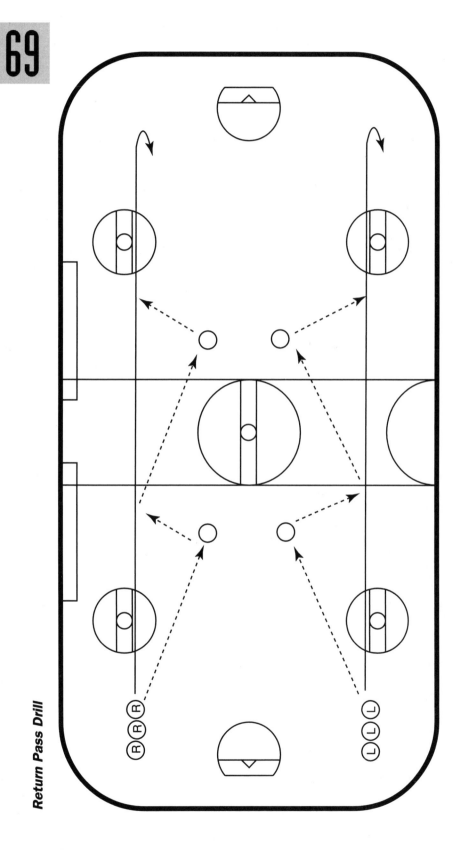

Return Pass Drill

70

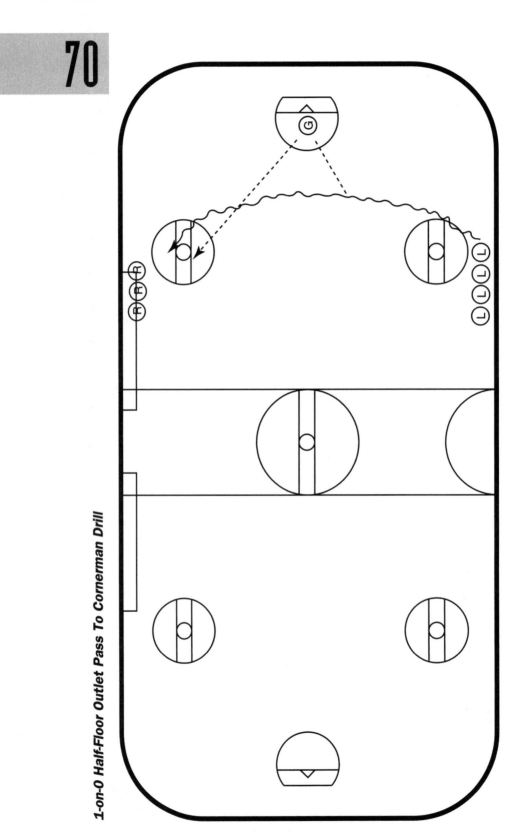

1-on-0 Half-Floor Outlet Pass To Cornerman Drill

71

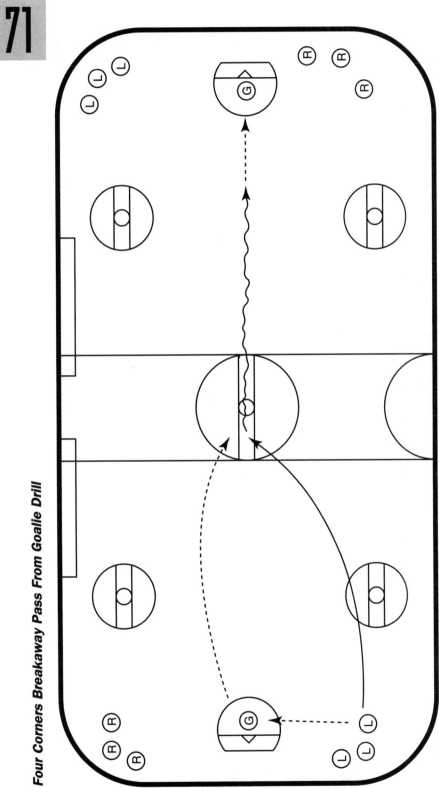

Four Corners Breakaway Pass From Goalie Drill

Variation: Run as a passing drill with no shot. Also run all players from one end of the floor first, then run them all from the other end.

Stress: The goalie, in practicing breakaway passes, must learn to lead the player with a "rainbow" pass. This pass should end up around the center area of the floor. To help the goalie focus on throwing the perfect breakaway pass stress to him that "it is not a mistake if he over passes, but it is a mistake if he under passes to the breaking player." The player should catch the ball over his inside shoulder with the stick's face open to the ball and pointing straight ahead.

9. 2-on-0 Drills
a. 2-on-0 Up The Floor Passing Drill (Opposite Shots) (see diagram 72)
Form two lines behind the extended goal line, one line of right shots and one line of left shots. Start with all the lefts having a ball. The first left-handed shot passes to the opposite right-handed shot, and they continue passing back-and-forth down the floor, before ending with a shot on net. There are two rules to follow. First, "the ballcarrier should not take more than two steps with the ball." This rule encourages players to throw lots of passes as they run up the floor. Second, "the ballcarrier must call out the receiver's first name." This encourages communication on the floor. The whole team tries to beat the last objective; i.e., the number of goals in relation to the number of shots in 3 to 5 minutes.

Variation: Run the drill narrow (same width as the crease) or wide (players run up beside the side boards). Do-It-Again Drill—if a pair drop the ball, they run back, go to the back of the line, and start again.

b. 2-on-0 Breakout Drill (Opposite Shots) (From Goalie)
Start the drill with all the lefts having a ball. The ballcarrier rolls the ball into the goalie. The goalie passes to one of the partners. They both then run up to the other end of the arena passing back-and-forth with a shot on net. The partners then wait for the whole team.

Variation: The coach starts the drill by standing in front of the goalie and rolling the ball at him. Insist that each partner gets a shot on net at each end. The coach can restrict the number of passes down the floor to four.

c. 2-on-0 Sideline Breakout Drill (Same Shot) (From Goalie) (see diagram 73)

d. 2-on-0 Sideline Breakout Drill (Same Shot) (From Player in Crease)
   1) The cornerman passes up to the creaseman immediately (see diagram 74).
   2) The cornerman passes up to the creaseman at the end of the break.

e. 2-on-0 Sideline Breakout Drill—"Hit the Trailer" (Same Shot) (From Goalie) (see diagram 75)

f. 2-on-0 Sideline Breakout Drill—"Hit the Trailer" (Same Shot) (From Player in Crease) (see diagram 76)

10. Four Corner Drills
a. Four Corner Drill—2-on-0, Two Pass Breakout (see diagram 77)
Four groups of players stand in the four corner areas of the arena. Two players break at the same time from one end of the floor, then two players from the other end break as soon as the former players have taken a shot on net. The goalie makes an outlet pass to one of the players, who in turn makes a long pass to the opposite partner breaking long. The drill continues with two players breaking at the same time but alternating from one end to the other. The following are outlet pass options: go to all the left cornermen; go to all the right cornermen; or alternate sides. The objective is to run

2-On-0 Up The Floor Passing Drill

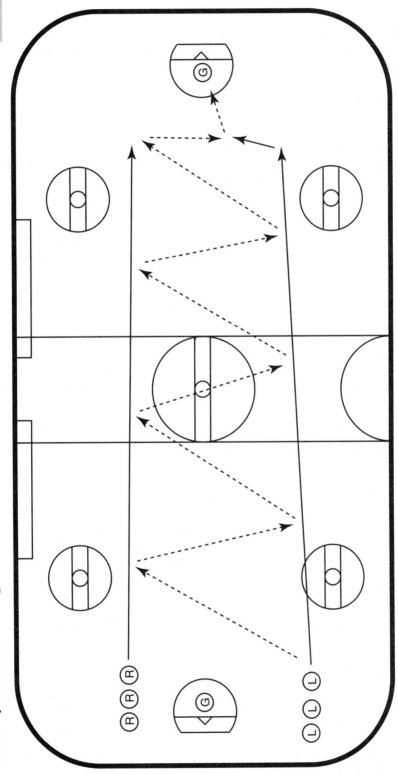

73

2-0n-0 Sideline Break Drill (Same Shot)

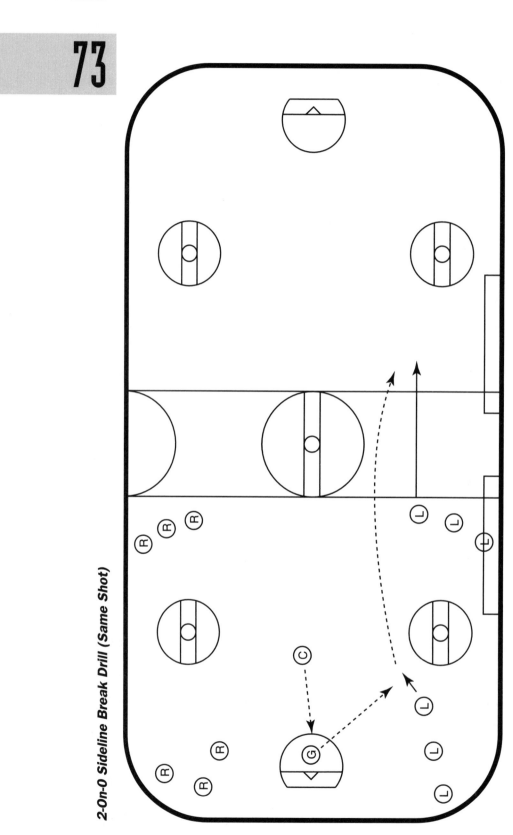

74

2-On-0 Sideline Breakout Drill

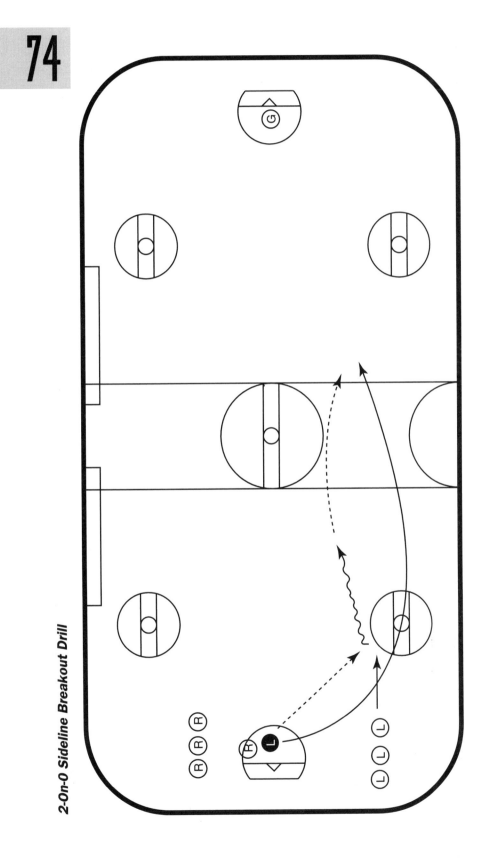

75

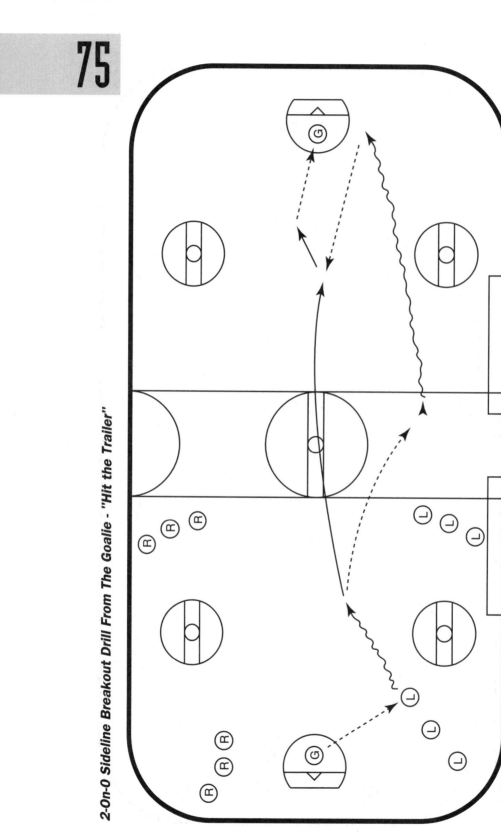

2-On-0 Sideline Breakout Drill From The Goalie - "Hit the Trailer"

76

2-On-0 Sideline Breakout Drill From The Crease - "Hit the Trailer"

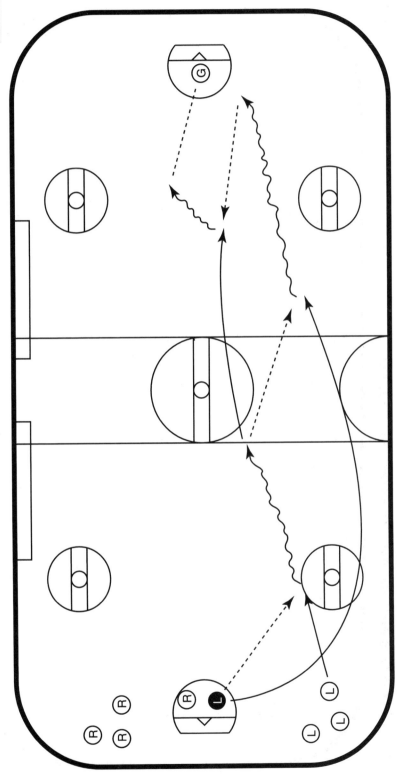

77

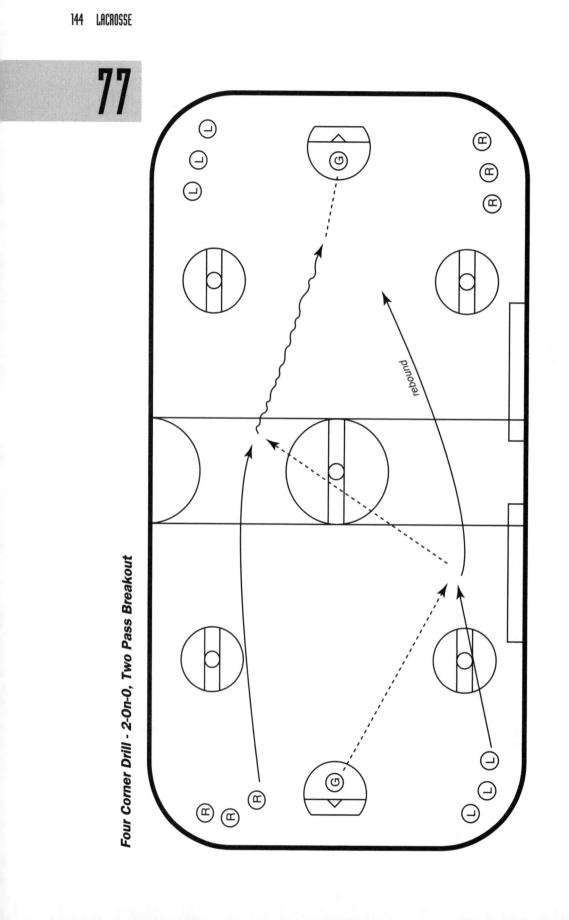

Four Corner Drill - 2-On-0, Two Pass Breakout

the drill for 5 minutes, record the number of goals in relation to the number of shots (or just the number of shots), and then try to better this objective every time the drill is run.

b. Four Corner Drill—2-on-0, Three Pass Breakout

   1) The player on the second pass takes the ball to the crease and hits the trailer (see diagram 78).

   2) The player on the second pass hits his partner on the fly.

11. 1-on-1 Chaser Drill

The players line up as such: the ballcarrier at the top of the Face-Off circle and the defender (the chaser) at the bottom of the Face-Off circle. On the whistle both players break with the defender trying to stop the ballcarrier from scoring. The drill is run from both ends of the arena.

Variation: (1) The same as above except the ballcarrier rolls the ball into the goalie who then passes to the breakaway player. The defender tries to intercept the pass or stop the receiver from scoring. (2) In this variation the ballcarrier faces the goalie while the defender takes a defensive position accordingly. The shooter, after he has taken a token shot, reacts back on defense. The defender breaks as the goalie makes the save to receive the breakaway pass.

12. 3-on-0 Up the Floor and Back Drill

   1) Run the drill wide where the players make sure the Outside Lanes are filled.

   2) Run the drill tight where all three players stay in the Middle Lane.

13. 3-on-0 Weave Drill (Full-Floor)

Stress: Pass and go behind; 5 passes and a shot.

Variation: (1) Again, run it tight or wide. (2) On the fourth pass, the player must shoot.

14. 3-on-0 Fast-Break Drills

a. 3-on-0 Fast-Break—5 Passes Up and 3 Passes Back (see diagrams 79a, 79b)

Three players jog in a circle and then roll the ball into the goalie. They then go to their spots for the break. Counting the goalie's pass they make five passes and take a shot on net. After the shot, they cross sides and break out again coming back down the floor. This time only three passes are made before the shot.

Variation: Three passes up and three passes back can be used.

b. 3-on-0 Fast-Break—Cross-floor Pass

The whole team starts at one end. The three players make three passes and take a shot. The cornerman's option is to headman the ball; i.e., pass the ball up the floor by throwing a cross-floor pass to the opposite creaseman. The three players shoot until they score. The players remain at the other end until the whole team has gone.

c. 3-on-0 Fast-Break—Sideline Pass

The cornerman's option is to headman the ball by throwing a sideline pass up to the creaseman on his side of the floor. Again, the three players make three passes and take a shot.

d. 3-on-0 Fast-Break—Cornerman Runs the Ball

The cornerman's option is to run the ball into the Offensive Zone and then pass to the opposite creaseman. The three passes are still required.

Variation: The cornerman can pass to the creaseman on his side of the floor.

e. 3-on-0 Fast-Break—Creaseman "Hits the Trailer"

The cornerman, after passing to the opposite creaseman, gets a return pass from the creaseman on his side of the floor.

78

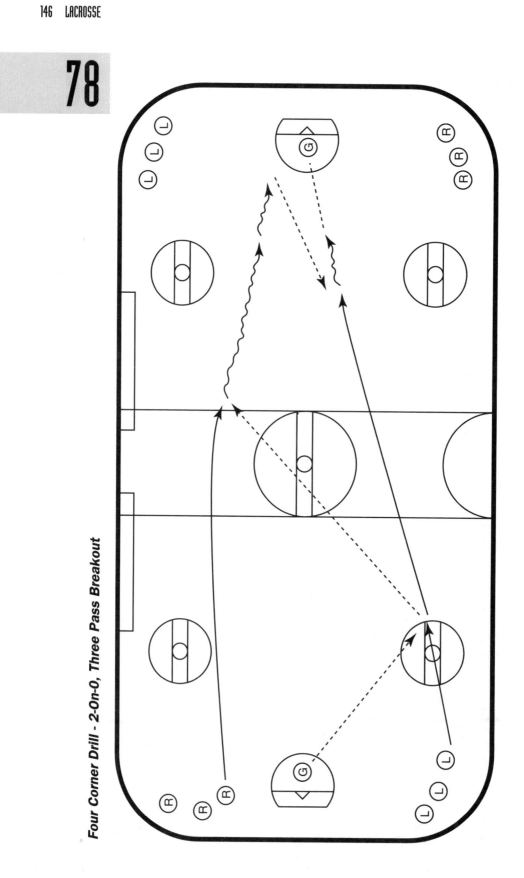

Four Corner Drill - 2-On-0, Three Pass Breakout

79a

3-On-0 Fast-Break Drill - 5 Passes Up

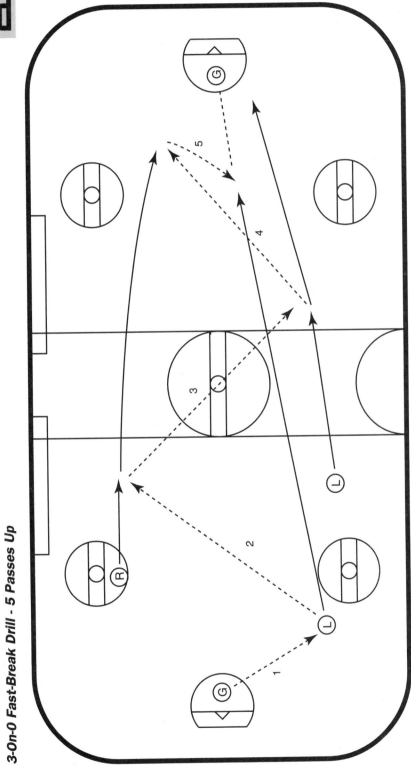

79b

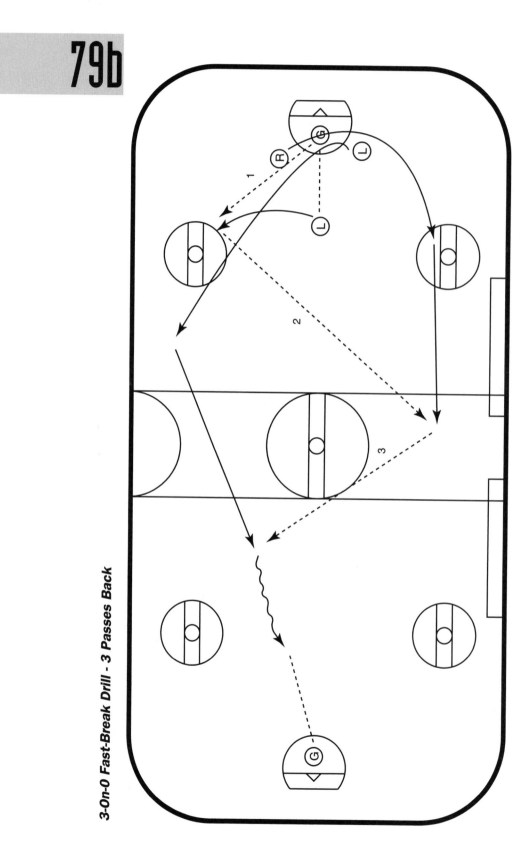

3-On-0 Fast-Break Drill - 3 Passes Back

15. 5-on-0 Up and Back Conditioning Drill
Use this drill as a conditioner—one time, two times, three times.

D. PRIMARY BREAK DRILLS

16. 2-on-1 Half-Floor Drill (Teaching Drill)
Start the drill from center floor. Players form three lines: two offensive lines in the Outside Lanes, and a defensive line in the Middle Lane. The coach starts the drill by passing to one of the offensive players. As soon as he passes, the offensive players break, while the defensive player retreats back. There is no defensive pressure from behind to hurry the play, but the offensive players must shoot within four seconds.

17. 2-on-1 Full-Floor Drill
The whole team starts at one end of the floor. Again, start with three lines. A middle line player (defensive) steps out and puts the ball down on the floor and starts to run back on defense. One of the offensive players attacks the loose ball, yells "Ball," picks up the loose ball, and runs up the floor. The ballcarrier runs the ball up the floor until he is challenged by the defensive player at which time he will pass off.

Variation: To work on their passing on the run, the offensive players must pass the ball back-and-forth all the way down the floor until the defensive player starts to challenge.

18. 2-on-1 Full-Floor Drill with Defensive Pressure (Chaser) (see diagram 80)
Two offensive players face up the floor and two defensive players face them. The coach passes to one of the offensive players who breaks up the floor. The defender opposite this offensive player, who the coach passes to, must touch a cone near the net area and then get back into the play to play defense.

Variation: (1)The coach calls the chaser's name. (2) The coach shoots at the goaltender and calls out the chaser's name who must touch the cone. (3) One of the defenders just goes and touches the cone to initiate play.

19. 3-on-0 Up, 2-on-1 Back Reaction Drill
The last offensive player to touch the ball goes back on defense.

20. 3-on-2 Half-Floor Drill (Teaching Drill)
The team forms two groups: a group of three forward players at center floor and a group of two defensive players near the Defensive Zone Line. From the center area the three forwards run against the two defensive players. Again, there is no defensive pressure from behind and they must execute within four seconds.

21. 3-on-2 Half-Floor Drill with Defensive Pressure (see diagram 81)
Three offensive players at center face three defensive players. The coach yells the defensive player's name who must go and touch the cone at center and then becomes a chaser. When the coach yells the defender's name, the three offensive players with a ball break towards the goal on the two defensive players.

22. 3-on-2 Full-Floor Drill with Defensive Pressure
The same drill as above except it is begun at the far end of the arena. The defensive player whose name is called must run and touch the cone near the net while the offensive players break up the floor against the other two defensive players.
Variation: The defensive player opposite the offensive player, who the coach passes to, must go and touch the cone.

80

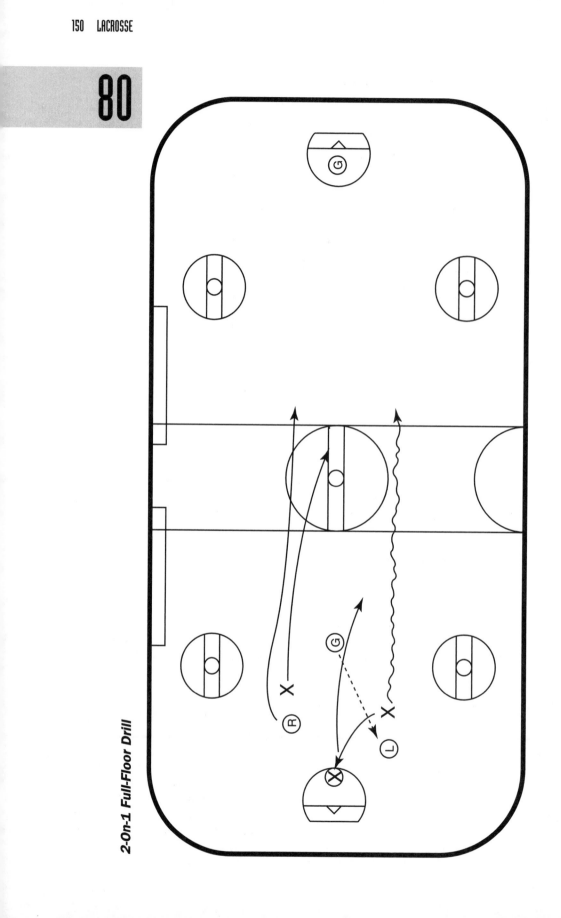

2-0n-1 Full-Floor Drill

81   *3-On-2 Half-Floor Drill*

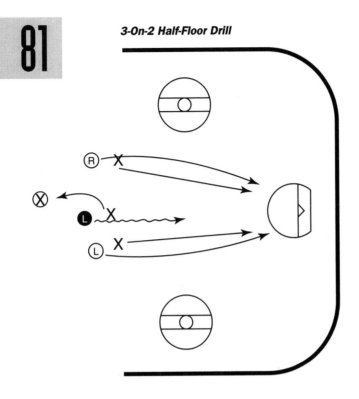

23. 5-on-0 Up to 3-on-2 Back Reaction Drill
Usually, the three offensive players are made up of the cornerman and the two creasemen, while the two defensive players are the other cornerman and the pointman.

24. 3-on-2 Drill From Center Face-Off Circle
The opposing centerman gives token resistance and stays at the Face-Off Circle.

25. 3-on-3 Loose Ball Drill
This drill involves two groups of three players. The two groups stand with their backs to the coach facing the corner area. When the coach rolls the ball into the corner and yells "Ball," the players chase and fight for the loose ball. The group that obtains the ball breaks on offense while the other group gets back on defense to defend the net.

26. 3-on-2 Continuous Drill (Two Teams) (see diagram 82)
Divide the team into two teams. Each team lines up on opposite sides of the floor. Three offensive players break out from their goalie with a ball. As soon as the offense get possession of the ball, two defensive players from the other team touch the Center Face-Off Circle and get back on defense. As soon as the ballcarrier passes over the center of the floor, a third defensive player gets into the drill by touching the Center Face-Off Circle. Make sure the third defender is an opposite shot to the other two defenders to keep offensive balance when they break out to come back the other way. If this third defender gets back in time, the situation becomes a 3-on-3; if not, it remains a 3-on-2. Once the defense gets possession or is scored upon, the three defenders now break on two new defenders from the other team. The teams play to 5 goals with the losers doing sprints.

82

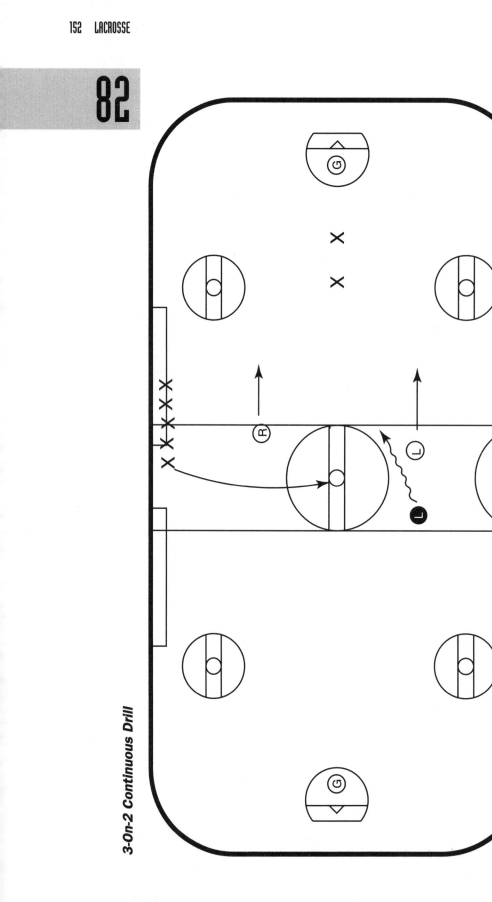

3-On-2 Continuous Drill

27. 3-on-2 Up to 2-on-1 Back Reaction Drill
Starting with the whole team at one end, run a 3-on-2 situation to the other end. Have a rule that the offensive player who shoots the ball, or the last one who touches it, reacts back on defense. When the two former defenders get possession, either from a loose ball or from the goalie, they then break out on the former offensive player.

Variation: Just tell a certain cornerman that he reacts back on defense when they lose possession of the ball.

28. 3-on-2-on-2 Drill
The same three offensive players break up the floor on two defenders and come back on two other defenders at the other end.

29. 3-on-3 Game Drill (Two Teams) (see CHAPTER I: MAN-TO-MAN TEAM OFFENSE - Team Offensive Drills, Drill 7)
Split the whole team equally in two. The two teams are further divided into groups of three players who play full-floor and run continuously for 45-second shifts. On the whistle, three players from each team run off the floor while three new players from each team run on the floor. The ballcarrier, on hearing the whistle, must drop the ball right where he is and run off the floor. The game is played to a designated score with the losers running sprints. This is more a conditioning drill than a true Fast-Break drill.

30. 4-on-3 Half-Floor Drill (Teaching Drill) (see diagram 83)
This drill involves a group of three defensive players and a group of three offensive players who are standing in their primary fast-break positions. At the center area, the rest of the team is in a single line with a ball each. The first ballcarrier runs in yelling "Odd" and fills in the open cornerman's spot in the box formation. It doesn't matter what shot he is. The three offensive players in the box basically stay stationary, with the exception of the non-ballcarrier cornerman who might take a step into the middle for an anticipated pass and shot. This is a great reaction drill for the offense as they must learn "to read the defense"; i.e., the defense will tell them, especially the ballcarrier, what play they are going to make. Again there is no defensive pressure from behind and the offense must execute within four seconds.

Variation: The coach can begin the drill with the defense having no sticks.

31. 4-on-3 Half-Floor Drill with Defensive Pressure
Four offensive players at center face four defensive players. The coach yells the defensive player's name who must touch the cone at center and then become a chaser. When the coach yells the defender's name, the four offensive players, with a ball, break towards the goal on the three defensive players.

32. 4-on-3 Half-Floor Drill with Full-Floor Pressure on Ballcarrier
This drill is similar to drill 30, except the ballcarrier starts at the other end of the floor and he gets defensive pressure all the way down. The ballcarrier cannot pass the ball until he gets into the Primary Scoring Area.

33. 4-on-2 Continuous Drill (Two Teams) (see drill 26)
This drill is similar to the 3-on-2 Continuous drill. The coach divides the team into two. Each team lines up on opposite sides of the floor. Four offensive players break out from their goalie with a ball. As soon as the offense gets possession of the ball, two defensive players from the other team touch the Center Face-Off Circle and get back on defense. As soon as the ballcarrier passes over the center of the floor, two other defensive players get into the drill by touching the Center Face-Off Circle.

83

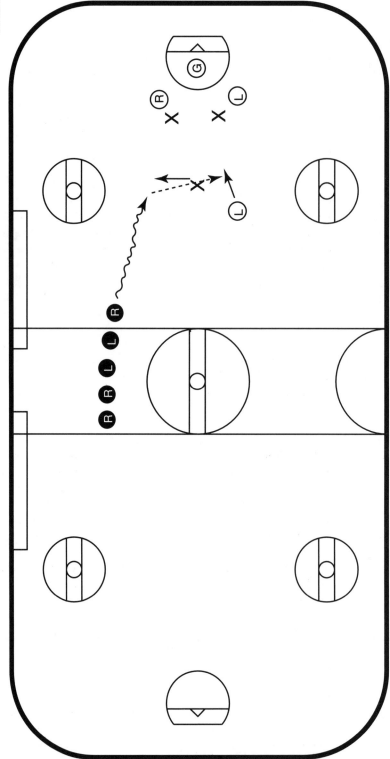

4-On-3 Half-Floor Drill

Make sure the two new defenders are opposite shots to the other two defenders to keep offensive balance when they break out to come back the other way. If these two new defenders get back in time, the situation becomes a 4-on-4; if not, it remains a 4-on-2. The teams play to 5 goals with the losers doing sprints.

34. 4-on-3 Continuous Drill (Two Teams) (see diagram 84)
The drill is the same as the one above except the offense runs a 4-on-3 with only one defensive player coming into the drill for defensive pressure.

Variation: Rather than having the defense drop back into the Defensive Zone, have the defense pick up the offense in the center area to force bad plays. This forces the ballcarrier to keep his head up to see what is happening.

35. 4-on-3 Fast-Break Drill (Three Lines) (see diagram 85)
Start at center with four offensive players with a ball. They break on a defensive team of three players. The extra defensive player is on the side boards ready to enter the drill when the defensive team gains possession of the ball. Once the defensive team gains possession of the ball they break with the extra player on another group of three defensive players at the other end of the floor. This drill keeps the players of the same line together so they get used to playing with each other.

Variation: (1) The offense is allowed one shot only. The goalie keeps extra balls in his net to start the break. (2) The offense is allowed one offensive rebound off the goalie or off the boards. (3) The offense continues until they score. If the goalie stops the ball he must throw it into the corner or to the coach who passes it back to the offense. If the defense obtains the ball, they throw it into the corner or pass it back to the coach who passes it to the offense. This creates persistence; i.e., it conditions players to never give up on a missed shot and to pursue all rebounds. (4) The defense can drop back and play regular defense in the Defensive Zone or the defense can force the play at center floor trying to pressure the ballcarrier into mistakes.

36. 4-on-3 Up to 3-on-2 Back Reaction Drill (see diagrams 86a, 86b, 86c)
Use three lines of five players. For simplicity call the lines A, B, and C. Start the drill at one end of the arena with lines A and C. The first line up, A, will consist of four offensive players who will break on three defensive B players at the other end. The extra A player waits in the Offensive Zone while the extra two defensive B players stay at the starting end. Once the 4-on-3 situation is over, i.e., the defensive team has obtained possession of the ball or was scored upon, the former three defensive B players break on the top two offensive A cornermen who have reacted back on defense.

Once the 3-on-2 situation is over, the next group of four offensive C players break out on the next three defensive players. The former two offensive A creasemen who held in the Offensive Zone, along with the extra A player, become the next three defensive players.

Then, the next group of four offensive B players break and the drill just continues.
Remember: The extra C player just goes down to the other end to become a defensive player with the two C creasemen.

37. 5-on-4 Continuous Drill (Three Lines)
The same as the 3-on-2 Continuous, 4-on-2 Continuous, and 4-on-3 Continuous Drills.

38. 5-on-4 Fast-Break Drill (Three Lines)
The same as the 4-on-3 Fast-Break Drill.

84

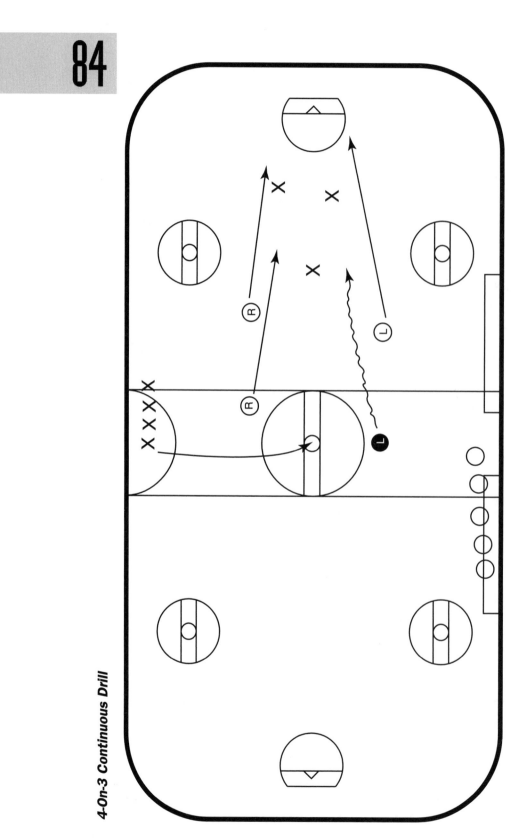

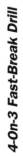

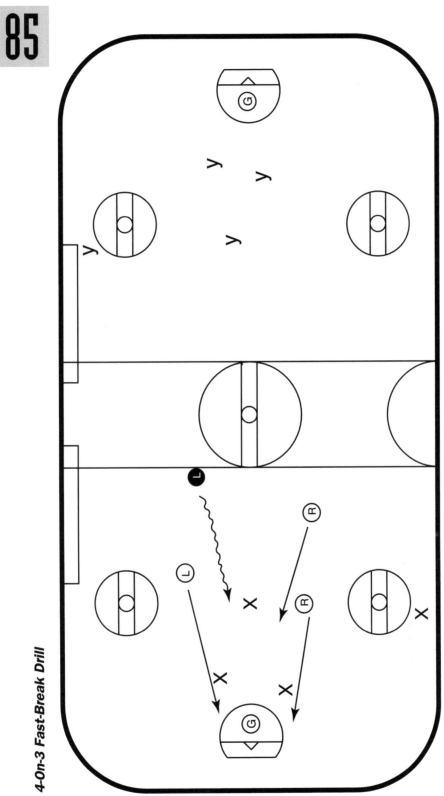

85

4-On-3 Fast-Break Drill

86a

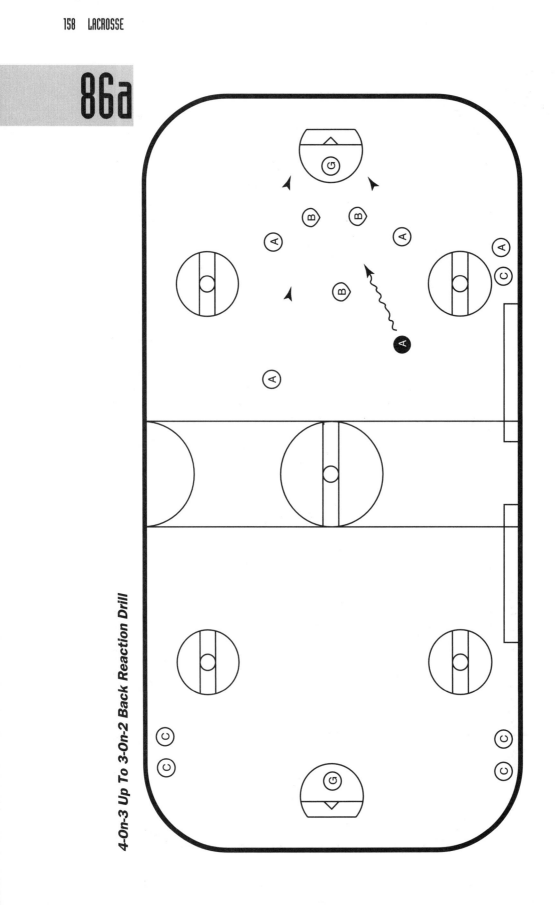

4-On-3 Up To 3-On-2 Back Reaction Drill

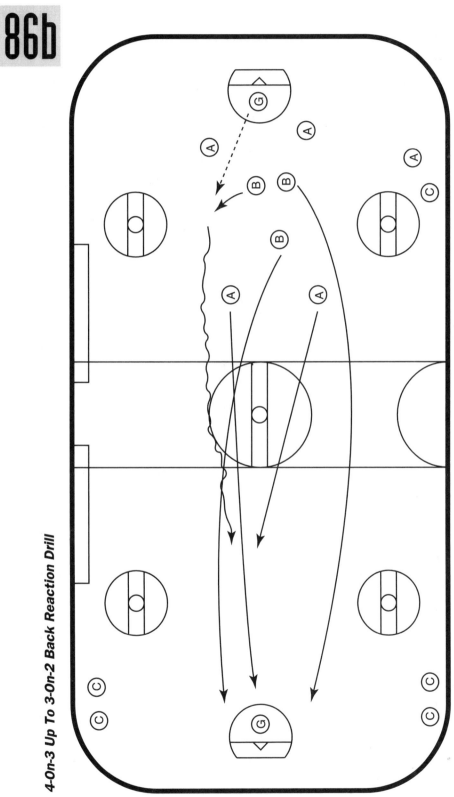

86b

4-On-3 Up To 3-On-2 Back Reaction Drill

86c

4-On-3 Up To 3-On-2 Back Reaction Drill

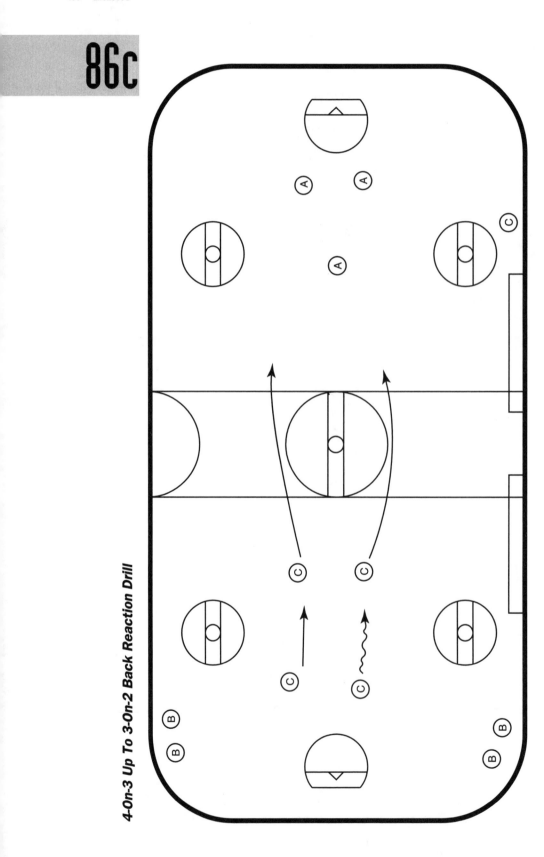

39. 5-on-4 Up to 4-on-3 Back Reaction Drill (see diagrams 87a, 87b, 87c, 87d)
This drill is similar to the 4-on-3 Up to 3-on-2 Back Reaction Drill. Start line A with five offensive players breaking on four defensive B players. The 5-on-4 situation is over when the defensive team obtains possession of the ball or is scored upon. The back three offensive A players react back on defense, the two offensive A creasemen hold, while the four former defensive B players break out.

When the next five offensive C players break, there will be four defenders back—the two offensive A creasemen who held, plus the extra B player, plus another extra D player. Once this mixed group breaks on the three C defenders, start the drill over again with the five offensive A players breaking on the four defensive B players.

E. SECONDARY BREAK DRILLS

40. 5-on-0 Fast-Break Drill (Up and Back)
The five players run up the floor and back. Everybody must handle the ball on the way up the floor. They score off the secondary break. They can run up the floor and back one time, two times, three times, four times.

41. 5-on-0 Fast-Break Up Drill
The same drill as above except the five players run to the other end and hold after they shoot. As soon as the first group goes, the next group goes, and so on.

42. 4-on-4 Fast-Break Game Drill (Three Lines)
This is a great intensity drill. Three lines just keep running their secondary break on each other. Start the drill at center with four A players. They run their break on another group of B players, who in turn break on the other group of C players at the other end of the arena. Players work on "headhunting," i.e., on setting their Down Picks. The first team to score three goals win.

43. 5-on-5 Fast-Break Drill
   1) Team A will run in a circle in front of their net, roll the ball into the goalie, break to the other end against team B, and try to score off their Secondary Break. This is a controlled drill because now team C runs in a circle and breaks against team A that ran the first break.
   2) Players run the floor four times. The line that scores the most goals in their four chances wins.

44. 5-on-5 Fast-Break Game Drill
This game involves three lines running their secondary break against each other. Team A breaks against team B; team B breaks against team C; team C breaks against team A; and then the cycle starts again. The defense can pick up in their Defensive Zone or in the Neutral Zone. The offense must shoot within 5 seconds once in the Offensive Zone and is allowed only one shot. The teams play "live" with a team getting one point for a score and two points for scoring off the Secondary Break.

Variation: A team is allowed one shot plus a rebound. In this case a team gets two points for scoring off an offensive rebound.

45. 5-on-5 Borden Ball Drill (see CHAPTER I: MAN-TO-MAN TEAM OFFENSE; CHAPTER IV: MAN-TO-MAN TEAM DEFENSE)
Play this game 5-on-5 (either full-floor or half-floor).
   The rules are:
   1) The ballcarrier can only take three steps with the ball before he must pass it.
   2) The ballcarrier must pass the ball in three seconds. Any violation of these two rules gives the other team the ball.

87a

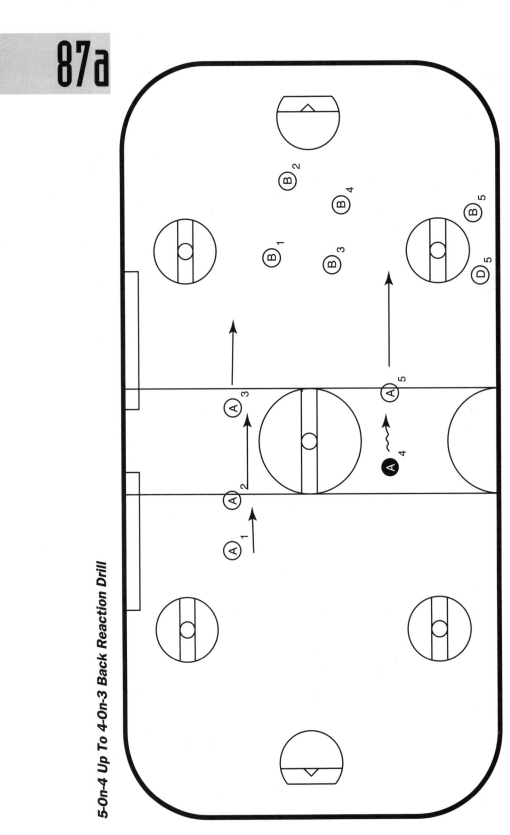

5-On-4 Up To 4-On-3 Back Reaction Drill

87b

5-On-4 Up To 4-On-3 Back Reaction Drill

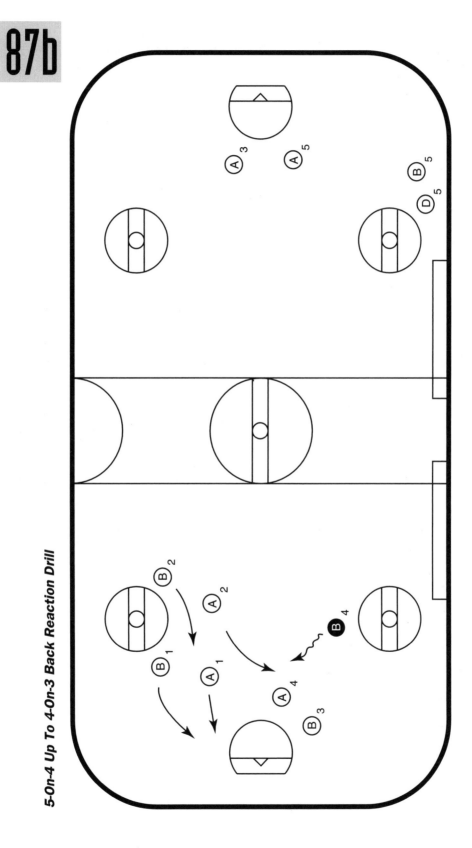

87c

5-On-4 Up To 4-On-3 Back Reaction Drill

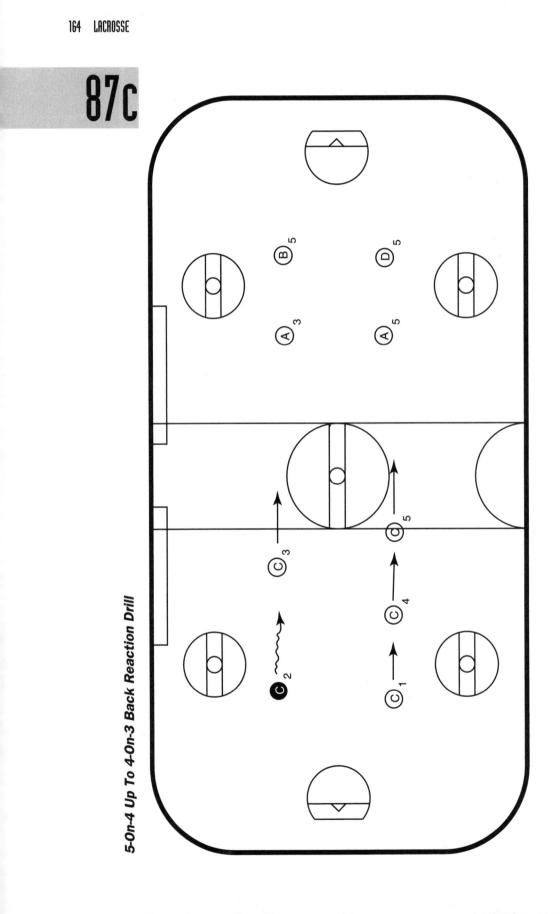

87d

5-On-4 Up To 4-On-3 Back Reaction Drill

3) If the offensive team drops the ball, it loses possession. This game reinforces the give-and-go play; the work ethic needed to get open for a pass; the need for the ballcarrier to see the whole floor; and the need to remain calm (avoid panicking) when being pressured.

F. LINE CHANGE DRILL

46. "On-The-Fly" Line Change Drill (see diagram 88)
Team B starts the drill by taking a shot on team A. Once possession of the ball is obtained, team A breaks to the bench and team C players break out from the bench down the floor on defensive team B. Team B, after getting possession, then brings the ball up the floor in a controlled manner against team C. Team B takes a token shot on net, then team C breaks to the bench on a line change with the A players coming on the floor.

G. BREAKOUT VERSUS PRESSURE DRILLS

The basic rule on a breakout with no pressure is "a player never runs back for a pass." But the basic rule against pressure is "a player should come back to meet the ball." This is to avoid any interceptions by the pressuring defensive team.

47. 1-on-1 Versus Pressure Drill

48. 2-on-2 Versus Pressure Drill

49. 3-on-3 Versus Pressure Drill

50. 4-on-4 Versus Pressure Drill (see CHAPTER III: THE FAST-BREAK SYSTEM - Parts of the Fast-Break, Breakout Versus Pressure Defense)
(see diagrams 49, 50, 51)
Five options: (1) The Outside Exchange; (2) The Inside Exchange; (3) The Up Pick-and-Roll; (4) The Safety Valve; (5) Off-the-Bench Play.

Variation: The two back men cannot run the ball out of the Defensive Zone. They must pass.

FAST-BREAK SPOT SHOOTING DRILL

51. 5-on-0 Spot Shooting
Players run up the floor and back five times. Everybody must shoot once. Record the number of goals and how long it took the players to run five times. Put this drill to music.

52. Stationary Creaseman Spot Shooting Drill (see diagram 89)
This drill consists of a shooter, two passers, and two buckets of balls. The shooter shoots for one minute, and the coach records the number of goals. Passers feed the shooter as fast as they can.

53. Stationary Cornerman Spot Shooting Drill (see diagram 90)
The same as above, except the shooter shoots from the cornerman's position.

54. Creaseman On-the-Move Spot Shooting Drill (see diagram 91)
The same as above, except the shooter moves up and down the side of the floor.

55. Cornerman On-the-Move Spot Shooting Drill (see diagram 92)
The same as above, except the shooter shoots while moving from the middle of the floor to the side.

88

"On-The-Fly" Line Change Drill

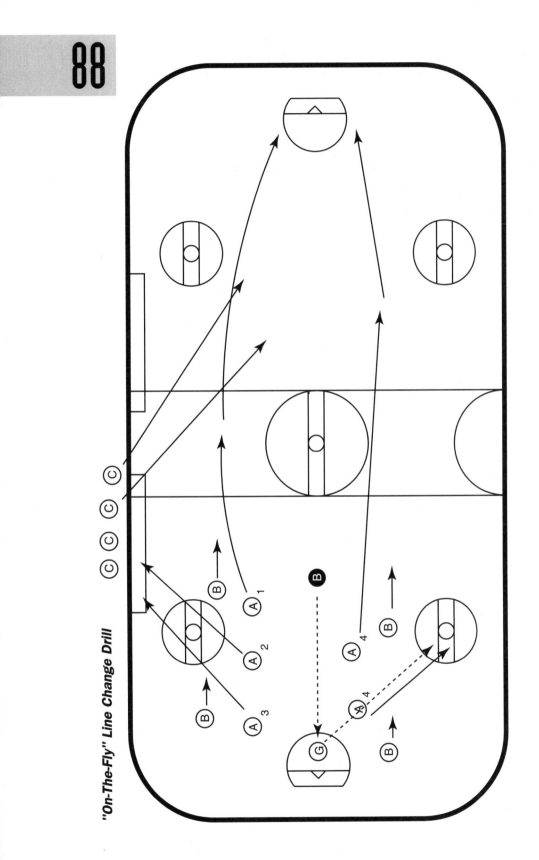

Stationary Creaseman Spot Shooting Drill

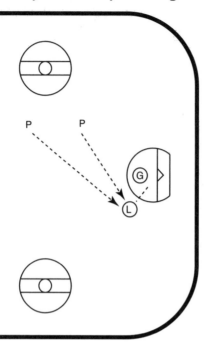

Stationary Cornerman Spot Shooting Drill

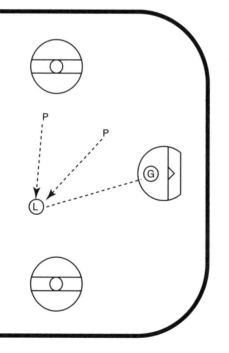

91 *Creaseman On-The-Move Spot Shooting Drill*

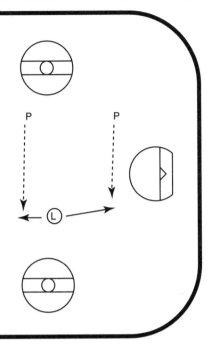

92 *Cornerman On-The-Move Spot Shooting Drill*

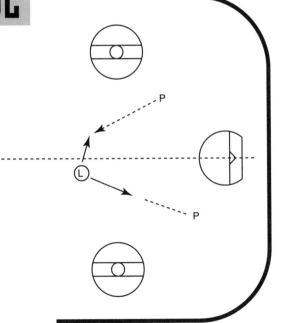

56. Creaseman On-the-Run Shooting Drill (see diagram 93)
Players, all with balls, form two lines (lefts and rights) and run to the creaseman's spot for a shot.

57. Cornerman On-the-Run Shooting Drill
The same as above, except the players shoot from the cornerman's spot.

58. Creaseman On-the-Run, Off the Pass Shooting Drill (see diagram 94)
Two players (opposite shots) run up the floor to the creaseman's and cornerman's spots. The cornerman is the ballcarrier and he makes a diagonal pass to the player on the creaseman's spot.

59. Cornermen On-the-Run, Off the Pass Shooting Drill (see diagram 95)
Two players (opposite shots) run up the floor together. Once they both reach the cornerman's spots, the ballcarrier makes a cross-floor pass to his teammate for a shot.

93 *Creaseman On-The-Run Shooting Drill*

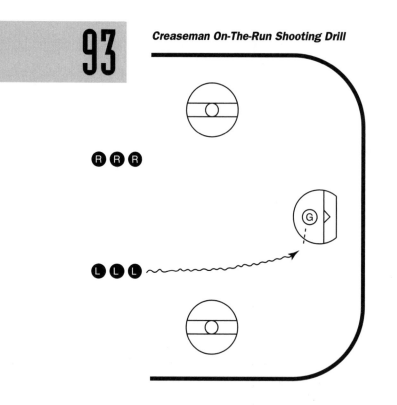

94

*Creaseman On-The-Run, Off The Pass
Shooting Drill*

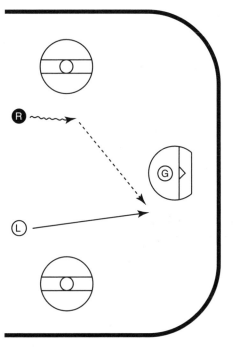

95

*Cornerman On-The-Run, Off The Pass
Shooting Drill*

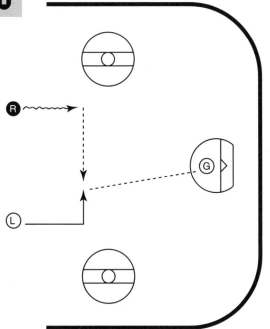

CHAPTER IV: MAN-TO-MAN DEFENSE

I. DEFENSIVE TERMINOLOGY

1. Prime Scoring Area—is an area in the Offensive Zone which is the best position to score from. This area is located:

a) Within an imaginary outside boundary line from the side of the crease to the inside edge of the Offensive Face-Off Circle.

b) Across the top of the Imaginary Semicircle Line (15 feet).

c) Within an imaginary inside boundary line from the far goal post out to the Imaginary Semicircle Line which is parallel to the outside boundary line of the Prime Scoring Area for the opposite shot (see CHAPTER I: MAN-TO-MAN TEAM OFFENSE, diagram 5).

2. Secondary Scoring Area— is an area located between the far outside boundary line and the inside boundary line of the Prime Scoring Area.

3. Three Imaginary Lanes—divide the length of the floor into three lanes: the Middle Lane consists of two lines as wide as the goal crease and the two Outside Lanes from these two lines to the boards. These lanes help teach team defensive positioning and fast-break positioning (see CHAPTER II: THE FAST-BREAK SYSTEM - Filling the Lanes). The defensive players will know whether they are on the "ball side" (in the Outside Lane) or on the "help side" (off-ball side, just inside the Middle Lane).

4. Defensive Zone Line—the line across the width of the arena from side board to side board to distinguish the defensive area.

5. Defensive Zone—where the defense defends the net area inside the Defensive Zone Line.

6. Ball Side—the side of the floor the ball is on.

7. Help Side (Off-Ball Side)—the side of the floor opposite to the ball.

8. Cross-Check—the main way to stop the ballcarrier from scoring.

9. Ball-You-Net—the best position for defending the ballcarrier.

10. Ball-You-Man Position—the best position for playing the non-ballcarrier. The defender plays between the ballcarrier and his check to deny him the pass. He can play him in a closed stance or open stance, depending on his check's relationship to the ballcarrier.

11. Closed Stance—when playing an offensive opponent the defender is between his check and the ballcarrier, and in front of his check belly-to-belly to stop him from getting the ball. He makes body contact on any cut to the ball while looking partially over his shoulder to peripherally see the ball. Usually, this position is taken against a cutter from the off-ball side.

12. Open Stance—in an "open stance" position the defensive player is facing up the floor in a position to see both the ball and his check who is on the off-ball side of the floor. In this position, by seeing both the ball and his check, he can either defend a pass to his check or help the ballcarrier if necessary. If his offensive check cuts to the ballcarrier for a pass, the defender plays him in a "closed stance."

13. "Cheat" Position—a position a defender takes in anticipation of helping out a teammate. "Cheat" here means the defender moves early from his original check one step over (into the middle), one step back, or one step up in order to rotate to help out a teammate.

14. Closing Out (Attack Step)—occurs when a defender has to rush the ballcarrier to maintain pressure and to stop the ballcarrier from scoring. The checker "closes out" quickly, usually on a cross-floor pass, by sprinting hard towards the ballcarrier, then shuffling his last two steps while maintaining a good defensive stance. On these last two steps he pushes off with his back foot and steps with his front foot to be balanced and under control when he makes contact.

15. Retreat Step—the defender takes a staggered stance with the inside foot forward. When the ballcarrier starts to go one-on-one, the defender pushes off with his front foot and steps with his back foot to cut off the ballcarrier from going to the net.

16. Drop Step—when the ballcarrier changes direction to go across the top of the floor, the defender swings his inside foot backwards to be parallel with his outside foot and then moves laterally to cut off the ballcarrier from going to the net.

17. Shuffle Step—the defender, staying in his defensive stance, shuffles sideways with quick, short, side steps to stay with the ballcarrier.

18. Switch—when two defenders exchange offensive players.

19. Jump Switch—same as a "switch" except done more aggressively.

20. Double-Team—two defenders attacking the ballcarrier.

21. Tandem Defense—one defender playing behind another defender.

22. Passing Lane—the path the ball will take between passer and receiver.

23. One Pass Away—when the offensive team moves the ball around the outside of the defense, and the ballcarrier makes a pass to the next player beside him (either down the side of the floor, back to the top of the floor, or across the floor, but not to a cutting player).

24. Two Passes Away—when the offensive team passes the ball around the outside of the defense and the defender is playing the offensive player two passes away. He plays him usually in an "open stance" position.

25. Penetrating Pass—a pass towards the net or into the Prime Scoring Area.

26. Non-Penetrating Pass—a pass into a non-scoring area, such as the side or corner area of the floor; across the floor on the outside of the defense.

II. TYPES OF DEFENSES

1. Helping Man-to-Man Defense
This is the most common type of defense played by teams. The players play their man and the ball equally, i.e., 50 percent concentration on their check and 50 percent concentration on the ball. Usually, the players are in a defensive position to help a teammate stop the ballcarrier from going to the net.

2. Contain Man-to-Man Defense

This is a more man-oriented defense. The defender will try to prevent his check from cutting across the floor towards the ball by using some kind of interference. The players are a little more concerned with their check than the ball, i.e., 60 percent concentration on their check and 40 percent concentration on the ball. There is less helping out by teammates and thus more pressure and work for the defender on the ballcarrier to stop the ballcarrier from beating him. This defense is more concerned with taking away the off-ball plays.

3. Pressure Man-to-Man Defense

This defense is a more ball-oriented defense, i.e., 60 percent concentration on the ball and 40 percent concentration on the check. The key here is to pressure the ballcarrier, forcing him into mistakes. The defender's teammates look to intercept bad or forced passes. The help side defense plays zone principles.

4. Gambling Man-to-Man Defense

This type of defense either tries to steal the ball from the ballcarrier or double-team the ballcarrier. This defense is usually executed in certain situations (for example, when losing late in the game and the team has to get the ball back) rather than as a "bread-and-butter" defense. Techniques used in this defense are:

a) Gambling to get the ball from the ballcarrier by stick checking.
b) Gambling to intercept passes.
c) Gambling with a "Run-and-Jump" Defense.
d) Gambling on all picks and screens by jump switching.
e) Gambling by double-teaming or trapping the ballcarrier.

5. Switching Man-to-Man Defense

This defense resembles a zone defense because players switch on all up and down picks and screens, thereby remaining in their areas. By switching, a team can keep their fast men at the front of the defense for quick breaking purposes, or a team can keep their better checkers at the front of the defense to pick up the top scorers, depending on the team's philosophy.

6. Zone Defense

Most teams play a 2-1-2 Zone or a 1-2-2 Zone defense. In this defense each player is responsible for a certain area rather than a specific opponent. Zones are a ball-oriented defense because the players keep an eye on the ball more than their man.

7. 1-4 Zone Defense

This defense is a combination of a zone defense and a man-to-man defense. Basically one man pressures the ballcarrier while the rest of the players back him up by playing a four-man zone.

8. Camouflage Defense

The team fakes a man-to-man defense but plays a zone defense. Or, the team fakes a zone defense but plays a man-to-man defense.

9. Full-Floor Man-to-Man Defense

As soon as the team loses possession of the ball in the Offensive Zone, they pick up the opposition in a man-to-man defense and pressure the opposition all the way down the floor.

10. Full-Floor Zone Press Defense

As soon as the team loses possession of the ball, they go into a full-floor 2-1-2 zone picking up the opponent in the Offensive Zone. In this defense, the team's options are: just contain the ballcarrier (play off him to slow him down); pressure the ballcarrier up the floor (play him tighter to force him to run); trap the ballcarrier to steal the ball from him or force bad passes from him for interceptions.

11. Full-Floor Run-and-Jump Defense
Basically, in this defense defenders run at the ballcarrier to make him pass or run with the ball.

Note: When losing, a team will have to take some chances to get back in the game by gambling:
a) Using a full-floor zone press looking for the trap.
b) Double-teaming the ball out of the regular defense.
c) Looking to intercept any pass thrown.
d) Looking to steal the ball off the ballcarrier by stick checking.

Note: One reason minor/youth coaches play and teach zone defenses is because it is easier to teach and easier to play an area rather than a man. When teams play man-to-man defense the problem for younger players occurs when they interpret this literally; that is, if the defender's check goes into the corner of the arena, the defender will follow him because he is supposed to be playing him man-to-man. Another reason minor/youth coaches play zones is because most youth teams have only one good offensive player on each line and one player will have a tough time beating a zone by himself. At the higher level of competition there are usually three or four good players on a line, and by working together they can beat a zone defense much easier.

III. QUESTIONS A COACH SHOULD ASK WHEN PUTTING A DEFENSIVE SYSTEM TOGETHER

> Do you want the players to fit the defensive system? Do you want the defensive system to fit the players? Does it matter?

> Do you give the defensive positions names, numbers, or nothing?

> Do you put together the lines thinking of the better defensive players?

> What area of the floor do you want to start your defense?

> How do you start your defense?

> Do you work on defensive floor positioning and floor balance?

> Do you want to be a man-oriented or ball-oriented defense, or both?

> Do you want to play man-to-man, zone, or a combination defense?

> Do you teach your players to move with their check and still know where the ball is, or play their check tough and not worry about the ball?

> Do you have "keys" or signals to run different defensive systems?

> Do you play just one type of defense?

> Do you gamble on defense so that if you are losing in the third period you can get the ball back to score?

> Do you practice the basic defensive responsibilities everyday? (One-on-one checking the ballcarrier, one-on-one defensing the cutter, defensing the pick on the ball, defensing the pick off the ball.)

> Do your players play hard on defense? How do you get your players to play hard on defense?

> Do your players concentrate on defense? How do you teach your players to concentrate?

> Do your players communicate on the floor? How do you get your players to talk on the floor?

> How do you get your players to play together (as "one")?

> Do your players pressure the ball or protect the goal?

> Do you want your players just to stop the ball or force the ball in a certain direction?

> Do you want the ballcarrier to go one-on-one?

> Do you want the offense to pass the ball around?

> Do your players know how to play the non-ballcarrier on the ball side?

> Do your players know how to play the non-ballcarrier on the off-ball side?

> Do your players know how to defend the ballcarrier who goes one-on-one; i.e., do they know how to cross-check properly?

> Does your defender know what to do if he is beaten one-on-one by the ballcarrier?

> Do your players know how to help the defender on the ballcarrier if he is beaten?

> Do your players know how to defend the "Give-and-Go" play?

> Do your players know how to defend the "Go" play (cutter)?

> Do your players know how to defend a Pick-and-Roll on the ball?
   a) Cross Pick-and-Roll on the ball?
   b) Up Pick-and-Roll on the ball?
   c) Down Pick-and-Roll on the ball?

> Do your players know how to defend an off-ball Pick-and- Roll?
   a) Cross Pick-and-Roll off the ball?
   b) Up Pick-and-Roll off the ball?
   c) Down Pick-and-Roll off the ball?

> Do your players know how to defend a screen on the ball?

> Do your players know how to defend a screen off the ball?

> Do your players know how to defend the Cross Pick-and-Roll on the ball from the off-ball side?

> When getting back on defense what do you stress to your players?

er "who picks up who" except for the standard rule of right shot checking left shot or

> Do you assign special checking assignments, thereby keeping your best checker at the top of your defense? The trade-off for this situation is that you might give up speed at the front of your fast-break to keep your best checker on the better offensive players.

> Do you make sure your creasemen are at the top of the defense for the fast-break? The trade-off for this situation is that you might give up your better checkers on the better offensive players to keep your speed at the front of the break.

> When getting back on defense, what do you stress to your players: finding their man first or finding the ball first?

> Do your players know how to play a great player as a special checking assignment?

> Do your players know how to play a breakaway player?

> Do your players know how to defend the odd-man situation (2-on-1, 3-on-2, 4-on-3, 5-on-4)?

> Do your players know when to come off the floor?

IV. THE STRENGTHS AND THE WEAKNESSES OF PLAYING DEFENSE

A. EIGHT TIPS FOR PLAYING GOOD TEAM DEFENSE
1. Players working hard—being aggressive and putting pressure on the ballcarrier.

2. Players using a good defensive technique to stop the ballcarrier from going to the net, which includes no slashing, no stick checking, and no rushing the ballcarrier. Players making sure their opponents take no shots at all, or at least they take only forced shots (molested or pressured).
3. Players taking a good defensive position and forcing the ballcarrier to the boards.

4. Players concentrating on both their check and the ball.

5. Players anticipating what is going to happen before it happens.

6. Players playing good "team" defense by helping out their teammates, especially the teammate who is checking the ballcarrier.

7. Players playing with poise under pressure.

8. Players communicating with their teammates.

B. THE EIGHT SINS OF PLAYING POOR DEFENSE
1. Players not working hard on defense (not fighting through picks, trailing a cutter through the middle of the floor).

2. Players not stopping the ballcarrier from going to the net or at least not forcing bad shots or pressured shots.

3. Players taking poor defensive floor positioning.

4. Players losing their concentration while on the floor, especially taking their eye off the ball or their check.

5. Players reacting to everything by the offense rather than anticipating.

6. Players not helping out to stop the ballcarrier.

7. Players panicking under pressure.

8. Players not communicating on the floor.

V. BUILDING THE "UMBRELLA" DEFENSE

> "Offense wins games, defense wins championships."

> "You always win the big games on defense."

> "Defense is all work and no glory."

The "Umbrella" Defense is called this because the opening and closing action of the defensive players is similar to the opening and closing of an umbrella. The defensive player moves out on the ballcarrier, but if he passes the ball the defensive player sags to the middle of the floor to be in a position to help any teammate.

A. DEFENSIVE OBJECTIVE OF THE "UMBRELLA" DEFENSE
1. The main objective is to stop the opposition from scoring.

2. A defensive team cannot stop a team completely from shooting at the net, but it can force low percentage shots by the opposition; i.e., shots that are interfered with from pressure of a cross-check or a stick in the way, or forced shots that are taken from a bad angle.

3. This defense is just not content to try to stop the ballcarrier, which is a tough thing to do with all the great offensive players. Instead, the defense wants to get the ball back so that the team can initiate the fast-break.

B. DEFENSIVE PHILOSOPHY OF THE "UMBRELLA" DEFENSE
1. It Is A Pressure Defense
This defense believes that pressure causes errors and creates mistakes. The defense puts pressure on the ballcarrier all the time wherever he goes.

2. It Is A Combination Of Two Defenses
The defense is a combination of a pressure, man-to-man defense and a zone defense. It has a ball side of man-to-man pressure and the help side principles of a zone. The defense puts pressure on the ballcarrier and contests or denies all opponents from receiving the ball that are "one pass away". If the opponent is "two passes away" from the ball, i.e., on the help side, the defender plays zone principles by taking an "open stance" position to deny the pass to his check with the ability to collapse on the ball if his teammate needs help on the ballcarrier.

3. It Is A Ball-Oriented Defense
The team plays a ball-oriented defense. If a player takes his eye off anything, he takes it off his check, not the ball. Always see the ball on defense!

4. It Stresses "Team" Defense
The team must play defense with five playing as one. The team stresses togetherness: moving together, reacting together, thinking together, and helping out one another.

The team assumes that "one defensive player cannot go out and stop an offensive ballcarrier." Therefore, each player has to help each other and play as a unit.

A team cannot play good team defense playing as individuals; i.e., every player being concerned only with his check. Team defense stresses looking after the other guy: "If I get beaten, somebody will help me; if my teammate gets beaten, I will help him."

The team objective in this defense is two fold:
1) The defense stresses not to keep just your man from scoring, but to keep the other team from scoring.
2) The defense stresses that the opposition must beat them as an offensive unit rather than individually with their great players; i.e., the defense will not let one player beat them.

5. It Is A Gambling Defense
The players will gamble and take chances on defense, but only when it's a surprise or it's backed up. The team sometimes has to take risks to give itself a chance to win.

6. It Is A Defense That Dictates
The defense takes the initiative. It sets the tempo of the game. It does not sit back and let the offense attack; rather the defense attacks the offense. The defense does not let the offense do what they want, but what it wants. Thus, the defense does the acting, the offense does the reacting.

7. If It Is Beaten, It Is Only Beaten By The Opposition's Weaknesses
If the team gets beaten, it wants to get beaten by the opposition's weaknesses, not its strength. The team is going to try to stop the opposition's most dangerous players and their best plays.

8. If It Is Beaten, It Is Only Beaten From The Outside
If the team gets beaten, it gets beaten from the outside around the Imaginary Semicircle Shooting Line, not from the inside of the Prime Scoring Area, and especially not around the crease area.

9. It Is A Defense That Is Always Consistent
The team believes that its defense can keep it in any game regardless of its goal production. The defense is consistent because the team is willing to work hard, even though on certain nights the offense might be inconsistent. Everything can break down in the game plan, but the team knows the defense will always be there.
Remember: A team does not dominate without a great defense. If it is a great defensive team, it can take more risks on offense.

C. TWENTY-ONE DEFENSIVE RULES OF THE "UMBRELLA" DEFENSE
To help defensive players work as one they must have some idea what they are trying to accomplish on defense other than just trying to stop the opposition from scoring. One of the philosophies of this defense is to get the players to think as one, so that they will all know what is going to happen before it happens. This is done by giving the players some guidelines or rules.

Rule #1—Maximum Intensity

This defense demands maximum intensity, persistence, and aggressiveness. The defense sets the tone of the game so the players must play as hard and as physical as they can. Players must know that if they do not play their utmost, they will be benched. "The team will work and play harder than any other team."

Rule #2—Communication

All players must talk on the floor during the game to build team unity and to get rid of any indecision. Defensive players must call out their check's number and point with their sticks to designate their checks so there is no confusion in assignments. Teams who are constantly warning and alerting each other—before picks are set, for example—play in a more unified way. Players must know they will be benched if the opposition scores off a pick or screen without any communication between teammates. Usually the back defenders do more talking, acting as defensive floor generals, because they can see better what is developing out in front.

Rule #3—Concentration

Players must be able to concentrate 100 percent of the time during a game and be in a constant state of readiness. They must stay mentally alert on defense at all times, i.e., they must be totally involved in the game. They cannot lose concentration for one minute by losing their checks or getting picked off. It takes hard work and concentration to watch a man and back up the ball at the same time.

Rule #4—Pressure the Ball

(see book: *Lacrosse Fundamentals,* CHAPTER 7 - INDIVIDUAL DEFENSE, Cross-Check Stance)

This team defense starts with the checker pressuring the ballcarrier (cross-checking or bothering him with his stick, but not stick checking or slashing), so that the latter has a hard time scoring, a hard time getting a good shot off, or a hard time making a perfect pass. The result of this pressure might be a bad pass, a dropped ball, or a turnover, resulting in the defense getting the ball back.

Coaches do not want the checker on the ballcarrier to worry about getting beaten and, thereby, putting only medium pressure on the ballcarrier. So coaches take the "monkey off the checker's back" (worrying about getting beaten) by stating that they do not care if he is beaten, as long as he is pressuring the ball. Then the checker will go all out and check the ballcarrier aggressively.

The ballcarrier must be pressured when he is at the top of the floor in the Prime Scoring Area, when he is on the side of the floor, or when he is in the corner area. Even if he is not in the Prime Scoring Area, the defense still pressures him all out. Even if the ballcarrier goes behind the net, the checker still puts pressure on him.

"Closing out" occurs when a defender has to rush the ballcarrier to maintain pressure and/or to stop the ballcarrier from scoring. The checker "closes out" quickly, usually on a cross-floor pass, or when meeting the ballcarrier at the top of the floor, or when firing out to put pressure on the ballcarrier on the side of the floor. The checker sprints hard towards the ballcarrier, then shuffles his last two steps to be balanced, under control, and in a good defensive stance when he makes contact. These last two steps are called "Attack Steps" and are short, choppy steps. The individual pushes off with his back foot and steps with his front foot.

The players are aware of teams who try to draw the checker out, then dump the ball off, trying to get the defenders running around. The question with this defense is whether the defense is chasing the ball or forcing the ball in trying to maintain pressure on the ballcarrier. To prevent the maneuver of getting defensive players to chase the ball, the defensive players stop the offense from moving the ball around by cutting off the passing lanes, giving the checker time to put pressure on the ballcarrier. If the ballcarrier passes off before the checker has a chance to get pressure on him, the checker drops off immediately to help his defensive teammate on the new ballcarrier or to prevent a Give-and-Go play.

Rule #5—Force the Ball to the Boards

To get this team unity it is important the players know in which direction to force the ball when pressuring; i.e., the defense is going to tell the offense where to go.

If the ballcarrier is at the top of the offense, the defense wants to force the ballcarrier to the outside (by overplaying his inside shoulder) towards a spot on the side boards near the Face-Off Circle. The defender forces him to the side boards because this gives him a target to aim for; the side boards become an extra defender; and his teammates, by knowing what direction the checker is trying to force the ballcarrier, can now get into a position to help him if he needs it (see diagram 96a).

If the ballcarrier is along the side of the floor, the defense wants to force the ballcarrier to a spot on the end boards and keep him in this alley (see diagram 96b).

The exception to Rule #5 occurs if the ballcarrier is in the corner area of the arena. The checker wants to force the ball to the middle of the floor or back towards the target of the side boards near the Face-Off Circle. This side board target gives him something to aim for and his teammates know what he is trying to do so they can be in a position to help.

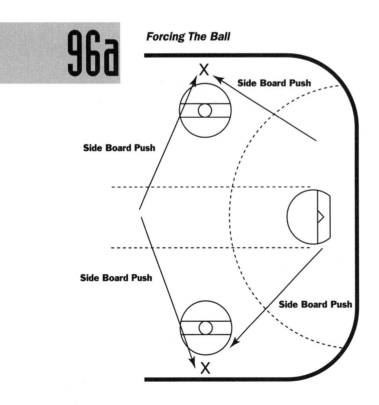

96a   *Forcing The Ball*

X

Side Board Push

Side Board Push

Side Board Push

Side Board Push

X

96b

Forcing The Ball

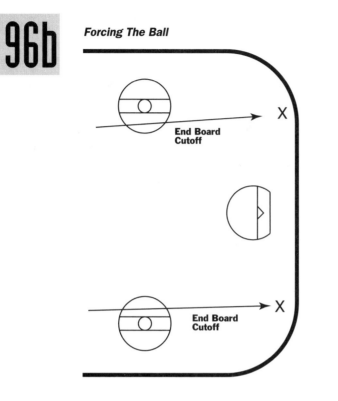

End Board Cutoff

End Board Cutoff

Rule #6—Denying One Pass Away

Note: The term "one pass away" refers to the offensive team moving the ball around the outside of the defense. The ballcarrier makes one pass away to the next player beside him either down the side of the floor, back to the top of the floor, or across the floor, but not to a cutting player. (Diagram 97a)

"Denying" means stopping your check from receiving a pass by playing him in a "closed stance" position.

"Closed Stance" means a defender is playing his check belly-to-belly, looking over his shoulder slightly to see the ball and his man. When some defenders lose sight of the ball and want to search for it, they use their stick as a "feeler" to keep contact with their check by placing the stick over the check's stick, or just by touching the check's body with their stick to tell when the check cuts or moves.

"Backdoor" cuts occur when the offensive player without the ball is being overplayed and prevented from cutting in front of his defender to receive a pass. He must then cut behind his defender to the net to get in the clear for a pass and shot.

The checker needs time to put pressure on the ballcarrier. This time is given by the checker's teammates expanding and playing their checks in a "closed stance" to deny the pass. Once the checker has pressure on the ballcarrier, his teammates will drop off the passing lanes or sag into the middle of the floor to be ready to help him on the ballcarrier if he needs it (see diagram 97b).
Remember: It is much easier to defend a player without the ball than defending him when he gets it.

This defense wants the offense to go one-on-one rather than move the ball around. To force this one-on-one, the defenders checking the non-ballcarriers overplay the passing lanes so the ballcarrier cannot

97a

Denying One Pass Away

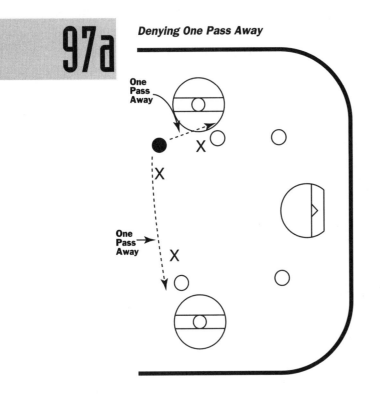

97b

Denying One Pass Away

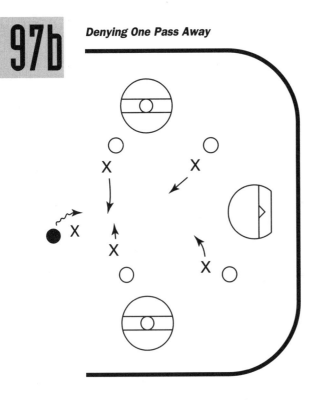

pass to his teammates. In other words, the defense makes it tough, but not impossible, for the offense to pass the ball around. Because the ballcarrier cannot make a pass, he attempts to go one-on-one; this is the time the four defenders sag into the middle of the floor ready to help and possibly gang-tackle the ballcarrier. Once he is being pressured, and even though his teammates are open, it is tough to make a good pass when he is being checked.

Defenders should not be concerned about playing a tough denial with the result of being beaten on the "backdoor" cut. The offense will have a hard time trying to execute a "backdoor" play especially when the ballcarrier is being pressured. But if his opponent does cut "backdoor," the defender should still play him in a "closed stance" (face guard him), turn his back to the ball, and run with him, playing his stick for a split second to take away the initial cut. Once the cutter is not a scoring threat, he will open up to find the ball again.

Rule #7—Floor Positioning

In teaching defensive floor positioning, draw the Three Imaginary Lanes down the floor, and talk to the defensive players about "ball side" positioning (in the Outside Lane) and "help side" positioning (just inside the Middle Lane).

Good floor positioning is very important for a good defense.

a. Ball Side Positioning Rules

1) When playing the ballcarrier, play him ball-you-net position; i.e., always play between the ballcarrier and the net.

2) When playing the non-ballcarrier one pass away on the ball side, the defender plays him ball-you-man and must contest all penetrating passes (passes towards the net) by overplaying the passing lane in the "closed stance," trying to force his check to go "backdoor."

Remember: Once the checker begins his pressure on the ballcarrier this defender takes an "open stance" and sags towards the Middle Lane to help the defender on the ballcarrier and forgets about denying the pass to his check.

3) When playing the non-ballcarrier two passes away on the ball side, this defender still plays his check ball-you-man, but plays in an "open stance" and sags right away towards the Middle Lane as it is difficult for the ballcarrier to make a good pass through all the bodies.

b. Help Side Positioning Rules

1) When playing the non-ballcarrier one pass away on the off-ball side, the defender positions himself just inside the Middle Lane and plays the ball-you-man position, but in an open stance (intercept position), i.e., facing up the floor, in a position to see both the ball and his check so that he can either defend a pass to his check or help on the ballcarrier if necessary. Here, a player must look straight ahead and use his peripheral vision to see ball and man.

Note: Most lacrosse defenses play a man-oriented defense where the help side players play their checks in a closed stance (belly-to-belly, turning their back to the ball). In this "closed stance," the defender is not in the best position to help on the ball.

2) The help side players form an imaginary triangle: with themselves, the ball, and their check. To form this triangle a defender plays one step off the passing lane and sags towards the Middle Lane. To help him maintain this proper positioning, while holding the stick with two hands, he points the tip of the stick towards the ballcarrier and the butt of the stick towards his check.

Some players like to hold the stick with one hand while playing the help side defense. In this situation he points the head of the stick at his check and his free hand at the ballcarrier. He is still in a good position to help on the ballcarrier or intercept any passes thrown to his check (see diagram 98). Poor help side positioning is one of the major problems defensively in lacrosse.

98   *Flat Triangle*

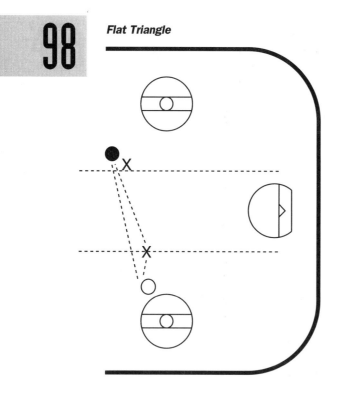

c. Retreat to Line of Ball Rule

If the ball is passed over a player's head, he must drop to the same level as the ballcarrier to be in a position to help. Here a player must adjust to the situation; if he drops totally level with the ballcarrier, the ballcarrier could then pass the ball back out to his check with a possibility of a score (see diagram 99).

d. Movement of Ball Rule

The defense moves and adjusts its position every time the ball moves. The defensive players must be constantly changing their angle and floor position as the ball is passed. On movement of the ball, if the defense can move before the offense can move in regards to the new position of the ball, the defense will be in good shape.

e. Pressure Rule

If there is pressure on the ball, the other defenders can sag off their checks thus becoming more ready to help on the ballcarrier. The help side players can sag into the Middle Lane to clog up the middle of the floor. They stay in this "open stance," almost playing a zone in the middle of the floor. If there is no pressure on the ball, the other defenders have to play closer to their checks (more man-oriented) because a lot of times their checks now become the focus of the offense.

f. Distance from the Ball Rule

"The further your check is from the ball, the further you can be from your check."

Rule #8—Help and Recover to Stop Penetration

Good team defense stresses helping each other out when in trouble. The defensive concept the team works on is that "a good ballcarrier can beat a good defensive player on a one-on-one situation." Therefore, the team stresses that teammates must be ready to help the checker on the ballcarrier and then recover back to their checks.

99 *Drop To The Level Of The Ball*

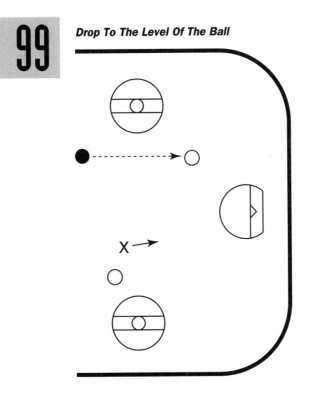

To reinforce that this is a helping defense the team uses the rule that "no ballcarrier can penetrate between two defensive players." In other words, "Someone helps you, you help him." This gives the defender checking the ballcarrier great confidence because he knows if he gets beaten, there will be a teammate ready to help him out (see diagram 100).

Note: Teammates help out by cross-checking the ballcarrier, not stick-checking the ballcarrier.

Remember: When the ballcarrier is in the corner of the arena, the defender forces him into the middle of the floor where the defender knows he will get help. The defender's help should come from the top of the defense, rather than from the bottom of the defense, which is harder from which to rotate. As well, if the help comes from the top, the defense gives up the long shot rather than the close-in shot. The close-in shot is more dangerous and results from the help rotating from the bottom of the defense (see diagrams 101a, 101b).

Sometimes a team has to do a complete rotation when helping and recovering. When teammates help each other, they must go into a "cheat" position; i.e., move early in case they have to leave their checks and rotate to help. They are either moving up early (one step), moving into the middle early (one to two steps over), or moving back early (one step back) in case they have to slide (rotate) over to help a teammate or to check another opponent (see diagram 102).

Rule #9—"Jump to the Ball" to Defense the "Give-and-Go"
If a ballcarrier is out of the scoring area and passes across the floor, his defender steps in the direction of the pass about two steps, takes an "open stance" to take away the Give-and-Go play, and steps back to the level of the ballcarrier to help on any penetration by the new ballcarrier.

100 *Help And Recover*

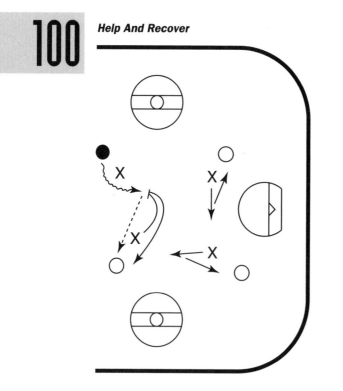

101a *Help And Recover - Do Not Help From The Back*

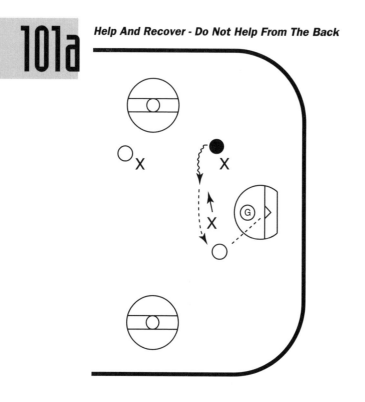

Help And Recover - Help From The Top

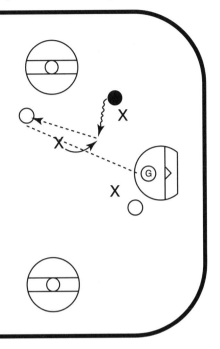

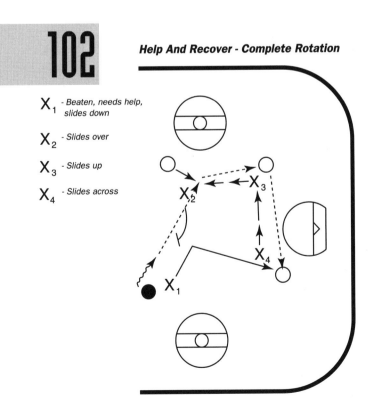

Help And Recover - Complete Rotation

X₁ - *Beaten, needs help, slides down*

X₂ - *Slides over*

X₃ - *Slides up*

X₄ - *Slides across*

If the ballcarrier is in the scoring area and passes across the floor, the defender steps to the ball in the direction of the pass taking an "open stance" to be in a position to help on the ballcarrier if he happens to beat his defender. Besides stepping towards the Middle Lane, he also steps up into the passing lane to defend the Give-and-Go play, now playing the cutter in a "closed stance," i.e., turning his back to the ball but looking over his shoulder, pushing and bumping the cutter and playing his stick. Because the cutter will have such a hard time trying to cut in front of the defender when moving to the ball, he will end up trying to cut behind the defender; i.e., going "backdoor." On this "backdoor" cut the defender will keep his back to the ball for a split second to play his opponent's stick (see diagram 103).

103   *Jump To The Ball*

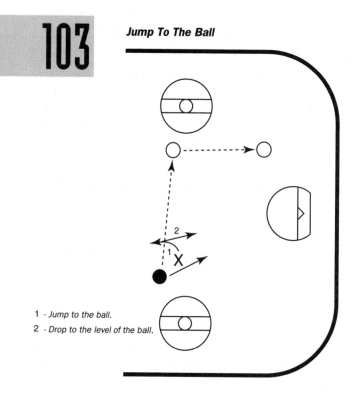

1 - *Jump to the ball.*
2 - *Drop to the level of the ball.*

Note: Playing the "backdoor" cut is the only time a defender loses sight of the ball while on defense.

Rule #10—Defensing the "Go" Play (Cutter)
If an offensive player cuts from the ball side of the floor, it is usually a clear-out maneuver for the ballcarrier to go one-on-one. As a result, the defender plays him accordingly: ball-you-man position; deny one pass away; play in a "closed stance."

If an offensive player cuts from the off-ball side of the floor, the defender should already be in an "open stance" position to deny a pass to his check and still be ready to help. On the cut the defender must always assume a pass is coming, so he plays him tough by moving into a "closed stance" to deny him the ball. The defender bumps him and tries to force him to go "back door."

Remember: In a "closed stance" position a defender is in front of his check (belly-to-belly) making body contact, yet looking partially over his shoulder to see the ball peripherally.

Recall: When playing the "backdoor" cutter, the defender turns his back to the ballcarrier for a split second and plays the cutter's stick.

Rule #11—Defensing the Screen on the Ball

The defender checking the ballcarrier can fight over top of the screen (see diagram 104a), especially if the ballcarrier is in the scoring area, or he can step back and go through the screen (see diagram 105). The defender checking the ballcarrier should never let himself get picked off (see diagram 106) or go behind the screen creating a gap for a good shot by the ballcarrier (see diagram 107).

The defender checking the screener can step out from behind the screen into the path (driving lane) of the ballcarrier to stop the ballcarrier, delay him, or make him go wide to give his teammate time to recover on the ballcarrier. He does this very quickly because he must recover back to his own check who will probably cut to the net (see diagram 104b). The other option is the defender can step back off the screener to give his teammate room to cut through the screen (see diagram 105).

Rule #12—Defensing the Off-Ball Screen

The defender checking the ballcarrier can go through the gap in the screen created by his defensive teammate who has taken a step back, or he can step up on the cutter before he gets to the screen and play him in a "closed stance" as he goes over the screen. The defender checking the screener is just concerned with not getting tied up by him. He wants to be in a position to give his teammate space, by taking a step back, to go through the screen if he has to use it (see diagram 108).

Rule #13—Defensing the Up, Down, and Cross Pick-and-Roll on the Ball

The general rule in defensing all picks is "do not let yourself get picked off." However, the tendency for defensive players is to let themselves get picked off without any fight or to just lazily call "Switch."

The defender checking the ballcarrier must anticipate opponents setting picks from behind or from the side. It is extremely important that the defender checking the ballcarrier hears the warning "Pick" called by his teammate before the actual pick is set.

Six options of defending the Up Pick-and-Roll on the ball:

#1: "Stop"
The first priority is for the defender checking the picker to stop him from setting the pick. In other words, push him out of the line of the path towards the ballcarrier's defender. If this is not possible, he then verbally warns his teammate of the pick before it is set.

The back defender calls most of the options because he can see the whole play developing (see Rule #2: Communication).

The other option for the defender checking the ballcarrier is not to let the ballcarrier use the pick at all. He overplays the ballcarrier in the direction the pick is coming to prevent him from using the pick (as an interference) to rub him out of the play. He really is forcing the ballcarrier to go the opposite way he wants to go.

#2: "Stay"
The second priority is for the defender on the ballcarrier to stay with him by stepping up and fighting over the top of the pick. This is only done when there is some space created by a poor pick set by the picker, especially when the ballcarrier is in the Prime Scoring Area.

Here the defender on the picker helps his teammate by showing himself to the ballcarrier, i.e., stepping out into his path (driving lane) from behind the pick. He tries to stop the ballcarrier, delay him, or make him go wide to give his teammate time to recover as he goes over the pick. As soon as he shows himself he must recover back to his own check who is likely now cutting to the net for a pass (see diagram 109a).

Defensing The Screen On The Ball
- Over Top Of The Screen

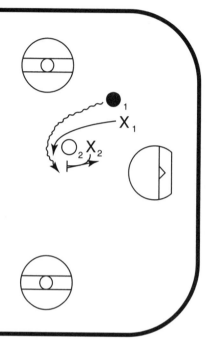

Defensing The Screen On The Ball
- Over The Top

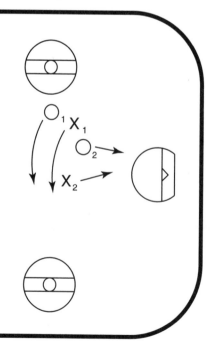

**Defensing The Screen On The Ball
- Through The Screen**

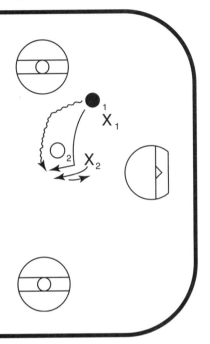

Defensing Screen on Ball

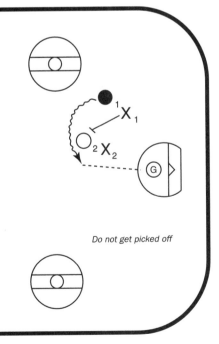

Do not get picked off

107   *Defensing The Screen On The Ball*

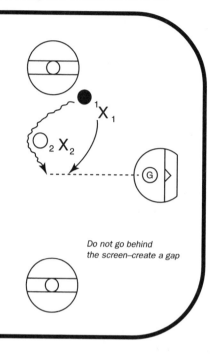

*Do not go behind
the screen–create a gap*

108   *Defensing The Off-Ball Screen
- Go Through*

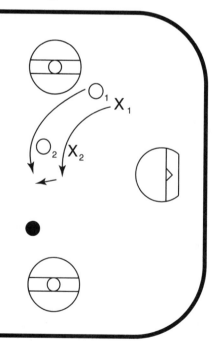

**Defensing The Up Pick-&-Roll
On The Ball - "Stay"**

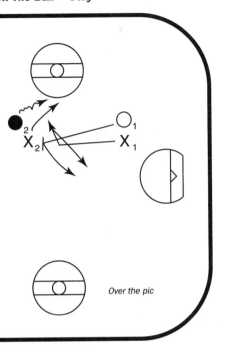

Over the pic

#3: "Space"
The third priority is for the defender on the ballcarrier to stay with him by stepping back and sliding through the pick. The back defender backs off his check and calls "Space" to tell his teammate he has space to go through the pick (see diagram 109b). Usually this is done because the picker has set a solid, physical pick at a good angle, and the defender would have a hard time getting over the pick.

Note: The defender on the ballcarrier does not want to go behind the pick, i.e., behind the picker and his own teammate, as this move will create an unnecessary gap between the defender and the ballcarrier. If this happens the ballcarrier can get a good shot off (see diagram 109c).

#4: "Switch"
The defender checking the ballcarrier on hearing the call "Switch" from the back defender will step back and around to get the inside floor position on the picker to take away his cut to the net.

The back defender, checking the picker, calls the switch, making sure he gives his teammate plenty of warning. He then fires out and fills the gap to stop the ballcarrier from going to the net and to maintain pressure on the ballcarrier (see diagram 109d).

Note: Good defensive teams don't switch because: they feel they lose their intensity and aggressiveness; they avoid creating mismatches; and they feel by constantly switching they will have a defensive breakdown where somebody does not pick up his new check, a teammate does not call out "Switch," or a teammate says he did not hear the call. The defensive team calls a "Switch" now and then for the element of surprise.

109b

Defensing The Up Pick-&-Roll On The Ball - "Space"

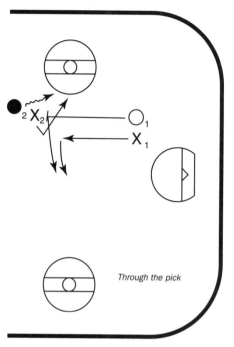

Through the pick

109c

Defensing The Up Pick-&-Roll On The Ball - "Behind"

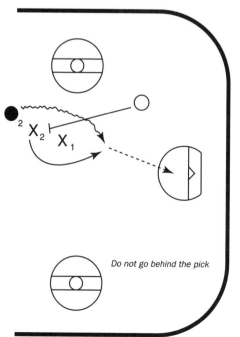

Do not go behind the pick

109d

**Defensing The Up Pick-&-Roll
On The Ball - "Switch"**

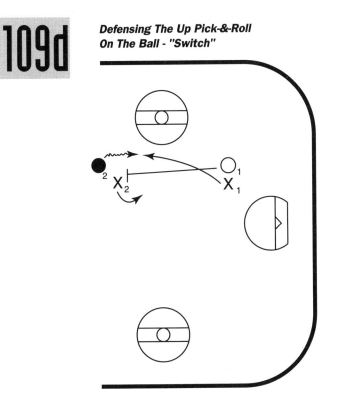

#5: "Jump"

The jump switch is keyed by the call "Jump" by the back defender. The normal switch is done more as a reaction to the Pick-and-Roll play of the offensive players to stop the ballcarrier, or if the back defender is not sure if the defender on the ballcarrier will get over the pick. On the other hand, the jump switch is a defensive play to attack and possibly surprise the ballcarrier with the result of dislodging the ball or creating some sort of turnover.

The defender checking the ballcarrier again steps back quickly and picks up the picker.

The defender on the picker switches players, jumps out, and attacks the ballcarrier.

#6: "Double"

On hearing the call "Double" the defenders will double-team the ballcarrier.

The defenders set up the double-team by having the checker on the ballcarrier overplay his stick side (by cross-checking), forcing him either to turn his back to protect his stick or to try to beat him to the outside.

The back defender comes from the ballcarrier's blind side and attacks his stick by stick checking while the original defender continues after his stick side by cross-checking.

As a backup during the double-team, the three other defenders form a triangular zone in case the ballcarrier is able to move out of the double-team or pass out of it. If the ballcarrier passes out of the double-team, the original defender on the ballcarrier stays with him while the double-teamer rotates by dropping to the middle of the floor to read the situation. He will either pick up his original check or pick up a teammate's check who has rotated and picked up his check (see diagrams 109e, 109f).

109e

**Defensing The Up Pick-&-Roll
On The Ball - "Double"**

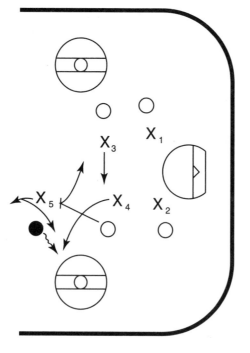

109f

**Defensing The Up Pick-&-Roll
On The Ball - "Double"**

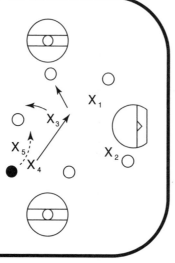

**Defensing The Up Pick-&-Roll
On The Ball - "Double"**

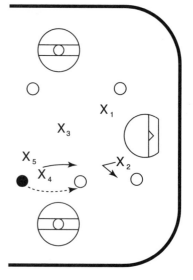

In defensing the Down Pick-and-Roll on the ball (see diagrams 110a, 110b, 110c, 110d) and the Cross Pick-and-Roll on the ball (see diagrams 111a, 111b, 111c, 111d) use the same six options.

Rule #14—Defensing the Up, Cross, and Down Pick-and-Roll on the Off-Ball
The two options are the same whether the play is an Up Pick-and-Roll, a Down Pick-and-Roll, or a Cross Pick-and-Roll.

#1: "Space"
a. If the back man's check starts to move upwards, he must anticipate that his opponent is going to set a pick. The back defender must yell "Space" to warn his teammate that a pick is coming and that he is creating space for him by playing off his check to go through the pick. As the picker approaches the top defender, he steps back and shuffles through the gap created by his teammate staying with his check (see diagram 112a).

b. If the top man's check starts to move downwards, he must anticipate that his opponent is going to set a pick. The top defender must yell "Space" to warn his teammate that a pick is coming and that he is creating space for him by playing off his check to go through the pick. As the picker approaches the back defender, he steps back as the pick is being set and slides up through the created gap, staying with his check (see diagram 112b).

#2: "Switch"
a. When the back defender sees that the picker is setting a solid Up Pick and there is no chance of warning his teammate, he must do the next best thing, which is call a "Switch." The back defender will pick up the offensive player coming down off the Up Pick, while the top defender has to step

110a

Defensing The Down Pick-&-Roll
On The Ball - "Stay"

110b

Defensing The Down Pick-&-Roll
On The Ball - "Space"

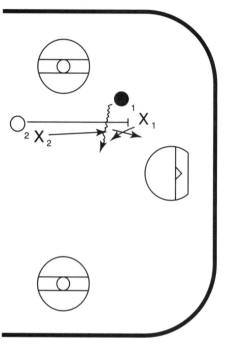

110c

Defensing The Down Pick-&-Roll
On The Ball - "Switch"

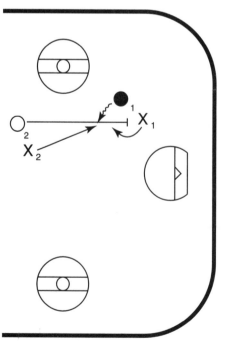

110d

**Defensing The Down Pick-&-Roll
On The Ball - "Double"**

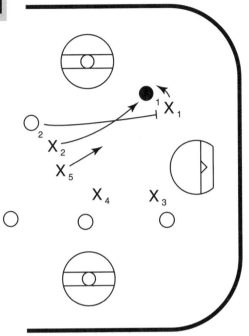

111a

**Defensing The Cross Pick-&-Roll
On The Ball - "Stay"**

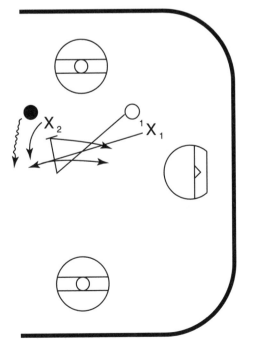

111b

Defending The Cross Pick-&-Roll
On The Ball - "Space"

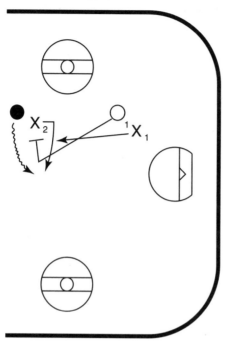

111c

Defending The Cross Pick-&-Roll
On The Ball - "Switch"

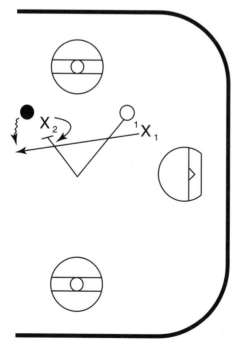

**Defensing The Cross Pick-&-Roll
On The Ball - "Double"**

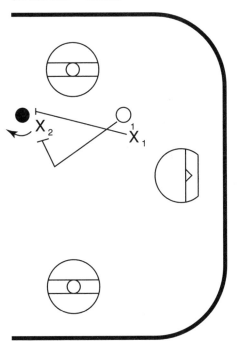

**Defensing The Up Pick-&-Roll
On The Off-Ball - "Stay"**

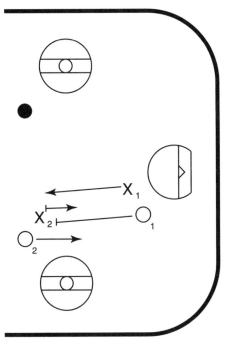

Defensing The Down Pick-&-Roll
On The Off-Ball - "Stay"

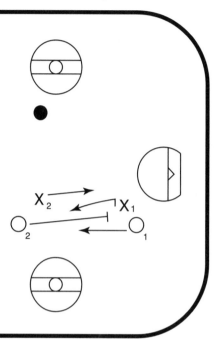

back and slide around the picker to get good positioning by staying between his new check and the ball (see diagram 113a).

b. When the top defender sees that his check is moving downwards to set a solid Down Pick and there is no chance of warning his teammate, again, he must do the next best thing which is call a "Switch." The top defender will pick up the offensive player coming up off the pick, while the back defender has to step back and slide around the picker to keep good positioning on him by staying between the ball and his check (see diagram 113b).

Rule #15—Defensing the Cross Pick-and-Roll on the Ball from the Off-Ball Side
The defensive team defends this play only one way by an automatic "Jump Switch." The defender coming across with the picker will attack the ballcarrier just as the pick is being set. The defender who was on the ballcarrier just switches to check the picker by stepping back and sliding around him to get good positioning between his new check and the ball (see diagram 114).

Rule #16—Defensing the Fast-Break
a. A team should never have a breakaway goal scored against them. The team should always have at least one or more defenders coming back on defense. Here are two ways to designate who is the defensive safety:
1) Tell a specific player that he is responsible for coming back first to protect the net from any clear-cut breakaways.
2) Or designate who comes back depending on what position they are in when a shot is taken:
   a) If the ballcarrier is in the cornerman's position and is only a passer, then his first priority is to react back on defense on the shot at the net.

113a

**Defensing The Up Pick-&-Roll
On The Off-Ball - "Switch"**

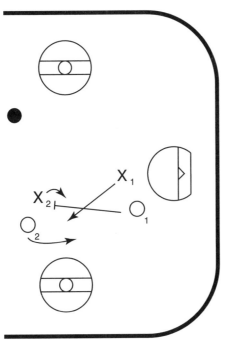

113b

**Defensing The Down Pick-&-Roll
On The Off-Ball - "Switch"**

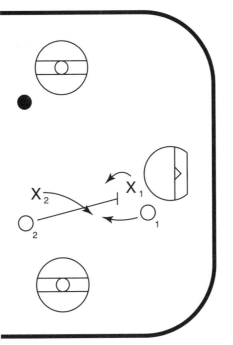

**Defensing The Cross Pick-&-Roll
On The Ball - "Jump Switch"**

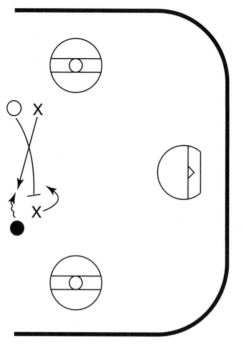

b) If the ballcarrier is in the cornerman's position and is the shooter, then the defensive man in the other cornerman's position (off-ball side) reacts back on defense on the shot.

Note: When playing against a team that sends a player up the floor early before the shot is taken or against a quick breaking team, a defensive team can delay this maneuver by assigning the closest man to the ball to put pressure on it. This will give his teammates time to get back and pick up the deep opponents.

b. Reacting back on defense requires mental quickness and mental discipline, which has to become a habit. When reacting back on defense, players must keep their eye on the ball all the time, find their check or at least point to their check, and run back from the Offensive Face-Off Circle to the Defensive Face-Off Circle.
1) The first priority on defensing the fast-break is to get back on defense.
2) The second priority is to stop the ballcarrier or delay him, whether he is your original check or not.
3) The third priority is to protect the net area.

c. Once in the Defensive Zone:
1) The first player back plays a one man zone.
2) The second player back plays the top of a tandem zone defense while bumping the first player down behind him. It is imperative the players communicate to each other so there is no confusion regarding who has the ball (top) and who is protecting the net (back).
3) The third player back bumps down the top defensive man and forms a triangular zone defense.
4) The fourth player back fills in the other top corner and forms a zone box defense.

d. Playing the odd-man situation:

1) Defensing the 2-on-1

The major rule here is not to let any ballcarrier go to the net without being checked. The lone defensive player stays in the middle of the floor or in the passing lane of the two offensive players. The lone defender can fake at the ballcarrier trying to force a pass and a possible turnover, look for an interception, or just try to delay the ballcarrier from making a decision for a few seconds until he gets defensive help. The defender eventually has to commit to the ballcarrier; however, he should not commit himself to check the ballcarrier too soon but wait until the last second, when the ballcarrier enters the Prime Scoring Area.

2) Defending the 3-on-2

The two defenders play a tandem zone defense, i.e., one player behind the other player. The top defender must call out the ballcarrier's number and stop him from penetrating. The other defender slides behind him to protect the net and also to be in a good position to rotate towards the ball on the pass. On the pass to one of the creasemen from the top offensive man, the bottom defender fires out to stop him from shooting, to force him to drop the ball, or to force him to hurry his pass across the crease to the opposite offensive creaseman, with the possibility of a turnover; i.e., the receiver drops the ball. At the same time the top defender rotates down to the opposite offensive creaseman to take away the crease-to-crease pass (see diagram 115). It is important that the top defender rotates in the opposite direction to the pass from the ballcarrier to take away this possible crease-to-crease pass from the ballcarrying creaseman to the opposite creaseman.

3) Defending the 4-on-3

The third defender back bumps down the top defender in the tandem zone to form a triangular zone defense. In this situation communication is very important. The top defender must physically stop the ballcarrier but only when he enters the Prime Scoring Area. He is mentally anticipating a

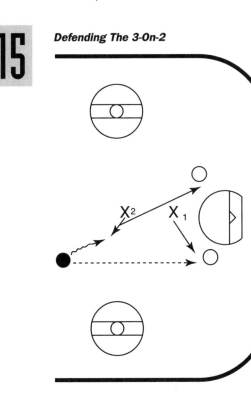

115 *Defending The 3-On-2*

pass across the floor to the open cornerman and his rotation movement is either to follow the pass if he has time to get to the other cornerman or to slide down to cover the creaseman on his side of the floor. He must learn to read the situation.

Usually, this defender on the original ballcarrier moves down on the first cross-floor pass (to the opposite cornerman). He goes into a "cheat" position; i.e., about half-way between the creaseman and the cornerman, to take away a diagonal pass to this off-ball creaseman on his side of the floor. On the second pass down to the ball side creaseman, he runs hard to cut off or intercept the anticipated cross-floor pass to this off-ball creaseman.

The off-ball back defender goes into a "cheat" position, i.e., about half-way between his check and the top offensive cornerman, anticipating a pass to this top offensive cornerman. He gets in front of his check and takes one step up, keeping the stick behind his body to take away any quick diagonal pass to this creaseman. If a cross-floor pass is made, he goes hard to this cornerman to force the play. It is important that he does not leave too soon.

On the first pass across the top, the original ball side back defender takes a "cheat" position, i.e., he moves one step over into the middle of the floor. On the second pass down to the ball side crease-man, he leaves and goes hard to this creaseman to force the play (see diagram 116).
4) Defending the 5-on-4
The fourth defender back fills in the corner of the box zone defense. There usually isn't much rotation in this setup, but if a defender commits to the ballcarrier, the rest of the defenders may have to rotate as previously explained.

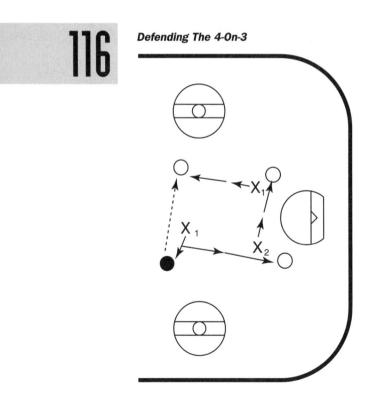

116   *Defending The 4-On-3*

Rule #17—Never Come Off the Floor while on Defense

Rule #18—Special Checking Assignments
When defending a dangerous offensive player, play him in a "closed stance" with your back to the ball, overplaying him to deny the pass.

Rule #19—Defending Set Plays
By scouting and preparing for the opposition teams, a coach can help anticipate the opposition's best offensive plays. He can teach players to learn to read certain keys that telegraph the coming play and, thereby, help to defend against it successfully.

Rule #20—Calling Out Your Check
As the players are running back they should always be looking around and over their shoulders for the ball and any opponents in the Defensive Zone. When getting back on defense, as the players run over the Defensive Zone Line, they should turn around and call out their checks as they point to them with their sticks. Usually, a left-handed shot picks up a right-handed shot and vice versa. This is so that the defender ends up in a stick-on-stick position, which makes it easier to interfere with the opponent's shot or pass.

Rule #21—Playing the Breakaway Player
In this situation the player is better off to play the offensive player's stick rather than going for the interception. Many players who attempt the interception are "burnt" because they miss the ball, while their opponent ends up with the ball and a pure breakaway. Although intercepting a pass to a breakaway player looks great, it still is a low percentage play. Remember to watch the opponent's stick, not the ball.

D. REMEMBER THE KEYS TO GOOD TEAM DEFENSE:
Players must:

#1 Have the right attitude. They must hustle, be aggressive, work hard, play with determination, fight through all picks, and be physically tough.

#2 Have good skill levels—good cross-checking techniques—and be physically ready.

#3 Take good defensive floor position.

#4 Play mentally ready, stay alert, and concentrate.

#5 Anticipate what is going to happen before it happens.

#6 Play together.

#7 Play with poise, especially under pressure and adversity.

#8 Communicate well on the floor.

VI. BUILDING THE "UMBRELLA" DEFENSE THROUGH DRILLS

A. TIPS FOR DEFENSIVE DRILLS

1. Remember: Defense is something that can be taught. Every player cannot be a great offensive threat, but everyone can be a great defensive player.

2. When teaching defensive drills control what the offense does so that the defense executes and gets confidence.

3. In the beginning when teaching defense, set up the defensive drill so that the defense always wins.

4. Encourage talking in all defensive drills.

5. Spend a large amount of the team defensive drills on the off-ball side.

6. As defensive skills improve, create drills as difficult as possible. Coaches want to set up tougher situations in practice than the players will be confronted with in a game.

7. With all 5-on-5 defensive half-floor drills, if the defense gets a steal, loose ball, or possession off a stopped shot, the defensive team has to run the fast-break to the other end of the floor for one shot.

8. Categorize the drills into teaching drills and competitive drills.

B. INDIVIDUAL DEFENSIVE DRILLS: DEFENSING THE MAN WITH THE BALL

1. Defensive Agility Drills (see book *Lacrosse Fundamentals*)

2. Defensive Stance Drill (see book *Lacrosse Fundamentals*)

3. Wave Drill (see book *Lacrosse Fundamentals*)

4. Shadow Drill (see book *Lacrosse Fundamentals*)

5. 1-on-1 Checking Ballcarrier Without a Stick Drill (see book *Lacrosse Fundamentals*)

6. 1-on-1 "Battle" Drill (see book *Lacrosse Fundamentals*)

7. "Showdown" Drill (see book *Lacrosse Fundamentals*)

8. 1-on-1 "Steal the Ball" Drill (see book *Lacrosse Fundamentals*)

C. INDIVIDUAL DEFENSIVE DRILLS: DEFENSING THE MAN WITHOUT THE BALL

9. 1-on-1 Denying One Pass Away When Your Check Is on the Ball Side Drill (see diagram 117)
This drill is to teach the defender to play his check in a ball-you-man position. He will contest any penetrating pass in a "closed stance," trying to force the offensive player to go "backdoor." The offensive man goes in and out trying to get in the clear for a pass from the ballcarrier.

10. 2-on-2 Denying One Pass Away When the Ball Is in the Middle of the Floor Drill (see diagram 118)

117

1-On-1 Denying One Pass Away Drill

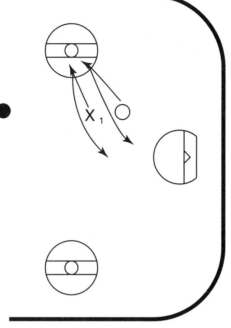

118

2-On-2 Denying One Pass Away Drill

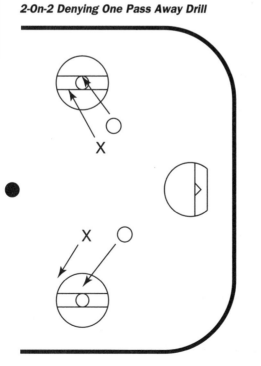

This drill is to teach the defenders to deny the first pass to their checks.

1) The offensive players go in and out slowly until the defenders get the right stance and positioning.

2) The coach times how long it takes the defenders to stop the first pass.

3) After one of the offensive players receives a pass, he can go one-on-one.

4) After one of the offensive players receives a pass, they can go two-on-two.

11. 1-on-1 Denying One Pass Away When Your Check is on the Off-Ball Side Drill (see diagram 119)

The defensive player plays ball-you-man position—the triangle principle (one step off the passing lane and sag towards the Middle Lane). The off-ball offensive player can't cut through the middle; he just moves up and down the Outside Lane to get in the clear for a pass and shot. The passer throws cross-floor passes with the defender trying to intercept.

12. 2-on-1 Interception Drill (On the Off-Ball Side)

Start two offensive receivers fairly close together on the same side of the floor in the Outside Lane. The lone defender plays between them. The passer on the opposite side of the floor from the receivers tries to get a pass to one of the two stationary receivers without it being intercepted or dropped.

13. 1-on-1 Defending the "Give-and-Go" Drill

This drill reinforces the concept "Jump to the Ball" when your check is around the Prime Scoring Area. After the ballcarrier throws a cross-floor pass, he will try to cut in front of his defender, either towards the passer or towards the net, trying to get one step ahead of him. The offensive player cannot cut "backdoor" yet to help build confidence in the defender. The defender, to counter this Give-and-Go move, in turn steps off the former passer towards the new passer. The defender gets in front of the cutter (former passer), not letting him cut in front of him but forcing him to cut behind him.

119   *1-On-1 Denying One Pass Away Drill*

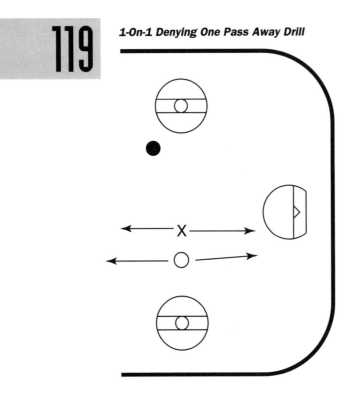

This is a tougher play to execute offensively.

Variation: Later in the drill the offensive player will be able to cut "backdoor." In this situation when the offensive player cuts "backdoor," the defender turns his back to the ball and plays the cutter's stick. To make it even tougher on the defense give the offensive player an advantage of one step to the goal on the "backdoor" cut, then two steps.

Variation:

1) The offensive player goes up and down the Outside Lane two times, then cuts.

2) The passer is allowed to throw only a pass on a "backdoor" cut.

14. 1-on-1 Defensing the "Go" Drill

Same principles as above.

15. 1-on-1 Attack Drill (Closing Out)

The defensive man plays in the help position, i.e., forming the imaginary triangle. On the cross-floor pass to his check, he attacks this new ballcarrier (closing out), staying low and shuffling the last few steps so he does not overcommit.

16. 1-on-1 Six Point Drill

The defender moves through six different defensive positions as the coaches move the ball around in a specific pattern.

1) In a "closed stance" he denies his check from receiving a pass on the ball side (see diagram 120a).

2) On a cross-floor pass, he moves into an "open stance" position.

3) Then, he denies the cutter in a "closed stance" (see diagram 120b).

120a *1-On-1 Six Point Drill - Denying The Pass*

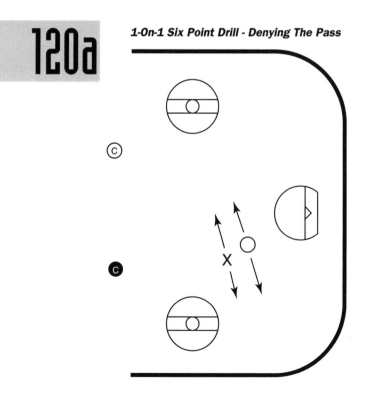

120b

1-On-1 Six Point Drill - Denying The Cutter

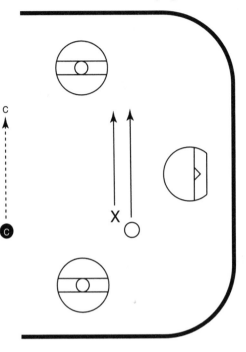

120c

1-On-1 Six Point Drill, Help Position
- Close Out

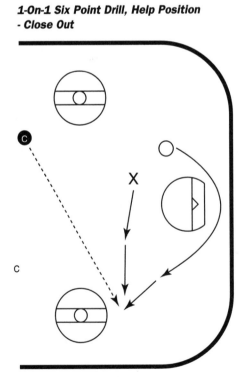

120d   *1-On-1 Six Point Drill*

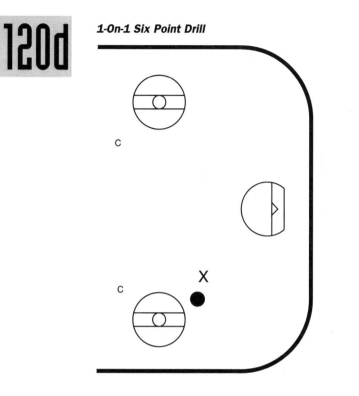

4) As the cutter goes behind the net, back to his own side, the defender moves into an "open stance" position.

5) The coach then throws a cross-floor pass to the offensive player, on which the defender "closes out" to put pressure on him (see diagram 120c).
6) The defender now stops the ballcarrier from scoring by cross-checking (see diagram 120d).

17. Live 1-on-1 Denying One Pass Away When Your Check Is on the Ball Side Drill

18. Live 2-on-2 Denying One Pass Away When the Ball Is in the Middle of the Floor Drill

19. Live 1-on-1 Denying One Pass Away When Your Check Is on the Off-Ball Side Drill

20. Live 1-on-1 Defensing the "Give-and-Go" Drill

21. Live 1-on-1 Defensing the "Go" Drill

22. Live 1-on-1 Attack Drill

D. TEAM DEFENSIVE DRILLS

23. 2-on-2 Defensing the "Up Pick-and-Roll" on the Ball Drill (see diagram 109)
Learning the rules of defensing the Up Pick-and-Roll and executing these rules takes a lot of time; don't get impatient and frustrated if the players don't pick them up quickly.
Teach the six options:

1) "Stop"—stopping the picker from setting the pick or preventing the ballcarrier from using the pick.

2) "Stay"—the defender on the ballcarrier steps up and fights over the top of the pick (usually a poor pick).

3) "Space"—the defender on the ballcarrier steps back and goes through the pick, i.e., the space created by his teammate. Never go around or behind the picker and his teammate.

4) "Switch"—the two defenders just switch checks. The back defender must shoot up and fill the gap on the ballcarrier.

5) "Jump"—the two defenders switch but do so more aggressively.

6) "Double"—on the pick the two defenders attack the ballcarrier.

Stress: Defenders do not wait to be "picked"; they step up or back right away. The back defender must talk to the top defender to warn him of the pick. Communicating and recognizing the pick is coming are the keys for defending a pick.

24. 2-on-2 Defensing the "Down Pick-and-Roll" on the Ball Drill (see diagram 110)
Teach the same six options for defending the pick.

25. 2-on-2 Defensing the "Cross Pick-and-Roll" on the Ball Drill (see diagram 111)
Teach the same six options for defending the pick.

26. 2-on-2 Defensing a "Cross Pick" on the Ball Drill (see diagram 114)
Defend this pick always with a "Jump" switch.

27. 3-on-2 Defensing the "Up Pick-and-Roll" on the Off-Ball Drill (see diagrams 112a, 113a)
One option only:
"Space"—as the bottom offensive player starts to move up towards the top defender to set a pick, the back defender yells "Space" and plays off his check towards the middle. The top defender steps over and back from the pick and slides through the space created by the back defender staying with his man. Both defenders play in an "open stance." Both defenders stay with their check.

28. 3-on-2 Defensing the "Down Pick-and-Roll" on the Off-Ball Drill (see diagrams 112b, 113b)
Two options:
1) "Stay"—this time the back defender goes through the space created by the top defender. The top defender yells "Space" and plays off his check to create the space for his teammate to slide through.
2) "Switch"—the two defenders switch assignments, but the back defender must stay between the ball and his new check. He must step around his new check rather than get sealed out of the play; i.e., the picker gets on the inside of the floor on the defender and thus has an unmolested path to the ball and net.

29. 3-on-2 Defensing the "Cross Pick-and-Roll" on the Off-Ball Drill
Three options:
1) "Stay"—top defender goes over the top of the pick.
2) "Space"—back defender plays off the picker giving space for the top defender to go through. The top defender steps back to go through the pick.
3) "Switch"—when the two defenders switch offensive players, the top defender must step back and around on his new check.

30. 2-on-2 Defensing Screens on the Ball Drill

31. 3-on-2 Defensing Screens on the Off-Ball Drill

32. 4-on-4 or 5-on-5 Shell Drill
Teach all the half-floor defense out of the Shell Drill. Make sure the Shell Drill is used every third practice.

1) Defensive Positioning:

When teaching defense be very position-conscious and understand that this takes a lot of time to get across to the players. To help explain positioning, draw the Three Imaginary Lanes down the floor, and talk to the players about ball side positioning (in the Outside Lane) and help side positioning (in the Middle Lane).

(a) In the beginning, the offense just passes the ball around slowly with offensive players remaining stationary. The defense moves accordingly as the ball moves. No shot is taken. The defense has no sticks to start with.

Stress: Defensive players "close out." Defensive players move together. The defense moves before the offense moves.

(b) Next, the offense can pass the ball around more quickly, the offense can look to shoot, and the offense can take two steps into their shot.

2) "Help and Recover" to Stop Penetration or 1-on-1:

The offense starts closer to the boards and moves the ball around systematically and slowly with the ballcarrier going one-on-one. The defensive man checking the ballcarrier lets him beat him. The nearest defensive man, following the defensive rule that "no ballcarrier can penetrate between two defenders," helps out by stopping the ballcarrier until the original defender picks up the ballcarrier again. Then the helper recovers back to his check. If the helping defender cannot get over in time to pick up his original check, everybody must rotate (see diagram 121).

3) "Jump to Ball" to Defense the Give-and-Go or Go (Cutter):

(a) Start the drill with the ballcarrier stationary and the rest of the offensive players moving and cutting. The defense moves accordingly.

(b) This time the ballcarrier can move by passing the ball then cutting to the ball (Give-and-Go). If the defender's check passes the ball, the defender must jump in the direction of the pass and back off.

121 *4-On-4 Shell Drill - Help & Recover*

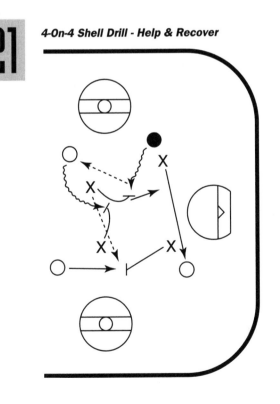

4) Defensing Picks:
Up, Down, Cross Picks—on the Ball
Up, Down, Cross Picks—on the Off-Ball
This drill is run more like a game situation. Players constantly run Down Picks on both sides of the floor, i.e., on the ball and on the off-ball. Then Up Picks and Cross Picks are run.
5) Collapse Drill with Man in Middle:
Run a 4-on-4 situation with an extra offensive player in the middle of the floor. When the offense passes the ball to the extra player in the middle, all the defenders collapse onto him to force him to pass the ball back out to one of his teammates. The defensive players learn to help on the ball and then quickly recover back to their own check.

33. 5-on-5 Collapse Drill
(a) Teammates just deny the pass to their check for five seconds while the ballcarrier tries to make a pass. By denying the passing lanes, the defense forces the ballcarrier to go one-on-one.
(b) Teammates deny the pass to their check for five seconds to give the checker time to put pressure on the ball. Once the checker is on the ballcarrier, his teammates drop off their checks to back up the checker on the ballcarrier. Once there is pressure on the ballcarrier, it becomes harder for him to pass to his teammates, plus the defender on the ballcarrier knows he has backup from his teammates.

Variation:
1) Once the checker is on the ballcarrier, he lets him beat him to see how quickly the defense can cut him off and how the four defenders react and rotate to playing the five offensive players.
2) The offense starts at the other end of the floor and runs the ball into the Offensive Zone. The defense works on denying the first pass.

34. 5-on-5 Fire Out and Drop Off Drill
The offense stands wide, does not move, and slowly passes the ball around. In the beginning, to work on positioning, start the drill with the defensive players with no sticks.

The defender on firing out on the ballcarrier:
1) Approaches at an angle to force him to the boards.
2) Stays in a low stance.
3) Stops one foot away from the ballcarrier.
4) Attacks or cross-checks in a controlled manner.

The defender on dropping off from the ballcarrier:
1) Sags to the middle of the floor and in the direction of the pass (as soon as the ballcarrier passes the ball). The defender does not wait to see what the ballcarrier is going to do.
2) Drops in the direction of the pass to back up his teammate checking the new ballcarrier.
3) Finds his check to see what he is going to do (once he has dropped).
4) Moves before the former ballcarrier does after the pass.
The defense works on how quickly players can drop off and fire out on the ballcarrier.

Variation:
1) The offense can go one-on-one upon receiving the ball.
2) The offense, upon receiving the ball, can pass and cut.

35. 2-on-2 Live Defensing Picks Drill
Up Pick-and-Roll, Down Pick-and-Roll, Cross Pick-and-Roll On the Ball and Off-the-ball
The defense cannot switch, yet must maintain pressure on the ball. The offense must create a switch before they can try to score. In this drill, somebody loses.

Variation: The defense can switch but must maintain pressure on the ball.

36. 4-on-4 Defensive Cut Throat Drill (also 5-on-5)
This drill stresses defense. The defense gets one point for stopping the offense from scoring. But if the offense scores, the former offensive line goes on defense, while the goalie passes to the coach, who in turn passes to the new offensive line coming on the floor from the rest station. If the offense does not score, the defense stays and gets one point, while the offense goes off to the side rest station, and the next line comes on the floor. The defense can only stay on the floor for a maximum of three times. First team to 5 points wins.

37. 3-on-4 Keep Away Drill
In this drill, four defenders try to double-team the ballcarrier, while the three offensive players try to keep the ball away from them for 15 seconds.
Variation: The offense tries to score.

38. 4-on-4 Defense with Offensive Restrictions Drill (also 5-on-5)
Offensive Restrictions:
1) The offense can only score off a cut.
2) The offense can only score off a 1-on-1.
3) The offense can only score off a Screen play.
4) The offense can only score off a Pick-and-Roll play.
5) The offense can only score after four passes.
6) A designated offensive player must score.
Each team gets five possessions. Losers run sprints.

39. 5-on-4 Scramble Drill (also 4-on-3 or 6-on-5)
The more difficult the drill, the better the defense will become. This is a good drill because the defense is at a disadvantage and is therefore required to develop quickness of body and mind, anticipation, and aggressiveness. The defense must talk to each other to get rid of any indecision, to pressure the ball, to help and recover to pick up the free offensive man, to remember to drop back when the ballcarrier passes, and to remember to leave open the farthest man away from the ball. The offense must run their normal offense and not set up as a Power Play. The defense must stop the offense two times.

40. 5-on-5 Borden Ball Half-Floor (see CHAPTER I: MAN-TO-MAN TEAM OFFENSE, Drill 14; and CHAPTER III: THE FAST-BREAK SYSTEM, Drill 45)
The rules are:
1) The ballcarrier can run only three steps with the ball before he must pass it.
2) The ballcarrier must pass the ball in three seconds.
Any violation of these two rules puts the ball over to the other team.
3) If the offensive team drops the ball, it loses possession.

Variation:
1) Play full-floor.
2) Count the number of completed passes. No shot is allowed.

41. 5-on-5 Scrimmage Drill
In this drill the coach gives feedback to the defense. Play a half-floor game. Each team is given five possessions to score. Play to five points.
Variation: Play full-floor.

42. Third Line Drill

To win games, the third line must play tough defense. This drill helps to make this line tougher, as the first line and the second line run their offense against them.

43. 5-on-5 Defense with Defensive Restrictions Drill

1) The defense has no sticks.
2) The defense uses their sticks the wrong way.
3) The defense plays "closed stance" with their back to the ball and switches on all picks.
4) The defense plays "open stance" to the ball and does not switch on picks.
5) The defense can only cross-check. No stick checking is allowed.

44. 5-on-5 Double-Team the Ballcarrier Drill

45. 5-on-5 "Change" Drill Half-Floor

The coach yells "Change"; the offense drops the ball and goes on defense, while the defense goes on offense.

46. Defending the Fast-Break Drills

1) Defending the 2-on-1
2) Defending the 3-on-2
3) Defending the 4-on-3
4) Defending the 5-on-4

CHAPTER V: 1-4 ZONE DEFENSE

I. INTRODUCTION

The 1-4 Zone Defense evolved from combining a simple zone defense and a man-to-man defense. Being an exponent of a tough, aggressive man-to-man defense and not wanting to use a passive zone defense, we (Jim Bishop and I) devised a zone that would be active and aggressive like a good man-to-man defense and still have good backup like a good zone defense. A coach might need this type of zone defense for certain teams or certain situations.

II. THE PHILOSOPHY OF THE 1-4 ZONE DEFENSE

1. Use both man-to-man and zone defensive principles. The one defender on the ballcarrier is playing man-to-man defense while the other four defenders are playing a zone defense.

2. The defense is aggressive and puts pressure on the ballcarrier at all times. The defensive player who takes the man with the ball, called the "chaser," plays him man-to-man. He must stay with him until he passes the ball.

3. The other four defenders must keep the four corners of the zone filled. They must be conscious of the offensive players in their area and where the ball is. Since the defenders will be reacting to the ball as much as their check, give the ball and their check the same priority.

Recall: A zone defense is basically ball-oriented (the ball is the first priority), while a man-to-man defense is man-oriented (the man is the first priority.)

4. The defensive players must learn to adjust to both the ball and to their check in the zone. It is important that the defensive players react to any movement of the ball or any movement of the offensive players before the offense does. If the defense reacts after the offense moves, they will be behind the play and therefore, in trouble.

5. Verbal communication is the key if all five defenders are going to work together. Verbal communication should come more from the two back defensive players than from the two top defensive players as they are in a better position to see what is going on. The key words players may use are: "chaser," "fill," "slide," "bump," "cutter," and "overload."

Recall:
The strong side of the offense is the side with three offensive players.
The weak side of the offense is the side with two offensive players.
The ball side is the side of the floor where the ball is.
The off-ball side is the side of the floor opposite the ball.
The overloaded side, defensively, is the side of the floor with three offensive players.

6. If the players get mixed up while playing the 1-4 zone defense, have a verbal key (call "black") to go back to straight man-to-man defense.

III. NAME OF POSITIONS OF DEFENSIVE PLAYERS (see diagram 122)

The Chaser—defensive player who pressures the ballcarrier.

Two Back Defenders—there is a ball side back defender and an off-ball side back defender.

Two Top Defenders—there is a ball side top defender and an off-ball side top defender.

Note: Some teams like to give the positions numbers so it is easier to communicate with the players and it is easier for the defensive players to remember. The beginning chaser is #5; #1 and #2 are the two top defenders; #3 and #4 are the two back defenders.

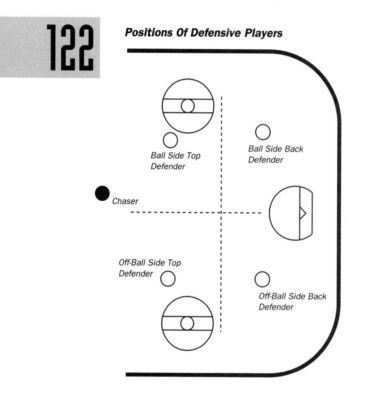

122   *Positions Of Defensive Players*

Ball Side Top Defender

Ball Side Back Defender

Chaser

Off-Ball Side Top Defender

Off-Ball Side Back Defender

IV. ALIGNMENT OF PLAYERS

In the early development of this defense, the team started out in a 2-1-2 zone but found there was too much sliding (movement) before they got organized and too much indecision about who took the ballcarrier. Does the defender in the middle of the zone or one of the top defenders in the zone pick up the ballcarrier when he penetrates down the center of the floor?

The team then decided to start out in a man-to-man defense but found the defensive players they wanted at the top of the zone (the better checkers) were not always there as they were following their checks deep into the corner area of the playing floor.

So, the solution was to start out in a basic 1-2-2 zone, with the defensive players matching up with the offensive player nearest them and in their area of the zone. They were now in a combination man-to-man and zone defense, but with the key defensive players where they were supposed to be (see diagram 123).

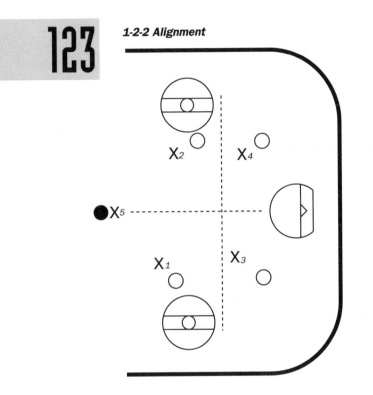

123 *1-2-2 Alignment*

V. ADVANTAGES OF THE 1-4 ZONE DEFENSE

1. Players are in good position for a quick breakout for the Fast-Break.

2. Forces the opposition to shoot outside.

3. There is pressure on the ballcarrier all the time.

4. This is a good defense to hide a weak checker. In this zone defense, the offense will have a hard time attacking the weak checker.

5. This defense helps to stop the good one-on-one teams. As a result, the offensive team has to play a more "team" game rather than relying on one or two players to carry the offense.

6. This defense is good for a change of pace.

7. The opposition has to prepare differently for this zone defense.

VI. DISADVANTAGES OF THE 1-4 ZONE DEFENSE

1. The center area of the defense is vulnerable.

2. The chaser has a tendency to overcommit on the ballcarrier.

3. Playing in a zone defense, players create bad habits, such as stick checking, standing flatfooted, and losing one's concentration.

4. The defensive players have to be aware of "chasing the ball" rather than "forcing the ball."

VII. TYPE OF PERSONNEL

The players in this defense have to be smart, aggressive, and mentally quick, along with being physically quick. The top three players in the zone are your key players as they have to do most of the work, be excellent checkers, be persistent, and be able to "read the offense." The back two players can be your weaker checkers, but they should be verbal.

Depending on your philosophy, you can put your faster players at the top of the zone for the Fast-Break.

VIII. RESPONSIBILITIES OF PLAYERS

The Chaser (#5)
He is the key player in the defense. He puts the pressure on the ballcarrier. His main concern is to first, stop the ballcarrier from scoring; second, to bother his opponent's stick to prevent him from making a good pass; and third, to force him to turn his back to the play so he cannot see the whole floor. Because this is an aggressive defense, the defensive player closest to the ballcarrier will react and start checking him. The chaser must learn to stop one and a half feet away from the ballcarrier, planting his feet and maintaining his basic defensive stance so that he does not overcommit. He also cross-checks under balance and control. He "closes out" and starts cross-checking the ballcarrier immediately so that the ballcarrier does not have the time to throw a nice pass. The chaser stays with the ballcarrier until he passes the ball and then reacts accordingly to the "positioning rules." A major fault can occur here if the chaser tends to overcommit on the ballcarrier.

The Ball Side Top Defender (#1 or #2)
His job is to back up his teammate checking the ballcarrier and to clog up the middle of the floor. He stays roughly in the middle of the floor in line with the chaser and the net. The chaser is not concerned about being beaten as he knows he has backup and therefore, checks all that much more aggressively.

The Ball Side Back Defender (#3 or #4)
He plays in an "open" position to his check ready to take away any thrown passes, deny any cuts, and help on the ballcarrier if needed.

The Off-ball Side Top Defender and the Off-ball Side Back Defender (#3 or #4)
They position themselves to intercept any passes thrown through the zone. They sink towards the middle and play with their sticks to the center of the floor to "pick off" any passes. If their check cuts to the ball, they play in a "closed stance" to stop their check from catching the ball. The off-ball

defender goes with his cutter to just past the middle of the floor, releases him, and then drops back into his area of the zone.

IX. RULES FOR THE 1-4 ZONE DEFENSE

A. DEFENDING THE BALLCARRIER RULES

Rule #1: Defending the Ballcarrier at the Top (see diagram 124)
"When the ballcarrier comes down the center of the floor, the four defensive players in the zone box play their checks in a 'closed stance' position at the beginning to discourage any passes." Because the ballcarrier has nobody to pass to, this gives the chaser (#5) the time he needs to get on the ballcarrier to pressure him. The other four defenders will float off their checks to back up the chaser once he is checking the ballcarrier.

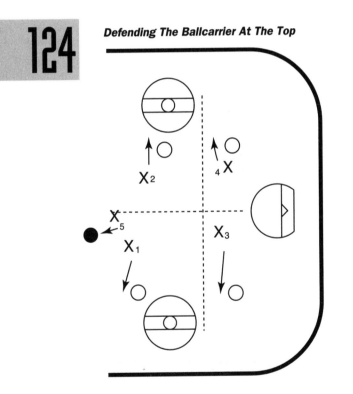

124 *Defending The Ballcarrier At The Top*

Rule #2: Defending the Ballcarrier When He Moves Around on Offense
"The chaser stays with the ballcarrier wherever he goes." The other defensive players adjust their positions according to where their check is and where the ball is. Once the ballcarrier passes the ball, the chaser fills in the zone depending on where he is in the zone (see diagram 125a, 125b).

B. POSITIONING RULES
The coach divides the Defensive Zone into quarters to help clarify the positioning rules. He draws an Imaginary Vertical Line (same as the Imaginary Center Line) down the center of the floor parallel to the sideboards and an Imaginary Horizontal Line across the floor just inside the Imaginary Semicircle Dotted Line (see diagram 126).

Defending The Ballcarrier

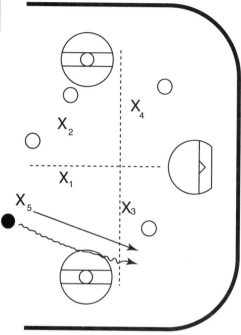

Defending The Ballcarrier

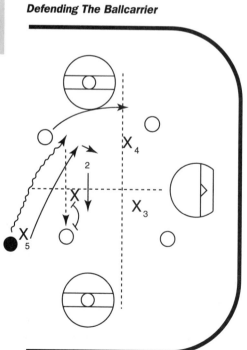

126

Positioning Rules

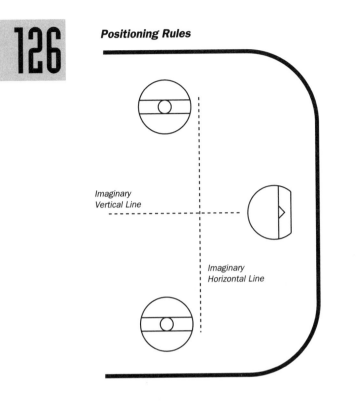

Imaginary
Vertical Line

Imaginary
Horizontal Line

Rule #3: Defending the Pass from the Top to the Side

"If the ball is at the top of the offense and in the center of the floor and then is passed to the side, the chaser will fill in the top vacant spot." In diagram 127, #5 fills in #1's spot in the zone box because he is closer to the Imaginary Vertical Line than #2. In other words, he follows the pass.

Rule #4: Defending a Cross-Floor Pass

"On any cross-floor pass, the defensive player closest to the Imaginary Vertical Line fills in the ball side top defender's spot." On this cross-floor pass in diagram 128, #5 will fill #1's spot. The ball side top defender (#1) is usually closer to the Imaginary Vertical Line than the chaser (#5), so he slides over and fills this new vacant spot (#2's spot). The new chaser becomes #2. The former chaser (#5) usually fills the off-ball side top defender's spot.

Recall: A cross-floor pass is a pass that goes from one side of the floor to the other side over the Imaginary Vertical Line.

In diagram 129, the chaser (#5) is closest to the Imaginary Vertical Line, so he slides and fills the ball side top defender's spot (#2's spot). Although this pass is not considered a cross-floor pass, the defenders react like it is.

Rule #5: Defending the Off-Ball Strong Side

Sometimes the two off-ball defenders have to check three offensive players at the same time. Depending on the situation, "the defender, farthest away from the ball, will play between the two farthest offensive players, while the defender closest to the ball plays his check accordingly." However, he must be aware of helping his off-ball teammate (see diagrams 130a, 130b).

127 Defending The Pass From The Top To The Side

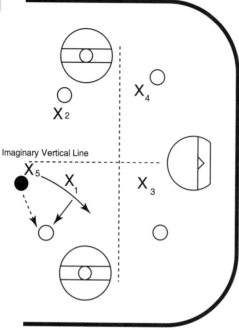

128 Defending A Cross-Floor Pass

129

Defending A Cross-Floor Pass

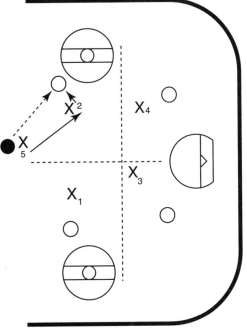

130a

Responsibility Of The Off-Ball Defender

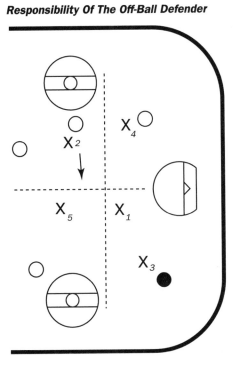

Responsibility Of The Off-Ball Defender

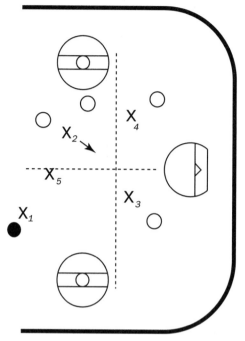

Rule #6: Defending the Pass Down the Side of the Floor
"If the ball is passed down the side of the floor, the defender closest to the Imaginary Horizontal Line fills in the vacant spot."

In diagram 131, the ball side top defender (#1) is backing up the chaser (#5). When the ballcarrier passes the ball down the side, #1 becomes the chaser and #5 becomes the ball side top defender. Then, #5 floats into the middle area of the zone, staying directly in line and slightly behind the chaser, but not in line with the net. Moreover, #5 cannot drop directly in line with the chaser and the net as this would collapse the zone, and all the ballcarrier would have to do is pass back out to the former ballcarrier for a good shot.

In diagram 132a, the defenders follow the rule "whoever is closest to the Imaginary Horizontal Line becomes the backup to the chaser." Therefore, on this sideline pass, because #1 is closest to the Imaginary Horizontal Line, he drops to become the ball side back defender. In addition, #3 shoots out on the ballcarrier to pressure him, and #5 drops slightly into the zone box but remains as the ball side top defender. But in diagram 132b, because the ballcarrier is higher, #1 is not the closest defender to the Imaginary Horizontal Line. Therefore, #5 drops, on the sideline pass, to become the ball side back defender.

In diagram 133, since the chaser (#1) is closer to the Imaginary Horizontal Line than #5, he fills the vacant spot in the zone when #3 fires out on the ballcarrier.

Note: In this situation #5 will not drop below the Imaginary Horizontal Line as it will collapse the zone. In other words, a quick pass out to the offensive player on this side of the floor would create a quick scoring opportunity.

131 *Defending The Pass Down The Side*

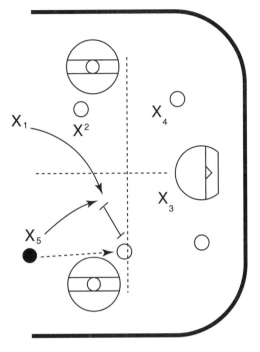

132a *Pass To The Corner*

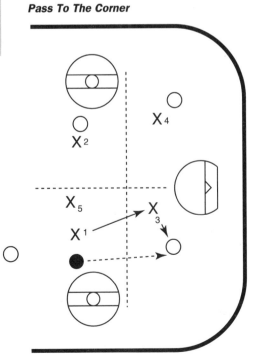

Pass To The Corner

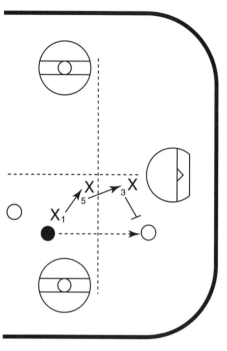

133 **Pass To The Corner**

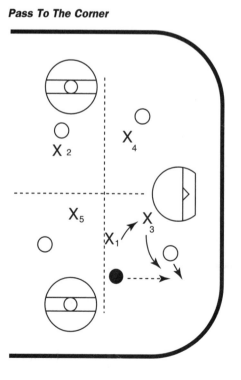

In diagram 134, the slides of the defensive players are shown but on the other side of the floor.

Note: The chaser does not always fill in a corner of the zone. He will always fill in the zone but not necessarily to back up the ballcarrier. Where he fills depends on where he is in relation to the two Imaginary Lines.

134

Pass To The Corner

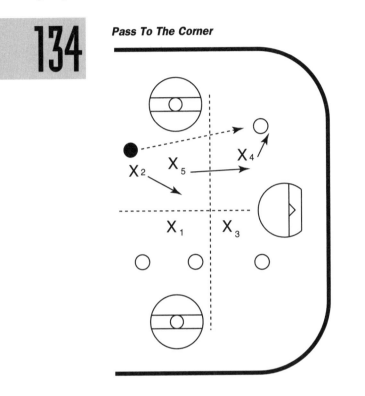

Rule #7: Defending the Pass Up the Side of the Floor
The rules are the same with regards to the Imaginary Horizontal Line (see diagram 135).

C. DEFENDING THE CUTTER RULES

Rule #8: Defending the Cutter
In any cutting situation, "the cutter becomes the first priority and filling the zone the second priority." The team feels the cutter is more dangerous than actually backing up the ballcarrier.

In diagram 136, the defender stays between the ball and his check, playing him in a closed stance (belly-to-belly). The defender goes with him until he is no longer an offensive threat (just past the Imaginary Vertical Line).

In diagram 137, if the former chaser's check cuts through the middle, the defensive player (#5) must go with him first until he is no longer a threat, then #5 fills in the vacant corner of the zone.

Pass Up The Side

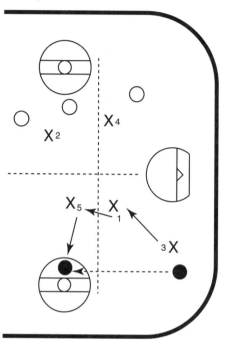

Defending The Cutter

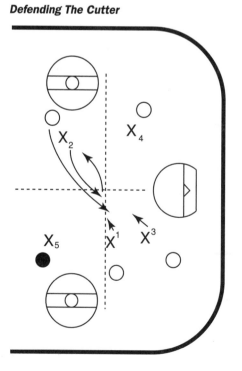

Defending The Cutter

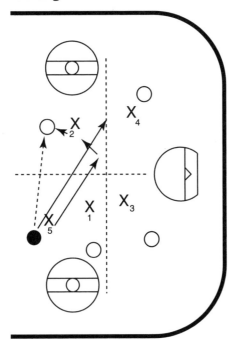

In diagram 138, on the cross-floor pass, #1 goes with the cutter, then fills in the zone backing up the ballcarrier.

In diagram 139, on the cross-floor pass, the cutter cuts down the off-ball side of the floor. Here, the defense makes the usual slides. Because it is a zone, the two off-ball defenders switch on any exchanges by the offensive players on their side of the floor.

In diagram 140, on the cross-floor pass, if an offensive player cuts, his defender will deny him until he is no longer an offensive threat.

D. DEFENDING PICKS AND SCREENS

Rule #9: Defending Picks and Screens
"On any pick, whether on the ball side or off-ball side, the defensive players stay in their area of the zone, i.e., they switch (see diagram 141)."

X. BUILDING THE 1-4 ZONE THROUGH DRILLS

Remember: Teach the whole-part-whole method.

1. 1-on-1 Attacking the Ballcarrier Drill
Teach that the man-to-man defensive stance as the whole concept of this defense is based on placing pressure on the ball.

138

Defending The Cutter

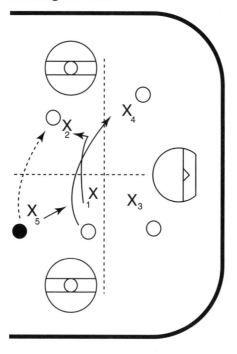

139

Defending The Cutter

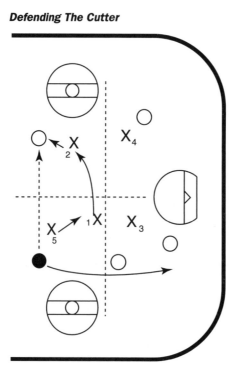

140   *Defending The Cutter*

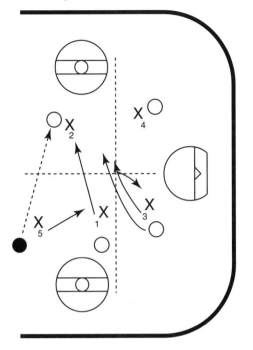

141   *Defending Picks*

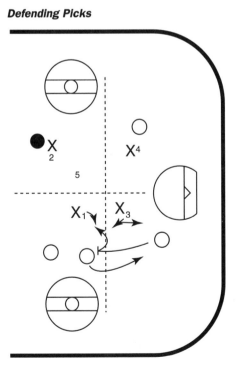

2. 5-on-0 Drill
Teach the philosophy and rules of the 1-4 zone defense, using chairs or pylons as offensive players.

3. 5-on-5 Positioning Drill
The offensive team passes the ball slowly around. There is no movement by the offense. The coach checks the floor positions of the defensive players.

4. 3-on-3 Drill with the Ball at the Top of the Floor
In this drill the ballcarrier moves around the top area of the offense, then makes a pass to one of his teammates on the side of the floor. The defenders react accordingly to the defensive rules (see diagram 142).

142   *3-On-3 Drill With The Ball At The Top*

5. 3-on-3 Drill with Ball at the Side of the Floor)
The same drill as above, except the ballcarrier either passes across or down to one of his teammates. The defenders again react accordingly to the defensive rules (see diagram 143).

6. 4-on-3 Drill
The same drill as above.

7. 5-on-4 Drill
The same drill as above.

8. 5-on-5 Pressure Drill
Place 1-on-1 pressure on the ballcarrier. The ballcarrier can make a pass, but the other four offensive players cannot move.

143 *3-On-3 Drill With The Ball On The Side*

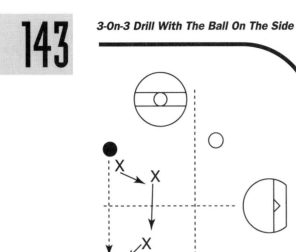

9. 5-on-5 Defensing the Cutter Drill
Token pressure is placed on the ballcarrier who cannot move while the other four offensive players can do anything they want—cut or run a pick-and-roll play.

10. 5-on-5 Offensive Restriction Drill
   The offense can try to score off:
   1) a 1-on-1 only;
   2) a cross-floor pass only;
   3) cutters only;
   4) or picks only.

11. 5-on-5 "Live" Drill

12. 6-on-5 Drill

13. 7-on-5 Drill

The question is now "How would you attack the 1-4 zone defense?"

CHAPTER VI: MAN SHORT (5-on-4 Situation)

I. SPECIALTY TEAMS TERMINOLOGY

1. Man Short—a specialty team that goes on the floor when the team gets a penalty to stop the opposition from scoring. This group of four players plays a zone defense.

2. Power Play—a specialty team that goes on the floor to score when the opposition gets a penalty. This group of five players attacks the zone with patience and ball movement.

3. Top Defenders—these two top defenders, on the man short, play the top three offensive players on the power play, trying to pressure or interfere with their opponent's shot.

4. Back Defenders—these two back defenders, on the man short, play mainly the offensive creasemen, but they do get involved with the shooters on the side of the power play in certain situations. Basically their job is to take away the pass to the offensive creasemen and prevent a shot from being taken by him.

5. Pointman—the top offensive man on the power play. The Pointman sets up the Shooters, passes the ball "around the horn," and must be a shooting threat.

6. Shooters—these are the two cornermen on the side of the power play. The Shooters' responsibilities are: to be a threat to score as soon as they get the ball; to look to pass the ball back to the Pointman; and to look to feed either Creaseman if they are open.

7. Creasemen—these are the two players on the crease of the power play. The Creasemen's job is to stay on the crease and wait for something to happen to the back two defenders to draw them out of the zone. If they become open, they have to anticipate a pass for a shot.

8. Penetration or One-on-One—the ballcarrier tries to beat his defender and go to the net for a scoring opportunity.

9. Press Breaker (Breakout)—if the team gets possession of the ball while on the man short, the man-short team must have a breakout against defensive pressure.

10. Ragging the Ball—once the man short gets the ball into the Offensive Zone, it tries to run around with the ball to kill clock time.

II. THE TYPE OF PLAYERS

We want our best athletes on the man short with these qualities: good anticipation, mental alertness, quickness, and mobility. They should be good ballhandlers, aggressive loose-ball players, talkers on the floor, physically and mentally tough, and endless workers.

III. THE PHILOSOPHY OF THE MAN SHORT

This philosophy is very simple and corresponds with the overall philosophy of our coaching—pressure. The man short does not sit back in a four-man box zone and react to the opposition's power play. Rather it attacks the power play and forces or pressures it into mistakes with hurried shots, bad passes, and turnovers. The man short initiates the action on defense and forces the offense to react to them.

IV. CHANGING DEFENSES OF THE MAN SHORT

The team uses a colored code to key the different types of man-short defenses. It has the "Blue" man short, the "Red" man short, the "Green" man short, and the "Yellow" man short. By changing defenses, the team will keep the opposition off balance and guessing.

A. THE "BLUE" MAN SHORT

The team starts and stays in a box formation. They are going to have the man-short players basically "freeze"; i.e., they are going to play four of the power-play players straight up and let the fifth power-play player shoot. Usually, the Pointman is the designated player, especially if the team does not know the opposition that well.

In the "Blue" defense, the goalie can move out and concentrate on the Pointman only. If the opposition Creasemen play wide, the two back defenders will move out with them. The two top defenders will fake movement towards the Pointman, but they will be concerned mainly with the Shooters shooting.

The man-short team will stay in the "Blue" until the Pointman looks as if he could be a threat to score or until he scores.

The "Blue" call could also indicate that the man-short players will play any of the four opponents tight and thereby dictate which power-play player they will want to shoot. This could be a weak offensive player other than the Pointman.

B. THE "RED" MAN SHORT

This is called the "Blitz" or "all or nothing" defense. The team starts in a box formation and rotates into a diamond formation. The players are going to shoot out hard on the ballcarrier to hurry the power-play players' passes and shots through pressure (via cross-checking or stick checking) and to keep constant pressure on the ball.

Before the full rotation, one of the back defenders will call "Red" so that everybody knows the rotation is on. The "key" for the rotation occurs when the ball is passed back to the pointman (pass #2) from one of the shooters. The players can anticipate this pass, and just before the pass they move into what is called a "cheat" position, i.e., one step towards the direction they are going to rotate. The players' bodies are in one place while their minds are in another.

Remember: The ball must be in the air on the full rotation.

The players should know if the Pointman is a right-handed or left-handed shooter. (It is easier to blitz a left-handed shooter coming from his blind side, i.e., coming from his right side.) They should know if the Pointman can swing the ball going from left to right, as well as from right to left.

The blitzing player should arrive at the same time as the ball arrives. This puts immediate pressure on the ballcarrier and does not give him the time he wants to think and be selective on his pass.

On the first pass (pass #1) from the Pointman to the Shooter, nobody moves; they stay in the box formation but start to anticipate the rotation.

Just before the return pass (pass #2) to the Pointman, everybody moves into a cheat position and starts to form a diamond formation.

On the reception of pass #2 by the Pointman, everybody has rotated into the diamond.

On the possibility of the swing pass (pass #3) to the other Shooter, everybody will rotate totally to the next player, returning to a box formation.

Half Rotation (Diamond Formation) Responsibilities (see diagram 144)
1) Player #1 (the top right player is a left-hand shot) on pass #2 "fires out" trying to put pressure on the ballcarrier. He must commit himself totally.

Half Rotation To A Diamond Formation - "Red"

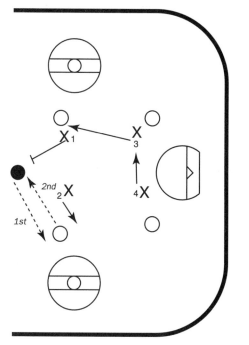

2) Player #2 (the top left player is a right-hand shot) on pass #2 stays in his original position. Once the pressure is on the ballcarrier, player #2 must anticipate a possible return pass back to the Shooter on his side of the floor, which is why he does not leave his position fully.

3) Player #3 (the back right player is a left-hand shot) moves into a "cheat" position; i.e., one step towards the direction he is rotating, halfway to the Shooter, as the ball is in the air on pass #2. He holds this position until the Pointman catches the ball and there is pressure on him. Once there is pressure on the Pointman, he commits fully to the Shooter. If player #3 leaves too early and there is no pressure on the Pointman, the Pointman is capable of throwing a diagonal pass to his offensive creaseman.

4) Player #4 (the back left player is a right-hand shot), when the ball is in the air on the return pass back to the Pointman (pass #2), goes into a "cheat" position, i.e., one step towards the direction he is rotating (moving halfway across the crease). He moves to the off-center position to cut off a possible diagonal pass from the Shooter to the opposite Creaseman. He should know beforehand what shot the Pointman is to anticipate the cutoff for a diagonal pass. It is easier for a left-hand shooting Pointman to make a diagonal pass to the left Creaseman.

Back Defenders' General Rule for Playing the Creases:
Anytime there is a question of which Creaseman to cover on the rotation (i.e., if the back defender is caught halfway on the rotation when the Shooter has the ball rather than the Pointman), always take away the diagonal crease pass from the Shooter as this is the most dangerous pass. The goalie will be out playing the Shooter with the ball and it is much easier for the goalie to play the pass to the Creaseman on his short side rather than the diagonal pass to the Creaseman on his long side. This is a general rule and may change depending on who the opposition players are.

Note: On this half rotation, if there is pressure on the Pointman with the ball, and he does not pass, all the man-short players should have now rotated into a diamond formation.

Full (Complete) Rotation Responsibilities (see diagram 145)
1) If the ballcarrier (Pointman) gets pass #3 off, player #1 must drop back quickly to cut off any cross-floor pass from the ballcarrying Shooter to the opposite Shooter. This is a very important and necessary move. He must drop back in the opposite direction to the pass as the ball is in the air. As he is physically playing the ballcarrier, he must be mentally anticipating, on pass #3, which direction he will go.

2) Player #2, at the beginning of pass #3, goes into a slight "cheat" position, i.e., one step towards the direction he is going to rotate. He drops halfway back to the crease. On pass #3, as the ball is in the air, he drops totally back to take away any diagonal pass from the ballcarrying Shooter to the crease. Remember: It is now player #1's responsibility to cover the off-ball Shooter.

3) Player #3, on pass #3, is either already on the Shooter or is blitzing out to the Shooter as the ball is in the air. He wants to arrive at the same time as the ball does to keep continuous pressure on the ballcarrier.

Back Defenders' General Rule for Playing Either Creaseman or Shooter:
Anytime it is a question of whether to take the Creaseman or the Shooter on the rotation (i.e., if the back defender again is caught halfway on the rotation when the Shooter already has the ball and he does not have time to pressure the ball), he must take the Creaseman and let the goalie move out and handle the Shooter. This general rule is an exception as the man-short philosophy is to keep pressure on the ball. But it does happen periodically where a man-short player cannot get out to put pressure on the ballcarrier in time so he follows this general rule.

4) Player #4, on pass #3, continues his rotation to the opposite Creaseman. On this complete rotation, if the ball gets to the Creaseman (pass #4), this player must shoot totally across and hit the offensive Creaseman.

145

**Full Rotation
- "Red"**

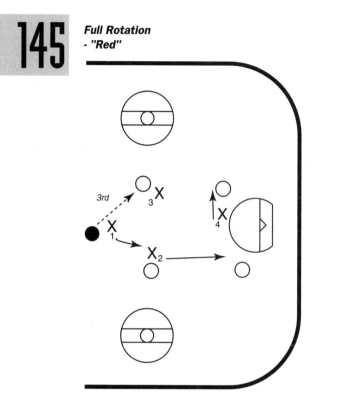

Summary:

The man short hopes to turn the ball over by forcing bad passes or forcing bad shots on two or three different opportunities. When the Pointman is pressured, his natural tendency is to pass from where the blitz came from, i.e., to the "open" Shooter. In attempting to throw pass #3 to the Shooter while being pressured, they hope he throws it away. If he does get a pass off to the Shooter, a back man-short player will be pressuring him immediately from the back. But if the Shooter has time to get pass #4 to the Creaseman, the Creaseman will also be pressured. The man short pressures until it gets a turnover; or until the opposition takes a bad shot; or until the power play resets their offense and the ball goes back to the Pointman.

C. THE "GREEN" MAN SHORT (see diagram 146)

In this rotation, there is no pass to key the blitz. After the call "Green," player #1 just blitzes the Pointman immediately. Again, we start in a box formation and rotate into a diamond.

D. THE "YELLOW" MAN SHORT (see diagram 147)

If the players call "Yellow," they are pulling the rotation off and playing the normal box man-short defense. The players call this when there is no pressure on the ball, i.e., the man-short players are chasing the ball versus forcing the ball, or when the ballcarrier is too far out to blitz him.

The players also call "Yellow" when the opposition is anticipating or waiting for the defensive rotation. If the offensive ballcarrier back-pedals from taking a hit, the man-short player also backs off in the other direction. Now the man-short players are playing a "cat-and-mouse" game, which they are winning because the power play has stopped attacking the man short in anticipation of the blitz.

146

***Full Rotation
- "Green"***

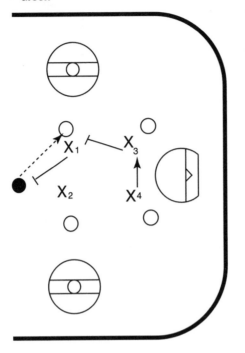

147

***Full Rotation
- "Yellow"***

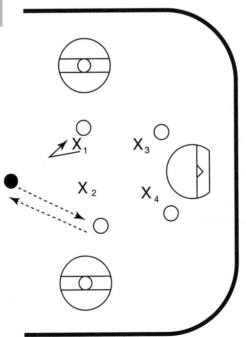

The man-short players can also automatically back off from the rotation when the power-play players start to back off in anticipation of the blitz.

The Man-Short General Rule Regarding Forcing or Chasing the Ball:
If the man-short players are forcing the power play, i.e., putting pressure on the ball, they stay in the "Red" Man Short. If the man-short players are chasing the ball, i.e., trying to catch up to the ball to put pressure on it, they go into the "Yellow" Man Short.

Later in the season as the opposition gets to know your team's color calls, they should be changed.

V. ADJUSTMENTS FOR SPECIAL SITUATIONS

1. Against a power play that likes to score by throwing diagonal cross-floor passes from the Shooter to the opposite Creaseman, the man short switch the two back defenders so that their sticks are now on the outside of their bodies (instead of being on the inside). This maneuver makes it easier for the back defenders to intercept the cross-floor pass or at least deny it.

2. Against a power play that likes to score from their Shooters and Pointman, start in a diamond formation and rotate into a box formation when the ball is passed to a Shooter or a Creaseman.

3. Against a power play that plays farther out than the normal positioning for long-ball Shooters, does the man short still rotate or not? Indeed, the man-short team still rotates to force the play.

4. Against a power-play team that puts a player in the middle of the power play (causing the man short a lot of trouble on the rotation), the middle man tries to interfere with the back defender coming across the crease on the rotation. This player must be aware of what is happening and take the shortest route by going over or under this screener (see diagram 148).

VI. OTHER TYPES OF MAN-SHORT SITUATIONS

A. THE "BOX" MAN SHORT
In this man short, the back two defenders start by playing the two offensive Creasemen. The top two defenders play the other three offensive players—the two Shooters and the Pointman. These top two defenders must try to interfere with passes and shots by these three players. If the Pointman is a right-hand shot and is going to shoot, player #2 must interfere with his shot and thereby force a pass to the left-hand Shooter. Player #4 might have to leave his crease check to help player #2 and delay the shot by the left-hand Shooter until player #2 can slide over to interfere or check him. If the left-hand Shooter passes to the ball side Creaseman because player #4 had to leave his check to help player #2, then player #3 now has to slide across to help player #4. If the left-hand Shooter reverses the ball back to the Pointman, either player #1 or player #2 has to play the Pointman (whoever is in the best and closest position to play him). In this man short, teammates help each other out a lot until they can recover to their original position. The goalie plays his normal position in his crease as he has to contend with shots from any of the power-play players (see diagram 149).

Another variation to the box man short occurs when the back two defenders play the two offensive Creasemen only. The top two defenders play the other three offensive players—the two Shooters and the Pointman. These top two defenders must try to interfere with passes and shots by these three players without any help from the two back defenders. If the Pointman is a right-hand shot and is going to shoot, player #2 must interfere with his shot and thereby force a pass to the left-hand Shooter (player #1

148

Adjustment Versus The "Man In The Middle"   *Adjustment Versus The "Man In The Middle"*

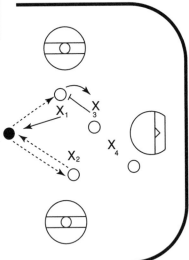

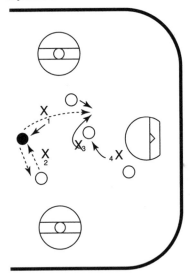

149

"Box" Man Short

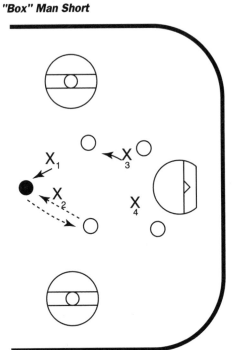

would interfere if the Pointman was a right-hand shooter). Player #2 then slides over to interfere with the left-hand Shooter. If the left-hand Shooter reverses the ball back to the Pointman, either player #1 or player #2 has to play the Pointman (whoever is in the best and closest position to play him). The goalie plays out a bit more on his crease as he has to contend with only the three top offensive players.

B. THE "DIAMOND" MAN SHORT

The players start in a 1-2-1 alignment to put pressure on the three outside shooters. This diamond man short is similar to the blitz except it starts already in the diamond formation and rotates into the box formation whenever the ball goes to the side of the power play, either to the Shooter or the Creaseman (see diagram 150). In this rotation, when any pass to the side occurs, the defender on the ballcarrying Shooter does not move and plays him. The lone back defender slides over to play the ball side Creaseman, while the defender on the off-ball Shooter drops and picks up the off-ball Creaseman to discourage any diagonal pass. The lone defender at the top, on the pass to the side, must drop opposite to the pass from the Pointman to the off-ball Shooter to take away any cross-floor pass from the ball-carrying Shooter and to cover for the defender who has dropped to cover the opposite crease. The four players have now rotated into a box formation. All players keep their sticks up to discourage any passes through the middle. Because most of the good scoring chances will come from the crease area in the diamond man short, the goalie sits back in his crease more to take away the quick crease shot.

C. THE "TRIANGLE-AND-ONE" MAN SHORT

Three players play a triangle zone while the other player covers his special check man-to-man. This offensive player is the most dangerous threat.

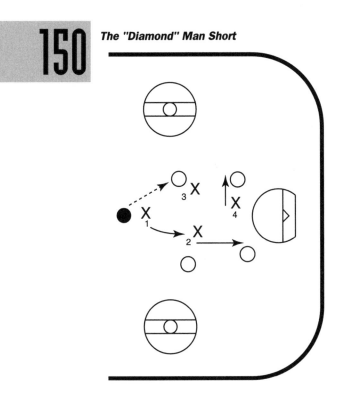

150 *The "Diamond" Man Short*

D. THE "TRIANGLE" MAN SHORT

This man short is played when down two players. The power play is a 4-on-3 or a 5-on-3 situation. The normal way of playing the triangle man short occurs when the top defender plays the top two offensive players, either trying to interfere with their shots or forcing bad passes to create a turnover. The back two defenders in the triangle play the two Creasemen. This is similar to the box man short where everybody will help each other out.

Also out of this alignment the team can play a blitz man short.

E. THE "INVERTED TRIANGLE" MAN SHORT

The power play is a 4-on-3 or 5-on-3 situation. The inverted man short is set up with two defenders playing the top two offensive players and the lone defender playing between the two offensive Creasemen. Similar to a "diamond" man short setup in the 5-on-4 situation, the players have to rotate when the ball goes to a Creaseman (see diagram 151).

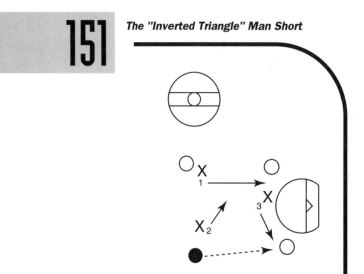

151   *The "Inverted Triangle" Man Short*

VII. PRESS BREAKER AGAINST THE 10-SECOND PRESS

As soon as the man short gets possession of the ball, it has 10 seconds to get the ball over their Offensive Zone Line or lose possession. Most power-play teams press to stop the man-short players from receiving an outlet pass from the goalie, to delay them, or to pressure them into turnovers.

If there is a loose ball, from a rebound off the boards or off the goalie, and a man-short player gets it, he can run the ball out or pass it up to a teammate.

If the goalie stops a shot, the man-short players have to have options to get the pass from the goalie against defensive pressure. Again, once the man-short player has possession he can either run the ball out or pass it up the floor.

Options to Get in the Clear Against Defensive Pressure:

1. Goalie calls "#1" or no call (see diagram 152)
This is the team's normal breakout. The two top defenders have three options: (a) Breaking straight up the floor for a breakaway pass from the goalie if in the clear; (b) Breaking up the floor to about center and seeing that the power-play checker is staying with him, he will then break out to the boards for a pass; (c) Breaking up the floor to about center and seeing that the power-play checker is staying with him, he will then button hook (stop suddenly) and come back to the ball to get in the clear for a pass from the goalie. There must be the offensive threat of at least one of the top defenders breaking out for a goal. This keeps the opposition power-play players a little edgy and a bit reluctant to take chances. The back defenders break two steps up, then break out to the boards to get in the clear for a pass from the goalie.

152   *"#1" Breakout*

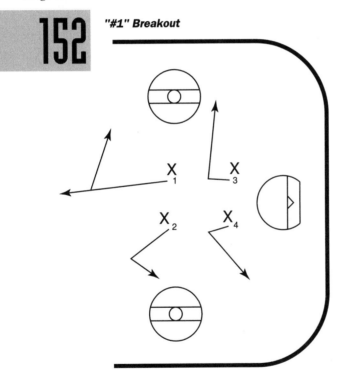

2. Goalie calls "#2" (see diagram 153)
In this breakout to get in the clear, the back defenders exchange positions with the top defenders. The back defenders go up the middle of the floor looking for the breakaway pass from the goalie. The top defenders come back towards the goalie, on the outside of the back defenders, looking for the short outlet pass from the goalie.

Note: With this option, when the top defender receives the first pass, he looks long immediately for the breaking back defender. It is amazing how often he is open on this interchange move.

153

"#2" Breakout

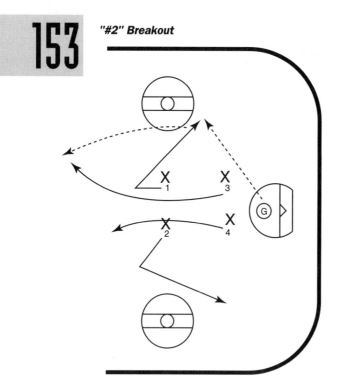

3. Goalie calls "#3"

On the right side of the floor, the back defender sets an up pick for the top defender to get in the clear. Another possibility is to work the play on the side of the best players. If the top player cuts to the outside towards the boards off the pick, the picker cuts opposite, so in this situation he would cut into the middle of the floor for the first pass. The picker reads off the cutter (see diagram 154a). If the top player cuts into the middle of the floor off the pick, the back defender, after setting the pick, cuts opposite. So in this situation he can either cut long to the outside (see diagram 154b) or cut to the outside of the floor for the first pass (see diagram 154c).

4. Goalie calls "#4" (see diagram 155)

Again, the top and back defenders exchange positions, but this time the back defender breaks up the floor on the outside and the top defender comes back on the inside of the floor for the first pass.

5. Goalie calls "#5" (see diagram 156)

In this situation, the power-play players will try to double-team the man-short player who gets the first pass. This breakout is for getting the ball out of their own end in a controlled manner. The ballcarrier runs the ball up the side boards to draw the double-team. Just before they arrive he passes to the goalie who has come out of his crease to stand in the middle of the floor. The goalie then relays the ball to the off-ball side man-short player. The off-ball man-short players can stay in their own positions or they can interchange positions to get in the clear.

6. Goalie calls "#6" (see diagram 157)

The back defender, on the same side as his players' bench, runs hard to the bench while a teammate on the bench comes out the offensive door. If the power-play checker stays with the back defender, his teammate will be in the clear coming out the offensive door. If the power-play checker leaves the back

154a

"#3" Breakout

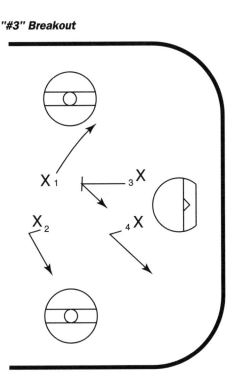

154b

"#3" Breakout Option

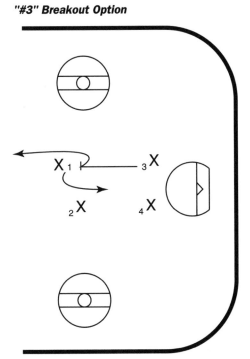

154c

"#3" Breakout Option

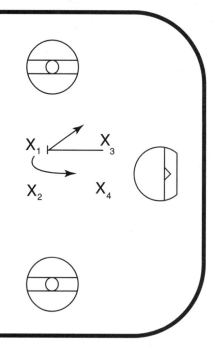

155

"#4" Breakout

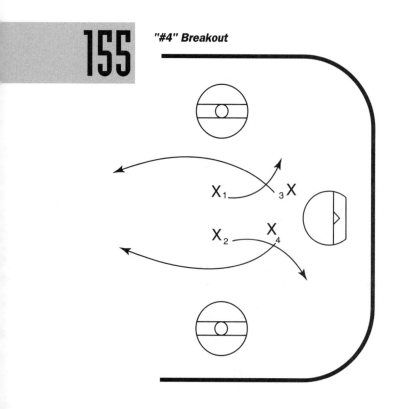

156

"#5" Breakout Versus The Double-Team

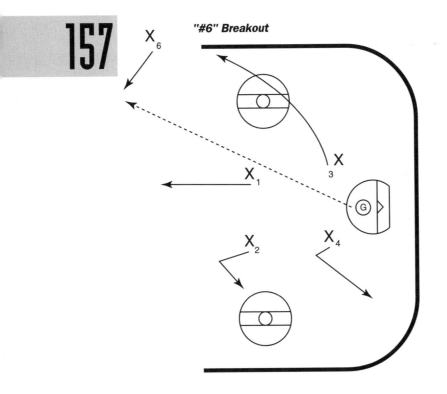

157

"#6" Breakout

man to cover the player coming out the offensive door, the back man has the option of coming back for the pass from the goalie, while the player on the offensive door stays on the bench.

VIII. MAN-SHORT OFFENSE OR RAGGING THE BALL

Ragging occurs when the man-short players try to maintain possession of the ball for the length of the penalty in their Offensive End.

The players set up in a box formation with two players in the corner area of the floor and two players near the boards and the Offensive Zone Line. This gives them plenty of room to run around and avoid double-teams. These players also stay on their own side of the floor for balance; to stay out of the way of the ballcarrier; and for a safety valve in case the ballcarrier gets into trouble.

The man-short players run continuous off-ball Down Picks to help themselves get in the clear for a cross-floor pass.

On receiving the Down Pick on the off-ball side, the cutter fakes a cut into the middle of the floor (to get a good angle to come off the Down Pick) and then cuts straight back towards the Offensive Zone Line. He must come hard off the pick (see diagram 158a).
Options for the picker:
He can run a Down Pick and just stay in the corner area as a safety valve.
He can run a Down Pick-and-Roll and cut into the middle for the pass.
He can fake an off-ball Down Pick and cut into the middle for the pass. This move works well as an element of surprise.
Or the picker can come from the off-ball corner area and come up the floor to set a Back Pick for his teammate (see diagram 158b).

Note: Do not set any picks on the ballcarrier as he already has two power-play checkers on him. One more checker in the area could create a lot of problems.

As the off-ball pick is being set, the ballcarrier throws the cross-floor pass so that the cutter coming off the pick runs into the pass. The passer must lead the cutter slightly on this cross-floor, semi-lob pass. The passer then goes down to set a Down Pick on his side of the floor. Timing is very important so the cutter must make sure the passer is ready to throw the cross-floor pass before he cuts off the pick. But the ballcarrier does not have to make a cross-floor pass if he is not being double-teamed; on the other hand, if he is a good one-on-one player he can go for a run with the ball.

The teammate in the corner area of the floor on the ball side must be ready to fake a cut to the net and then pop out as a safety valve. If he does receive a pass, he must run the ball out of the corner since it is easier to get into trouble as there are not as many options available.

The man-short players want to rag the ball for the first half of the penalty to frustrate and tire out the power-play players. Then, the man-short players can go for the score. So, unless, there is a clear cut break to the net by the ballcarrier, the man-short players do not go for a score immediately when ragging. Some teams like to rag the ball for the full penalty and forget about scoring; other teams like to look to score all the time. Again, the team's philosophy should depend on the type of personnel the team can put on the floor.

158a

Ragging Down Pick

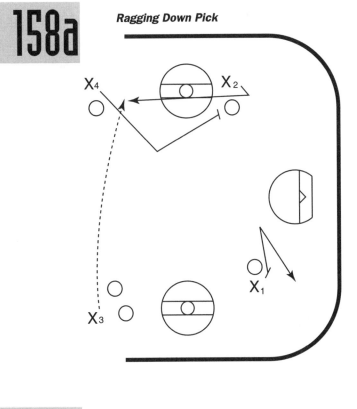

158b

Ragging Up Pick

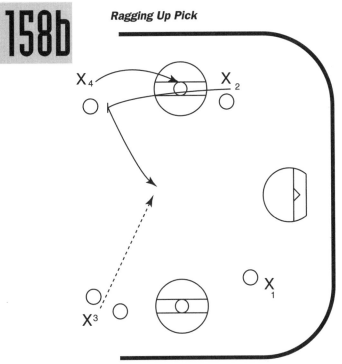

IX. MAN-SHORT FACE-OFF ALIGNMENT

The man-short players want to go for possession of the ball. Because one of the opponents will be open, the man-short players try to set up the face-off so that this open player thinks he will get the ball without any problems. The man-short players line up beside each of the other three opponents playing their sticks. Hopefully, this will be the same side of the opponent as the direction they will rotate. Although the man-short players are standing beside their opponent physically, they are mentally playing their next opponent they are going to rotate to. On the whistle two or three players rotate to the next opponent hoping to cut off a loose ball coming out of the face-off. If the centerman thinks he can win the draw or tie up the opposition centerman, he gives his teammates a signal so that they don't rotate but attack the loose ball coming to them.

The man-short players gamble that the power-play players will not go for a score off the face-off but will try to gain possession. Therefore, the man-short players align with one player (#4) always protecting their net (behind his own centerman) but ready to rotate to the next opponent. Another player (#2) takes a deep position where he can get a good opportunity to retrieve a loose ball if the opposition centerman knocks the ball back from the face-off to his own net. Here the man-short players gamble that if the opposition centerman wins the draw, he will usually knock the ball back towards his own net. The third man-short player (#5) aligns opposite to the side boards. If there is no opponent there he adjusts his position and moves until he is checking an opponent. The centerman's rule (#3), as in all face-offs, is "pursue all loose balls" (see diagram 159).

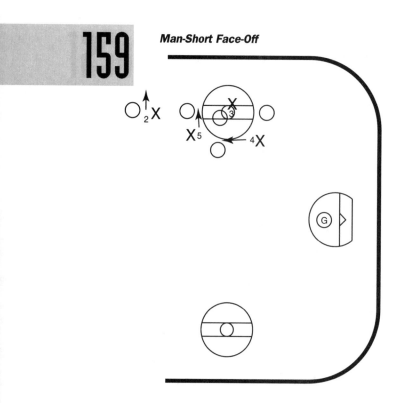

159 *Man-Short Face-Off*

X. MAN-SHORT DRILLS

A. TIPS FOR MAN-SHORT DRILLS

1. Teach the whole-part-whole method. Start with 4-on-0 and progress with breakdown drills of 3-on-2, 4-on-3, and end with 5-on-4.

2. Create drills that give players lots of repetition. Confidence is built through repetition.

3. Drills should be broken into teaching drills and competitive drills.

4. Encourage talking in all man-short drills.

B. BLITZ DRILLS

1. 4-on-0 Rotation Drill (see diagram 160)
The four players rotate against pylons or chairs.

2. 3-on-2 Back Man Fires Across Drill (see diagram 161)
The off-ball back defender should not leave too early and he should try to arrive at his check at the same time as the ball.

Remember to work both back defenders on firing across.

160   *4-On-0 Rotation Drill*

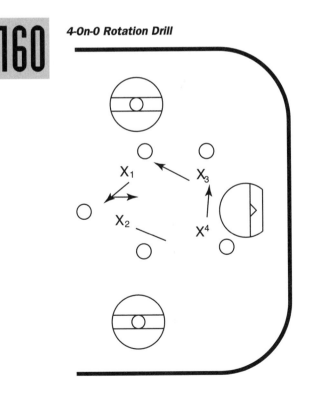

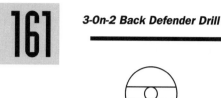

161 3-On-2 Back Defender Drill

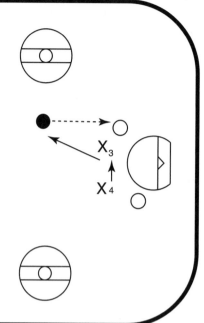

3. 3-on-2 Top Man Fires Out Drill (see diagram 162)
Remember to work both top defenders on firing out.

4. 3-on-2 Top Man Interception Drill (see diagram 163)
Here the power play must make a cross-floor pass, a Shooter-to-Shooter pass. Stress that once the top defender blitzes he must drop quickly to cut off this cross-floor pass.
Remember to work both top defenders on dropping to intercept.

5. 4-on-3 Back Man Fires Out Drill (see diagram 164)
Again work on the proper rotation. Stress that the back defender goes into the "cheat position" before he blitzes.
Remember to work both back defenders.

6. 4-on-3 Top Man Drops Down Drill (see diagram 165)
Stress that everybody rotates together.
Remember to work both top defenders.

7. 4-on-3 Rotation Drill (see diagram 166)
The four offensive players stand and pass the ball, holding it for two seconds—no shots. The coach checks the rotation and positioning of the man-short players. As the rotation gets better have the offensive players just pass the ball—no shots. Finally have the four offensive players try to score.

Stress that the man-short players go into a cheat position before they blitz; that they put pressure on the ball all the time; and that the top defender rotates down in the opposite direction to the pass.

3-On-2 Top Man Fires Out Drill

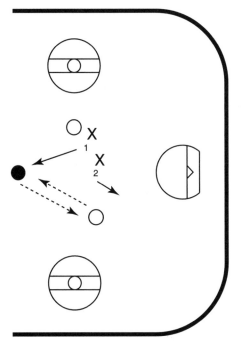

3-On-2 Top Man Interception Drill

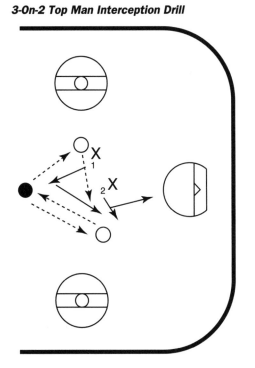

164

4-On-3 Back Man Fires Out Drill

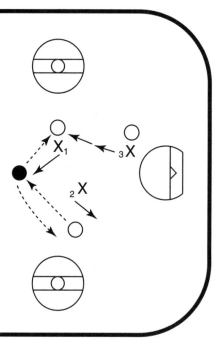

165

4-On-3 Top Man Drops Down Drill

166

4-On-3 Rotation Drill

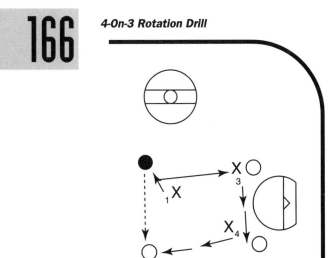

8. 5-on-4 Rotation Drill (see diagram 167)
In the beginning, the man-short players do not have sticks to reinforce the proper rotation and proper positioning. The power play cannot shoot. In the next progression, the man-short players have their sticks, but the power play can still not shoot.

Stress that the man-short players go into a "cheat position" before they blitz; that the top defender who fires out must pressure the ball; that the top defender must drop quickly and rotate in the opposite direction to the pass to cut off any cross-floor pass from the ballcarrying Shooter to the off-ball Shooter.

Recall:
If the power play can pass the ball at will, the man short will end up chasing the ball rather than forcing the ball. This is the time to call off the blitz.
If there is pressure on the Pointman with the ball, but he does not pass, everybody stays in the diamond formation.
If a man-short player is caught between letting the Shooter shoot or letting the Creaseman shoot, he should drop and stay with the Creaseman, letting the Shooter shoot.

9. 5-on-4 Specialty Game Drill
The power play has 10 possessions to score five goals. If the man-short holds the power play to four goals or less, the power-play players must run lengths.
Variation: The first specialty team to 10 points wins. The power play gets one point for a score. The man short gets one point for stopping the power play from scoring.

5-On-4 Rotation Drill

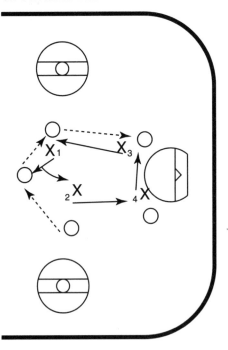

C. BREAKOUT DRILLS VERSUS PRESSURE

10. 1-on-1 Breakout Drill
The top defender breaks down the floor trying to get in the clear either by:
   1) Going long for a breakaway pass.
   2) Breaking out 10 steps, then button hooking back to the ball.
   3) Breaking out 10 steps, then cutting outside to the boards.

11. 4-on-5 Breakout Drill
   1) #1 or normal breakout (see diagram 152).
   2) #2 Exchange with the back defender going up the middle (see diagram 153).
   3) #3 Up Pick with only the left-shot side (see diagram 154).
   4) #4 Exchange with the back defender going outside (see diagram 155).
   5) #5 Versus the double-team (see diagram 156).
   6) #6 The back defender goes to the bench with a teammate coming on (see diagram 157).

12. 4-on-5 "10-Second" Drill
The man-short players try to get the ball into their Offensive Zone before 10 seconds elapse.

13. Man Short Versus Power Play Game Drill
   1) The power play is given 10 possessions. The power play gets one shot only. After the shot, no matter what happens, it gets the ball back. The power play gets one point for scoring; the man short gets one point for stopping the power play. The specialty team with the most points wins. The loser does push-ups.
   2) The power play is given five possessions for one minute each. The specialty team with the most points after the five mini-games wins. The loser does 10 pushups. The power play keeps shooting

and tries to keep getting the ball back as many times as they want for the minute. The man short wants to get the ball and rag the ball for the full minute.

3) The power play plays one-minute games until one of the specialty teams obtains ten points.

4) The power play plays a game for a two-minute penalty segment. Use the big score clock in the arena.

The point system for the power play:

If the power play scores, it gets one point.

If the power play doesn't score but gets the ball back from a loose ball, it gets one point plus another opportunity to score.

If the power play doesn't score but presses and gets the ball back, it gets one point plus another opportunity to score.

If the power play doesn't score but double-teams the ballcarrier in its Offensive Zone and gets the ball back, it gets one point plus another opportunity to score.

If the power play doesn't score, but double-teams the ball in the Defensive Zone (man short trying to rag the ball) and gets the ball back, it gets one point plus another opportunity to score.

The point system for the man short:

If the man short stops the power play from scoring, it gets one point.

If the man short stops the power play from scoring and gets the ball from a loose ball, it gets another point.

If the man short stops the power play from scoring and gets the ball into the Offensive Zone within ten seconds, it gets another point.

If the man short scores, it gets another point.

If the man short rags the ball for the length of the penalty, it gets another point.

Note: The man short can get four points maximum in one sequence. The power play can get two points maximum in one sequence. If the power play keeps scoring, it gets one point and the man short gets nothing.

D. MAN-SHORT RAGGING DRILLS

14. 1-on-2 Beating the Trap Drill
Near the Offensive Zone Line and the side boards.

15. 2-on-2 Working the Off-Ball Side Drill
    Options:
    a) Down Pick
    b) Fake Down Pick

16. 4-on-5 Down Pick Drill (see diagram 157)

17. 4-on-5 Down Pick-and-Roll to Middle Drill

18. 4-on-5 "Double" Pick-and-Roll Drill

19. Two-Minute Rag Drill
Keep records of the ragging time by each group.

Variation: Put six players on the four man-short players.

E. MAN-SHORT FACE-OFF DRILL

20. 4-on-5 Face-Off Drill

CHAPTER VII: POWER PLAY

I. THOUGHTS ON THE POWER PLAY

1. To have a good power play, a team needs three excellent outside (long-ball) shooters. Players that are usually the best ballhandlers and shooters are on the power play.

2. During the season, when the game "is over" or when the team is ahead, the coach plays his "lesser lights" on the power play. It is tough to win a scoring championship with this type of philosophy because a player cannot build up points against a weak opponent when playing time is given to weaker players on the power play. It is amazing, however, how much confidence players gain on the power play, especially at the minor/youth level.

II. POWER-PLAY STATISTICS

The team should average four power-play goals or more per game. The power-play shooting percentage should be 57 percent or 4 goals for every 7 shots a game. The power play should limit the opposition to one or less man-short goals per game.

III. PHILOSOPHY OF THE POWER PLAY

1. The first priority is to get a good shot (See Power Play Principles). Power-play players have to show composure and avoid forcing their shots or passes. Patience is very important because they are basically playing against a zone defense which has a tendency to "fall asleep" or to have mental lapses. Since zone defenses want power plays to shoot the ball quickly, the power play must learn to attack, yet take their time and take good shots.

2. The power play wants to attack the defense and make it react to the movement of the ball and the players. The old philosophy was just to pass the ball around and get a good shot. A power play cannot just pass, pass, pass, and then shoot. A power play must pass, penetrate, pass, penetrate, pass, swing the ball from side to side, make a cross-floor pass, and then shoot.

3. Because the power play outnumbers the man short, the power-play players must believe in working as a five-man unit to get the shot they want. They discourage any one-on-one moves except in certain situations where the ballcarrier fakes a shot and the defender totally "freezes" or plays the faked shot with his stick, in which case the ballcarrier can go around him.

IV. POWER-PLAY PLAYERS' RESPONSIBILITIES

1. The Pointman
He is the key person on the power play. He has to be an excellent shooter and a good ballhandler with the ability to move the ball quickly. He has to be unselfish, yet also selfish. This paradox means he has to be unselfish by setting everybody else up to score, yet at the same time he still has to score. Why must the Pointman be a scorer? A man short can play all the other four offensive players straight up defensively, leaving the pointman to do all the shooting. So he better be able to score if given the open shot.

Note: It helps his effectiveness on swinging the ball if he can throw the behind-the-back pass, but it is not necessary. When throwing this backhand pass, he cocks his stick back and flexes his top-hand arm, giving a little dump pass.

The Pointman's options:
a) Taking the shot on the return pass. Coaches do not like players on the power play who just go down and take a shot without even a pass. Even players who make one pass and then shoot do not help the power-play situation.
b) Reversing the ball from one side of the floor to the other, i.e., setting up the off-ball Shooter.
c) Making diagonal passes to either Creaseman.

2. The Shooters
The shooters also have to be excellent shooters and good passers. They have to step "down and in" behind the top defender to take the shot. They definitely have to cut in between the two defenders to be more of a threat.

The Shooter's options with the ball:
a) If open, take a shot.
b) Pass into the ball side crease.
c) Make a cross-floor pass to the opposite (off-ball) Shooter.
d) Make a return pass back to the Pointman.
e) Make a diagonal pass to the opposite (off-ball) Creaseman.

3. The Creasemen
These players have to be good in-close and excellent loose ball players in the corners. For the Creasemen to be effective the top three offensive players must score. Then, when the back defenders go out to stop these shooters from scoring, the Creasemen become open for the shot.

The Creaseman's options:
a) If he gets a pass (usually this occurs because he is open), he shoots. When he gets a pass from the ball side Shooter, he usually has to step out in front of the net to put himself in the best scoring position. When he gets a diagonal pass from the opposite Shooter, he just "quick sticks" the shot.
b) When he gets a pass, if he is pressured from the opposite back defender, he makes a cross-floor pass to the opposite Creaseman.
c) If nothing is available upon receiving the pass, he passes back to the ball side Shooter.

V. POWER-PLAY PRINCIPLES

1. Alignment (see diagram 168)
The Pointman stays in the middle of the floor at the top of the power play.
The Shooters align themselves in the gaps between the top defenders and the back defenders and stand out to receive the passes from the Pointman without fear of an interception.
The Creasemen align themselves beside the crease behind the back defenders.

On setting up the power play, the players do not line up beside the defensive players in the zone but stand behind the defenders in the gaps since it is harder for the defenders to see both the offensive player and the ball.
The power-play players also keep good spacing between each other by taking a position so that one defender has a hard time guarding two offensive players.

168 Power-Play Alignment

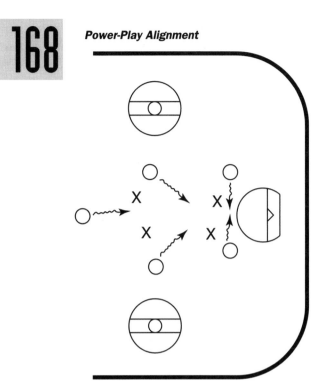

2. Ball Movement
The power play believes in moving the ball around the outside of the zone defense. They want the ball to do all the work. They don't believe in hanging onto the ball too long since this gives the man-short defense time to catch up and adjust. They want to force the zone defense to move and react. Types of ball movement: quick reversals of the ball; diagonal passes from shooter to crease; cross-floor passes from shooter to shooter; cross-floor passes from crease to crease; and fake passes to draw a defender or "freeze" him.

3. Reversal of the Ball
The ability to swing (reverse) the ball from one side of the floor to the other is very important. The power play sets up their ball side attack as a camouflage. They make it look like they are attacking on the ball side (the decoy), but everything is concentrated at attacking on the off-ball side. The main idea is to swing the ball quickly so that the off-ball Shooter just has to catch and shoot the ball all in one motion. Usually, if done quickly enough, the Shooter ends up shooting to the near side of the net because the goalie will still be moving across the crease.

When a power play is forced to play only 3-on-2 at the top of the man short, the ability to reverse the ball quickly is extremely important. That is against a man short where the two back defenders play the offensive Creasemen tight, and the two top defenders play the top three shooters. In this type of man short because the goalie does not have to worry about the creasemen, he can play out high on the crease concentrating only on the top three shooters.

4. Player Movement
a) On receiving the ball, the ballcarrier must look to penetrate the gaps, drawing two defenders and then dumping the ball off to a Creaseman or Shooter. Upon penetration, if the ballcarrier draws the

back defender up, he passes to the Creaseman. Upon penetration, if the Shooter draws the top defender down, he passes back to the Pointman.

b) The ballcarrier tries to draw a defender by stepping "down and in" towards the net looking to shoot.

c) The shooter can cut through the center of the zone defense looking for a pass from the opposite Shooter.

d) The Creasemen can cut from behind into the middle of the zone defense for a diagonal pass from the Pointman or opposite Shooter.

5. Good Shot Selection

Power-play players must know the difference between a good shot and a bad shot.

A bad shot is taken when the shooter is half checked or has a stick in his way; the goalie is set; the shooter shoots at a bad angle or "bombs" his shot.

A good shot is taken when the shooter is unmolested (not interfered with a stick) and has a good angle; the shot has an element of surprise (quick release); the goalie is moving (possibly to get into better position); and the shooter "picks" his shot.

Players must be disciplined in their shooting.

The ballcarrier should look at the net to be a scoring threat, to put pressure on the defense, and to see everybody on the floor. A power-play player must be prepared to shoot before the ball comes to him. He must be physically and mentally ready to shoot the ball so that he can catch and shoot in one motion.

6. Passing and Catching Principles

All passes must be "shooting" or "passing" passes, i.e., passes right in the stick pocket for a quick release. Players do not like passes that they have to catch and then move their stick into a shooting position to release the ball.

Types of passes players can throw are reversal passes, diagonal passes, and cross-floor passes.

Passing

Passes must be quick and accurate to the outside (stick side) of the receiving players so that defenders cannot interfere with the pass. Quick and accurate passes also allow for quick shots to be taken by the receiving players.

Catching

For the Shooter on the power play, the stick's target is back behind the body with both arms extended backwards almost parallel to the floor (the stick is in a cocked position ready to shoot). The shooter is ready to take a step into his shot. So as the ball is coming towards the Shooter, the stick is already back and he is starting to take a step into his shot. The Shooter should not move before receiving the ball. He must wait for the pass and, once he has the ball, move in for his shot. Remember: The player is in a position to catch and shoot all in one motion.

For the Creaseman, the stick's target can be in tight to the body and in front of his body so he can see the ball and the net. This position is good for receiving diagonal passes for a "quick stick" shot. The stick's target can also be extended out to the side (for a better target) for the pass from the ball side Shooter. In this situation before receiving the ball the Creaseman must remain stationary. He must wait for the pass before stepping in front of the net.

Coaches do not want a pass into the crease unless it is a scoring opportunity. Some teams like to throw the ball down to the crease to move the zone, but it is a waste of time.

VI. EXECUTION OF THE POWER PLAY

1. The Power Play Versus the Standard "Box" Man Short
The players do not make predetermined passes, except on set plays. They have to learn to read the defense and take what the defense gives them. The top three offensive players move the ball "around the horn" quickly. It is easier to make an accurate and quicker pass from an overhand shooting position into an overhand passing position, whereas it is tough to make an accurate and quick pass from an underhand or sidearm shooting position. Note: If a team has underhand shooters, it is much harder to pass the ball with quickness and accuracy from the underhand or sidearm position.

a) Some general rules for the power-play players to follow against a box man short:

Rule #1— "The Pointman must step in the direction of his pass." He always wants to stay directly between the two top defenders. Stepping towards his pass puts lots of pressure on the off-ball top defender who must decide whether to stay on his side of the floor or to come over to play the Pointman if he gets the ball back. If he stays in his original area the Pointman will step in for a shot upon receiving the ball. If he comes over to play the Pointman when he gets the return pass, the Pointman will pass to the off-ball Shooter for an open shot. This is why it is important for the Pointman to look to shoot every time. If he is open he has to shoot, and if he draws the off-ball top defender he can still pass to the open Shooter. The ballcarrier has to look to shoot first and pass second as this is easier to do both mentally and physically. If the ballcarrier looks to pass first and shoot second, the off-ball top defender may play off him because he does not look like a threat and then it might be too late to shoot (see diagram 169).

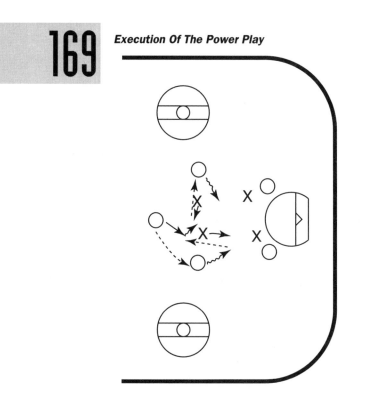

169   *Execution Of The Power Play*

Rule #2— "The Shooter, before receiving the ball, must be ready to shoot the ball."

Rule #3— "The Shooter, upon receiving the ball, must penetrate "in" or "down and in," depending on the situation, and look at the net."

The Shooter must draw the defensive top man down and then pass back to the Pointman. The Shooter takes him down as far as he will go. Sometimes the top defender doesn't play the Shooter strong and lets the back defender play him. In this case he still cuts in but ends up drawing the back defender, and therefore he passes to the Creaseman.

Rule #4— "The Creaseman, upon receiving the pass from the ballcarrying Shooter on his side, must read the defense."
If the opposite defender does not come across, the Creaseman steps in front of the net for a better shooting angle.
If the opposite defender comes across to check this Creaseman, he makes a cross-floor pass to the opposite Creaseman.

Remember: The pass is made to the crease only if the Shooter draws the back defender and only if there is a scoring opportunity.

Rule #5— "The Creaseman on the ball side plays 'tight' to the crease to receive the pass from the ballcarrying Shooter."

Rule #6— "The Creaseman on the off-ball side plays 'wide' to receive the diagonal pass from the opposite Shooter."
The opposition goalie will be playing out on his crease to play the ballcarrying Shooter, which gives this off-ball Creaseman a great shot if the Shooter can make this tough pass to him. The Shooter has to look at the goalie and still make an accurate pass to this off-ball Creaseman's stick.

b) Three set plays versus the standard box man short:

These predetermined plays help the offense get a split-second advantage on the defense, and allows teammates to anticipate what is going to happen. These plays are not run all the time but used occasionally as an element of surprise.

1) The "Cutter" Play (see diagram 170)
The power-play players call this play on the bench before they go on the floor. The key to start this play is that on the third pass the off-ball Shooter will cut either in front or behind the top defender for a pass and shot.

2) The "Swing" Play (see diagram 171)
Again, the play is called on the bench before the players go on the floor. On the first pass to the designated Shooter the off-ball Creaseman is going to cut in front of his defender looking for an imaginary pass. Hopefully, this player will draw the back defender. At the same time the off-ball Shooter slides to the open spot left by the Creaseman, ready to receive a pass and take a shot. They are following the concept of "cut and replace." If the Creaseman does not draw the back defender and is open, pass him the ball for a shot.

3) The "Pop" Play (see diagram 172)
This play is called on the bench. On the first pass to the designated Shooter, the off-ball Shooter cuts behind the top defender looking for an imaginary pass to draw or get the attention of the defender.

The "Cutter" Play

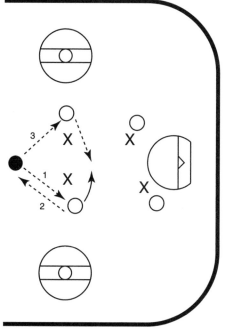

The "Swing" Play

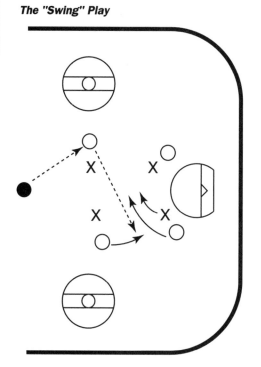

172 The "Pop" Play

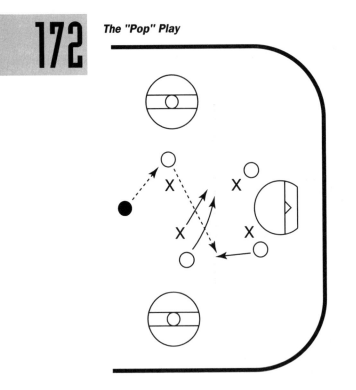

The off-ball Creaseman pops up to the open spot left by the cutting Shooter, looking for a cross-floor pass from the ballcarrying Shooter. This follows the concept of "cut and replace." If the top defender does not play the cutter and he is open, pass him the ball for a shot.

2. The Power Play Versus the "Blitzing" Man Short

Some general rules for the power-play players to follow against a blitzing man short:

Rule #1— "The ballcarrier 'backs off' against any pressure."
A ballcarrier does not pass the ball when being cross-checked or when bothered by a stick, i.e., the ballcarrier is being stick checked versus a stick just in front of him.

Rule #2— "On the blitz, i.e., when a defender is charging the Pointman, he passes opposite to where the pressure is coming from." The tendency under defensive pressure is to pass to where the pressure is coming from or to pass to the "open" offensive player. But the chances are very high that this receiver will also be pressured. That is why the best pass is a pass away from where the pressure came from. This gives the power-play receiver more time to make a selective pass as the man-short defenders are not ready to pressure him (see diagram 173).

The "open" man, the Shooter, takes one step out to the boards to receive the pass from the Pointman to give himself some time to make a play before being pressured. The Shooter's best option is to make a cross-floor pass to the opposite Shooter (see diagram 174) or swing the ball.

Remember: The hardest thing for a blitzing man short is for the top defensive man, who just blitzed the Pointman, to drop back to take away the cross-floor pass.

Pass Away From Pressure

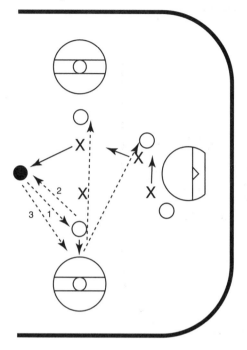

Cross-Floor Pass

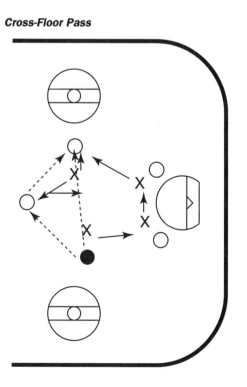

Other possibilities when a Pointman is being blitzed:

a) Send the Shooter behind the blitzer as a cutter through the middle to draw the back defender, and then have the Creaseman pop up for a pass. This is the "pop" play (see diagram 175).

b) The Shooter can set a down pick on the back defender for the Creaseman to pop up for a pass (see diagram 176).

175

Similar To The "Pop" Play

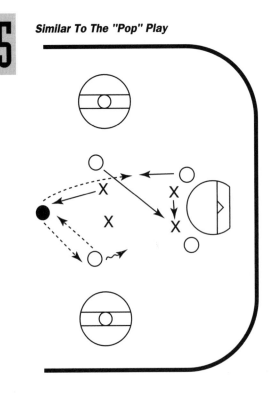

3. The Power Play Versus the "Diamond" Man Short

The objective of the diamond man short is to take away the top three offensive players and force the ball to the crease. In this man short the goalie usually plays back in the crease as most of the shots will come from the Creasemen.

The power play has to move the ball around to get the man short rotating or shifting. The power play must be aware that on the first pass to a Shooter the diamond rotates to a box formation on the off-ball side (see diagram 177). If the Shooter passes down to the Creaseman, the man short stays in the box formation. If the Shooter passes back to the Pointman, the man short rotates back to the diamond formation (see diagram 178). By moving the ball quickly and with a preconceived idea of what they are looking for, the power play feels it can move the ball quicker than the man short can rotate.

Some general rules for the power-play players to follow against the "diamond" man short:

Rule #1— "When the Shooter receives the ball, he should look for a diagonal pass to the off-ball Creaseman or a cross-floor pass to the opposite (off-ball) Shooter (see diagram 179)." The ballcarrying Shooter has to read the defense to see who moves slowly on their rotation. If he passes to the ball side Creaseman, the goalie is in a better position to move quickly to the short side as he is out slightly and ready to move sideways.

176

Down Pick

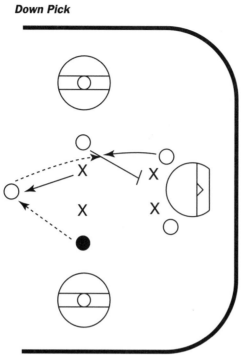

177

*Man-Short Rotation From A
Diamond To A Box*

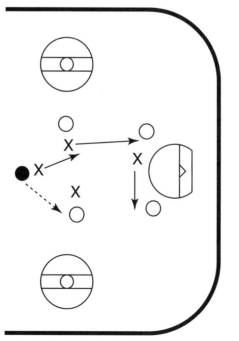

178

*Man-Short Rotation From A
Box To A Diamond*

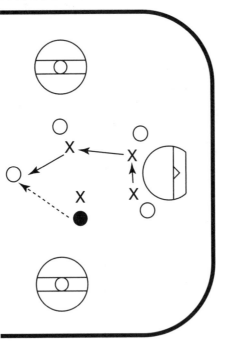

179

Attacking A Diamond Man Short

Rule #2— "When the Creaseman receives the ball, he should look for a diagonal pass to the opposite Shooter first or a cross-floor pass to the opposite Creaseman (see diagram 180)." Since the goalie sits back in his crease to take away the anticipated crease shots, the Creaseman looks for the diagonal pass to the opposite Shooter since he will have a better shot with the goalie back in his net.

180

Attacking A Diamond Man Short

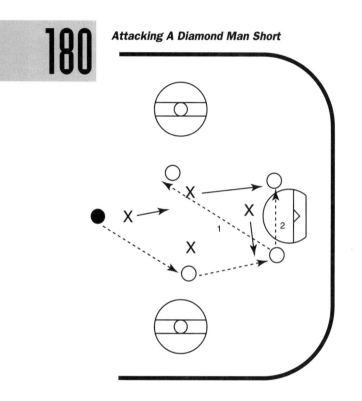

So, as the power play moves the ball around, the ballcarrier is looking a little more for diagonal or cross-floor passes rather than the standard passes around the outside of the man short.

Rule #3—"When the Pointman passes the ball to the Shooter he has to move towards his pass." On the return pass, the Pointman must look for the shot or pass to the off-ball Shooter. This movement by the Pointman makes the rotation longer for the defender to cover him (see diagrams 181a, 181b). Once the Pointman knows the off-ball top defender is coming after him, he can take some more steps with the ball which will pull this defender out of position. The off-ball Shooter can step up towards the ball to pull the defender in the diamond out of position again and to make the rotation longer. This Shooter makes the diagonal pass to the opposite Creaseman who either shoots or passes across to his partner. The defender on the ballcarrying Shooter has to drop to take away the cross-floor pass to the Creaseman which is a long slide (see diagram 181c).

Some other options are as follows:
1) When the ball is on the crease, send the opposite Shooter through as a cutter to get on the inside of the rotation (see diagram 182).
2) When the ball is on the crease, the off-ball Shooter sets a pick on the back defender for the opposite Creaseman (see diagram 183a).
3) When the ball is with a Shooter, the Pointman can set a pick on the opposite Shooter's defender for him to cut and receive the ball and shot.

Attacking A Diamond Man Short

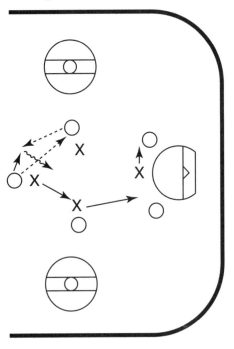

Attacking A Diamond Man Short

181c

Attacking A Diamond Man Short

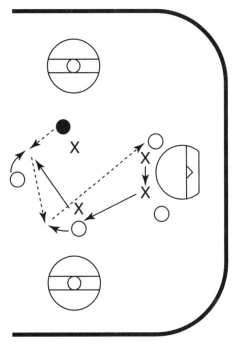

182

Attacking A Diamond Man Short

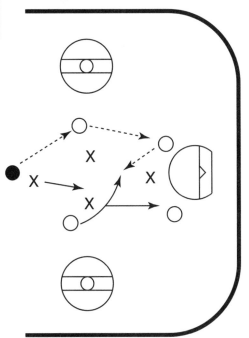

183a *Attacking A Diamond Man Short*

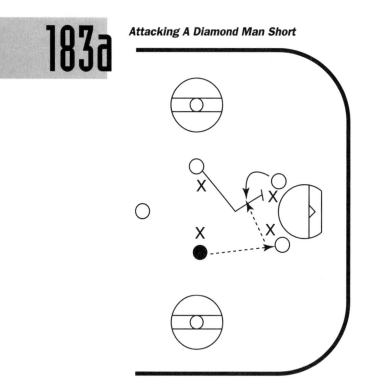

4) When the ball is with a Shooter, the opposite Shooter sets a down pick on the Creaseman's defender for him to pop back and receive the ball on a swing pass from the Pointman (see diagram 183b).

4. The Power Play Versus the "Triangle" Man Short
The team plays a 4-on-3 rather than the regular 5-on-3 situation. The fifth power-play player stays as a defensive safety valve. By playing the 4-on-3 situation the players can move and reverse the ball quicker without the extra pass to the fifth player.

VI. THE 10-SECOND POWER-PLAY PRESS

The purpose of the 10-second press is to deny the pass from the goalie to any of the man-short players. If the opposition receives the ball from the goalie, then the power-play players want to delay the ballcarrier and take away all passing outlets.

The power-play players follow these seven major rules for the 10-second press:

Rule #1— "Nobody presses the goalie unless he starts to bring the ball up the floor." Whoever is playing the defensive safety position will attack and check the goalie.

Rule #2— "If the Pointman does not shoot the ball, he drops back to size up the situation and will most likely pick up one of the two shooters' checks."

Rule #3— "Generally, in regards to the top three players on the power play, whoever shoots becomes the defensive safety."

Attacking A Diamond Man Short

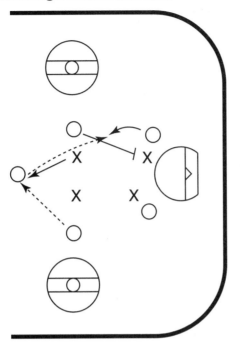

1) If the Pointman shoots the defensive assignments are as follows: the power-play Creasemen will press the two back defenders; the power-play Shooters will press the two top defenders; and the Pointman becomes the defensive safety.

The defensive safety drops back to size up the situation. If there is an unguarded opponent breaking up the floor, he will pick him up. If a teammate is checking the ballcarrier, he will help delay or double-team him.

2) If one of the Shooters shoots, the defensive assignments are as follows: the Pointman picks up this Shooter's check and the Shooter becomes the defensive safety (see diagram 184).

3) If one of the Creasemen shoots, the defensive assignments are as follows: the Creasemen usually picks up his check, but if he does not pick him up, everybody on his side of the floor will slide up one check and the Creaseman will then become the defensive safety.

Rule #4— "When pressing, the power-play player must play his opponent's stick, turn his back completely to the ball, and always assume a pass is coming to his check."

Rule #5— "When playing the breakaway pass the best play is just to stop the breaking opponent from catching the ball by playing his stick, stick on stick." It is a good idea to watch his eyes to get the general idea when the ball is coming. By playing the stick, the pass will go to the other end of the floor to his own goalie. When playing the breakaway pass most players want to turn around and go for the interception (the "grandstand play"), but if he misses the ball his opponent will have a clear cut breakaway with no defensive pressure.

Rule #6— "Once the man-short players get the ball the pressing team wants them to pass the ball out rather than run it out since there is a greater chance of a turnover if the ball is passed out."

184

"10-Second" Press

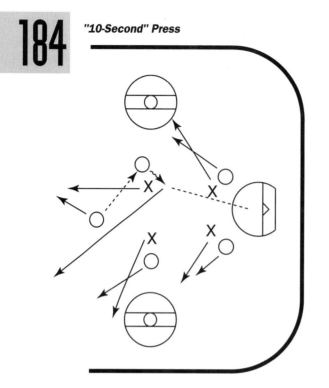

Rule #7— "Once a man-short player gets the ball, the pressing player must play him to stop the run." He does not try to intercept the pass up the floor off the ballcarrier as this move is usually a fake resulting in the ballcarrier going around the pressing player. He must stay down, ready to cross-check and assume the rest of the man-short players are covered.

Pressing Against a Team that Cheats a Player off the Bench
When defending the pass from the goalie to a player coming off the bench the power-play team must do two things:
1) Get pressure on the goalie. Usually one of the Creasemen does this.
2) Get the defensive safety to drop to the far offensive door on the opposition bench rather than playing the man-short player going to the defensive door on the bench. This situation can become a cat-and-mouse game as the opposition player can fake going to the bench, then cut back to the goalie for a pass or go straight to the bench where his teammate will fire out the offensive door. Between the two choices the defensive safety plays the opponent coming out the offensive door to take away the breakaway pass. But with good pressure on the goalie, the opposition will not have all that much time to make the right play (see diagram 185a).

Here in diagram 185b, the shooter who shot the ball picks up the Creaseman's defender while the Creaseman interferes with the goalie's pass. Everybody on the Shooter's side rotates up one check. This is an adjustment to the rule that "the player shooting drops as defensive safety" because the Creaseman is picking up the goalie. Therefore, the Shooter has to pick up his check.

Note: If the shot is from the opposition's bench side, the defensive safety picks up the man-short player going to the bench. If the shot is from the opposite side of the floor to the bench side, the defensive safety picks up the top man-short player while the shooter on the bench side plays the man-short player going to the bench.

185a

**Pressing Against A Team That
Cheats A Player Off The Bench**

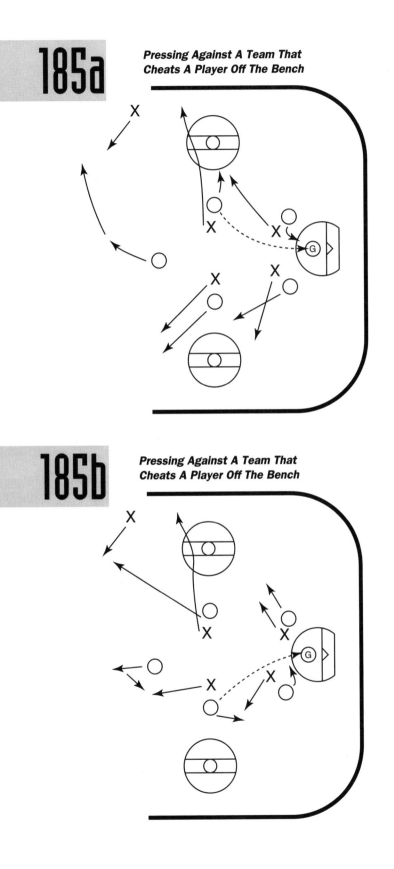

185b

**Pressing Against A Team That
Cheats A Player Off The Bench**

VII. POWER-PLAY DEFENSE

This is a defense against a man-short team trying to rag the ball in their Offensive Zone for the duration of the penalty.

The power-play players will try to double-team the ballcarrier while the other three teammates deny their check from getting the ball. The power-play defender on the ball side denies the pass to the man-short player in the corner area. The power-play defenders on the off-ball side overplay their checks also to deny them the pass. When these off-ball power-play defenders receive a down pick they give space so their teammate can go "through" the pick and thereby come out even with the cutter and thus deny the cross-floor pass to the man-short player. The power play wants to put the ballcarrier under extreme pressure by taking away all passing lanes while edging him into the corner area. When double-teaming, the two power-play defenders try to wedge the ballcarrier into a corner or along the boards, both cross-checking him rather than one cross-checking and the other trying to stick check. If the power-play players end up running after the ballcarrier or chasing after the ball as it is being passed around, they must get reorganized first by denying all passes, then gradually cornering the ballcarrier with the two defenders (see diagram 186).

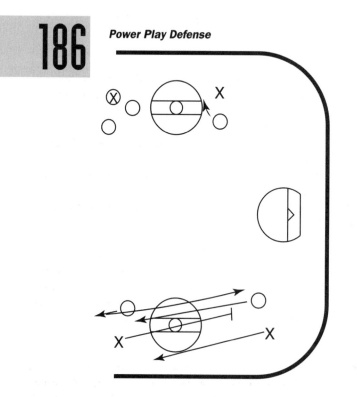

186 *Power Play Defense*

VIII. POWER-PLAY FACE-OFF

A team likes to send a special group of players (called "Chasers") on the floor who are aggressive loose-ball players and good defenders. The best centerman takes the face-off. This group's job is to get the ball for the offensive power-play players. When they align for the face-off, they make sure every opponent is covered on his stick side. The extra player plays back and reads where the ball is going.

IX. POWER-PLAY DRILLS

A. TIPS FOR POWER-PLAY DRILLS

1. The coach should have specialty team practices. He splits the floor in half, working with the number one power play at one end and the number one man short at the other end. This means the team has nine key players for specialty teams. The coach should not double-team any player on the specialty teams at the beginning of the year, i.e., playing on the number one power play and the number one man short. Players will be double-teamed on the number two power play and number two man short throughout the season. During special games and playoffs a player could be double-teamed on both of the number one specialty teams.

2. The head coach works with the man short while the assistant coaches work with the power play at the beginning of the practice as there is a lot of shooting in the power-play drills.

3. Teach the whole-part-whole method. Start with a 5-on-0 drill, progress with breakdown drills of 2-on-1, 3-on-2, 4-on-3, and end with a 5-on-4 drill.

4. Create drills that give players lots of repetition—high repetition builds confidence.

B. POWER-PLAY DRILLS

1. 5-on-0 Passing Drill
This is a warm-up drill for the power play. Players pass the ball around quickly like it's a "hot potato." Follow the rule that they cannot make the same pass twice in a row. This is a no shot drill.

2. 3-on-0 Pointman Shooting Drill (see diagram 187)
This is a high repetition shooting drill for the Pointman. Place a bucket of balls beside the Pointman. The Pointman passes to one Shooter, then gets the return pass and shoots. He then passes to the other Shooter and gets the return pass and shoots. Stress to the Pointman that he should take a step in the direction of his pass and, after catching the ball, step into his shot.
Note: In most of these power-play drills, the task of those power-play players not involved in the drill is to run around and pick up all the loose balls and put them in the bucket.

3. 2-on-1 "Monkey in the Middle" Drill (from Pointman to Shooter) (see diagram 188)
In this passing drill, the Pointman and the Shooter pass a ball back and forth while a defender tries to intercept it . The defender cannot stand in the middle of the two offensive players but goes after the ballcarrier to force the pass. This makes it more realistic. Work both sides of the floor. This passing drill teaches the ballcarrier not to panic and to pass around a defender's stick.

4. 3-on-2 Pointman Step-In Drill (see diagram 189)
This is a shooting drill for the Pointman. It starts with the Pointman passing to one of the Shooters, then getting the return pass back for a shot. He then passes to the other Shooter and does the same thing. The two defensive players give token defense to simulate a game situation. The Shooter, on receiving the pass, takes the defender down and in and then passes back to the Pointman.

5. 3-on-0 Shooter Shooting Drill (see diagram 190)
Start this high repetition shooting drill with the Pointman making a pass to one Shooter who then passes the ball back to the Pointman. The Pointman reverses the pass to the other Shooter who then shoots. The Pointman must reverse the ball quickly (with a step to the pass).

187

3-On-0 Pointman Shooting Drill

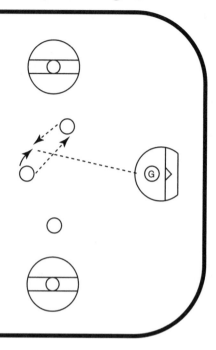

188

2-On-1 "Monkey In The Middle" Drill

3-On-2 Pointman Step-In Drill

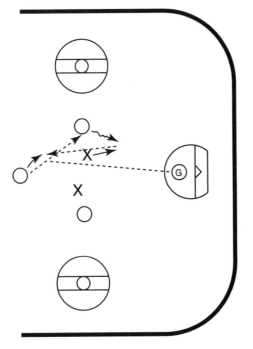

3-On-0 Shooter Shooting Drill

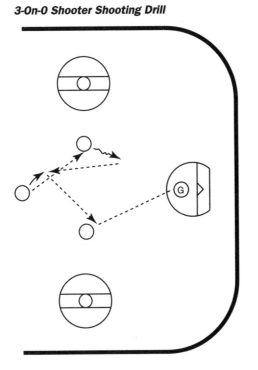

6. 3-on-2 Reversal Drill (see diagram 191)
This is the same as the above shooting drill, except this time there is token defense.
Stress swinging the ball quickly and shooting quickly.
Stress catching and stepping into the shot (all in one motion).
This is one of the "bread-and-butter" drills!

7. 3-on-4 Penetration Drill (see diagram 192)
This shooting drill consists of the three top offensive players and four man-short players forming a zone box. The Pointman passes to one of the Shooters who penetrates the gap to draw one or two defenders. Once he draws a defender, he passes the ball back to the Pointman who then penetrates the gap until played by one of the top two defenders. When he draws a defender, he continues the reversal of the ball to the opposite Shooter who shoots. Then the sequence starts over again.

8. 3-on-2 Shooter Step-In Drill (see diagram 193)
This shooting drill consists of the Pointman, a Shooter, and a Creaseman on the Shooter's side. The two defenders consist of the top and back defender on the same side of the floor. The Pointman starts the drill by drawing the top defender and then passing to the Shooter. The Shooter steps in and, depending on what the back defender does, either shoots the ball or passes into the Creaseman who shoots. The Shooter has to learn to read the defender. The defense gives only token defense. Run the drill on both sides of the floor.

191   *3-On-2 Reversal Drill*

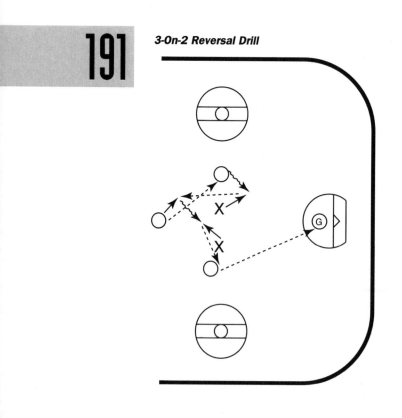

192

3-On-4 Penetration Drill

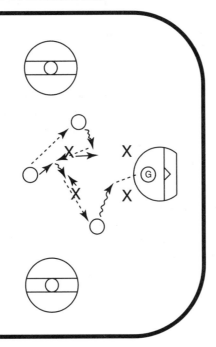

193

3-On-2 Shooter Step-In Drill

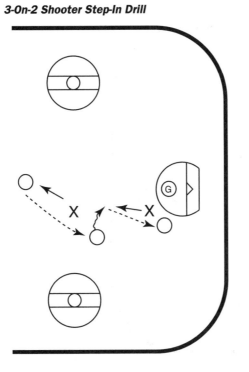

9. 2-on-0 Shooter to Creaseman Shooting Drill (see diagram 194)
This is a high repetition shooting drill for the Creaseman. The Shooter on the same side as the Creaseman feeds the Creaseman who works on his quick-stick (quick-release) shot. The Creaseman picks the short side of the net or tries to deflect the shot off the side of the goalie's body into the net. Work both Creasemen.

194 *2-On-0 Shooter To Creaseman Shooting Drill*

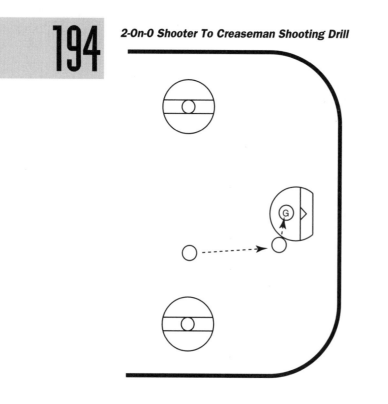

10. 2-on-1 "Monkey in the Middle" Drill (from Shooter to Creaseman)
The same setup as the above drill is used, except it is a passing drill between the Shooter and Creaseman with a defender in between. The defender tries to interfere with the pass from the Shooter to the Creaseman and back. The defender does not stay in the middle but charges the ball-carrier to force a turnover. This passing drill teaches the ballcarrier not to panic and to pass around a defender's stick.

11. 2-on-0 Creaseman to Creaseman Shooting Drill
This a high repetition shooting drill with one Creaseman feeding the other Creaseman. The goalie just plays token defense.

Variation: Use this drill as a speed shooting drill where a coach keeps time for one minute and records the number of goals in relation to the number of shots by one Creaseman. The goalie plays live but plays the shooter from his proper position.

12. 2-on-1 "Monkey in the Middle" Drill (from Creaseman to Creaseman)
The same drill as above, except it is a passing drill with a defender between the two Creaseman who will try to interfere with the passes back and forth. He does not stand in the middle but charges the ballcarrier to force a turnover. This passing drill teaches the ballcarrier not to panic and to pass around a defender's stick.

13. 3-on-2 Creaseman Step-Out Drill (see diagram 195)

This shooting drill consists of two Creasemen and a Shooter. The two defenders are defending the Creasemen. The Shooter starts the drill by penetrating towards the net. The back defender on his side must move out to interfere with his shot in which case he would dump the ball down to his Creaseman. Now if the Shooter sees the off-ball back defender start to cheat across to play this pass, he must then make a diagonal pass to the off-ball Creaseman.

Remember: The off-ball Creaseman has moved out from the crease to make himself available for a pass from the opposite Shooter. The two defenders give different movements so the power-play players react with the right decision.

195

3-On-2 Creaseman Step-Out Drill

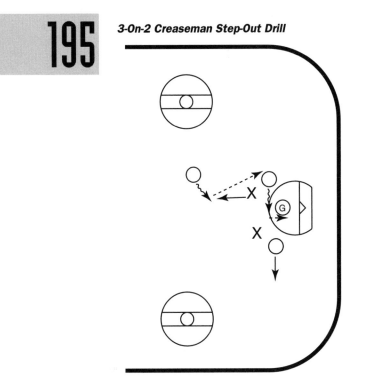

14. 3-on-2 Creaseman to Creaseman Shooting Drill (see diagram 196)

This is exactly the same drill as that above, except it is a high repetition shooting drill with an exact pattern. Therefore, the defense merely plays token defense. The Shooter passes to the ball side Creaseman who passes across to the off-ball Creaseman who shoots the ball.

15. 2-on-2 Pointman to Creaseman Shooting Drill (see diagram 197)

This a high repetition shooting drill. The Pointman feeds the Creaseman while the two defenders give token defense, i.e., they play their position and react as they would in a game but do not interfere with the pass or shot.

16. 2-on-2 Shooter to Creaseman Shooting Drill

This is similar to Drill 9 but with two token defenders.

3-On-2 Creaseman To Creaseman Shooting Drill

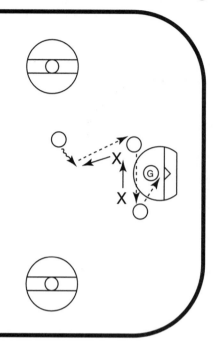

2-On-2 Pointman To Creaseman Shooting Drill

17. 2-on-2 Shooter to Opposite Creaseman Shooting Drill (see diagram 198)
This is a high repetition shooting drill. The Shooter feeds the opposite Creaseman who is playing wide so his defender cannot interfere with the pass. The two defenders are playing token defense.

198   *2-On-2 Shooter To Opposite Creaseman Shooting Drill*

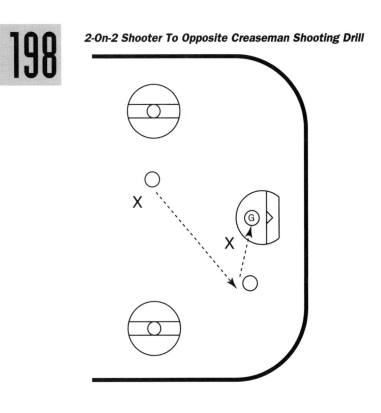

18. 3-on-2 Shooter to Creaseman Combination Shooting Drill (see diagrams 199a, 199b)
This drill reinforces the idea for the Creaseman to move out from the crease when on the off-ball side and to move in tight to the crease when on the ball side. If the opposite Shooter has the ball, the Creaseman moves out for a pass. If the Shooter on the same side as the Creaseman has the ball, the Creaseman moves in tight to the crease for a pass.

19. 3-on-2 Shooter to Shooter Shooting Drill
This is similar to Drill 6 with the ball reversal, but this time the Shooters are only looking for cross-floor passes and shots. Usually these passes are behind the top defenders.

20. 4-on-4 Cutting Drill
This is a power-play setup but with no pointman. When the Shooter has the ball, the opposite Creaseman cuts to the ball. When the Creaseman has the ball, the opposite Shooter cuts to the ball.

21. 4-on-3 Versus "Blitzing" Man-Short Drill
This is just a reaction drill by the power play. The defensive players just pressure the ball wherever it goes and the power play reacts accordingly. This is a great drill for minor/youth lacrosse teams because it teaches players not to panic under pressure.

3-On-2 Shooter To Creaseman Combination Shooting Drill

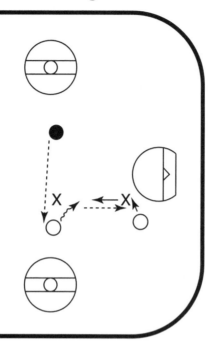

3-On-2 Shooter To Creaseman Combination Shooting Drill

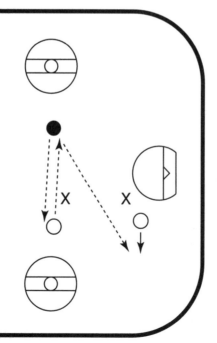

22. 5-on-4 Versus "Blitzing" Man-Short Drill
This is the same drill as above. This is also a great drill for minor/youth lacrosse teams.

23. 5-on-4 "Set" Plays Drill
Work on the "Cutter" play, the "Swing" play, and the "Pop" play.

24. 5-on-4 Versus "Box" Man-Short Drill
   Variations:
   1) The power play must make ten passes before taking a shot.
   2) The power play must make five passes before taking a shot.
   3) The power play is given five chances to score twice.
If the man short gets the ball, they give it back to the power play. Loss of possession or not scoring counts as one of their chances.
If the power-play players shoot and get the ball back, i.e., from a rebound or from the press, they just continue.
If the power play does not score twice after five chances, they do five push-ups each.
If the man short is scored upon more than twice, they do five push-ups each.
   4) One-Minute Power Play Versus Man Short Game
   On the big clock put up one minute. Play this game five times. Whoever gets the most points at the end of the fifth mini-game wins. The losers do 10 push-ups each.
The power play gets two points for a score.
The power play gets one point for a loose ball.
The power play gets two points for getting the ball back on the press.
The power play gets two points for getting the ball back in the Defensive zone.
The man short gets two points if they stop the score.
The man short gets one point for a loose ball.
The man short gets two points if they get the ball into their Offensive Zone before 10 seconds elapse.
The man short gets two points if they rag the ball for the duration of the minute or score.

C. POWER-PLAY PRESS DRILLS

25. 1-on-1 Denial Drill
Starting from their original positions on the power play and the man short, the power-play player denies the man-short player the pass from the goalie. Once the man-short players receive the ball the drill is over. The object is to deny him from getting the pass for 10 seconds.
The official rule is that the man short has to get the ball over their Offensive Zone Line in 10 seconds or lose possession of the ball.

26. 2-on-1 Trap Drill (see diagram 200)
A power-play player denies a pass to his check from the goalie for as long as he can. Once the man-short player gets the ball he is then cross-checked by the power-play player to delay him for the 10-second count. The Pointman drops back. Then once the man-short player gets the ball, he moves up to help his teammate double-team the ballcarrier.

27. 1-on-1 Denying the Breakaway Pass Drill
Two players set up on the face-off circle—one on top of the circle with a ball and the other at the bottom. On the whistle, the top player rolls the ball into the goalie and breaks long for a return pass. The bottom player tries to deny the pass to the breaking player by playing his stick. The coach should discourage any player from turning around and looking for the interception. Once the whole team has finished the drill going one way, they switch positions coming back the other way.

200

2-On-1 Trap Drill

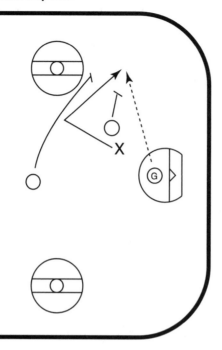

Variation: There is no pass by the top player on the circle. The goalie already has the ball. On the whistle, both players break with the top player looking for the pass from the goalie.

28. 3-on-2 Trap Drill (see diagram 201)
This drill consists of two shooters and the pointman, and the two top defenders. The Pointman initiates the drill by rolling the ball into the goalie. The two man-short players break to get into the clear for a pass from the goalie. The two Shooters work on denying the pass first, then delaying them from getting over the Offensive Zone Line in 10 seconds. The Pointman reads the situation: If an opponent gets the ball and starts to run it out, the Pointman helps to double-team; if the ballcarrier tries to pass it out, the Pointman drops back even farther looking to intercept it.
Remember: The power-play players want the man-short players to pass the ball out of their Defensive Zone rather than run the ball out.

Variation:
1) The ballcarrier can only run the ball out.
2) The ballcarrier can only pass it out.

29. 4-on-3 Delay Drill
The same as the drill above.

30. 5-on-4 Delay Drill
The same as the drill above.

3-On-2 Trap Drill

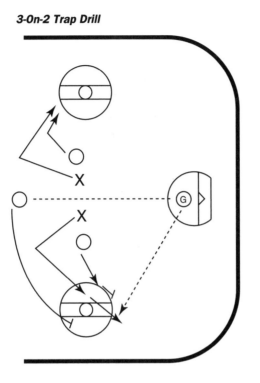

D. DEFENSIVE POWER-PLAY DRILLS

31. 2-on-1 Trap Drill
Two power-play defenders try to "wedge" the ballcarrier into a corner or the side boards where they will double-team him. They both must cross-check his body (not one player cross-checking and the other player going for his stick).

32. 4-on-4 Defending the Down Pick Drill
Both sides of the man short run down picks with the checkers avoiding the pick and going "through" the pick. The power-play players are learning to go "through" the pick so they can stay even with the cutter coming off the pick.

33. 5-on-4 Defending the Rag
The power-play players work on double-teaming the ballcarrier while the other three teammates work on totally denying their checks from getting the ball.

E. POWER-PLAY FACE-OFF DRILLS

34. 5-on-4 Face-Off Drill
Players work on face-offs in different areas of the floor.

F. 6-ON-5–"THE DELAYED PENALTY"

This is not really a power play, but the situation is similar to one as the team gets an odd-man situation for a few seconds. This is a one-shot deal where a team might get a good shot off and even score. Usually, the team that caused the delayed penalty will form some sort of a zone, either a 2-1-2 or a 1-2-2. Thus, the team that has the extra player is attacking a zone. It would be better if the players could get the ball on the side of the floor opposite the bench so that the team can create some action involving the player coming off the bench.

Also, it would be better if there were three players opposite the bench side so that, when the team sends on the extra player, it will be balanced: three right shots and three left shots.
1) The simplest play is to send the cornerman on the off-ball side through the middle to look for a pass. Hopefully, he will pick up a defender leaving an open spot. The sixth player then cuts in behind him for the pass and shot. Another idea is to send the sixth player through first and have someone fill in behind him (see diagram 202).
2) Another simple play is to screen one of the off-ball top defenders and then have someone come in behind (see diagram 203).
3) Some teams like to swing the ball back behind the net and look for cutters or make the back defender play the ballcarrier who passes to a teammate who slipped into the open spot (see diagram 204).

202   *6-On-5 Play*

203

6-On-5 Play

6-On-5 Play

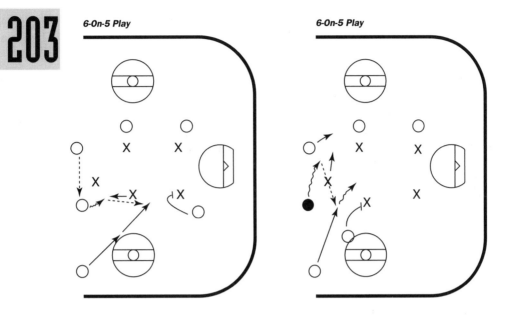

204

6-On-5

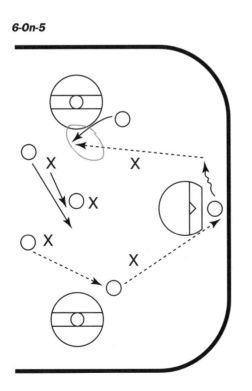

Acknowledgements

I'd like to thank the following people for taking the time to read this manuscript and give me some valuable feedback: Marty Gallas, Don Barrie, Mark Vitarelli and Jim Bishop.

My appreciation and thanks also go to my friend W. T. Westhead, Head of English at Stephen Leacock Collegiate Institute. His skills as an editor, proofreader, and English specialist has made my job much easier during the writing of this book and my earlier "Lacrosse Fundamentals."

I'd also like to thank Coach Roy Simmons Jr. for his introduction. It was perfect.

Many thanks to brian Drew for his professional picture of my kids and I for the back cover.

Thanks to Howard Gross for taking the time to help me out in copying and formatting my disks.

Major Lacrosse Stick Manufacturers in North America

1. BRINE Canada
    258 Lake Road
    Bowmanville, Ontario
    L1C 3K3
    Tel. (905) 623-5123
    Fax (905) 623-6906

    Manufacturer of lacrosse sticks for men and women field lacrosse, and men and youth box lacrosse; and protective equipment; and clothing.

2. NAMI SPORTS
    Northern Amerex Marketing Inc.
    400 Monarch Avenue, Unit 12
    Ajax, Ontario
    L1S 3W6
    Tel. (905) 427-6475
    Fax (905) 427-6790

    Exclusive Canadian Distributor of STX lacrosse sticks; and protective equipment.
    "The best goalies in the world use NAMI protective equipment!"
    (leg guards, upper body, pants, and gloves)

3. CANAM Lacrosse Limited
    19 Prince Charles Street
    St. Cathrines, Ontario
    Tel. (716) 297-2293
    Fax (716) 297-0318

    Manufacturer of wooden lacrosse sticks for men and women field lacrosse, and men and youth box lacrosse; and protective equipment.

4. Matthew Etienne
    1508 Ste. Philomene Street
    Kanesatake, Quebec
    J0N 1E0
    Tel. (514) 479-8447

    Manufacturer of wooden lacrosse sticks for men and women field lacrosse, and men and youth box lacrosse.

5. BRINE Inc.
    47 Sumner Street
    Milford, MA
    01757
    Tel. (508) 478-3250
    Tel. 1-800-227-2722
    Fax (508) 478-2430

    Manufacturer of lacrosse sticks for men and women field lacrosse; and protective equipment; and clothing.